MW01625687

HOVE
LEICA
BOOKS

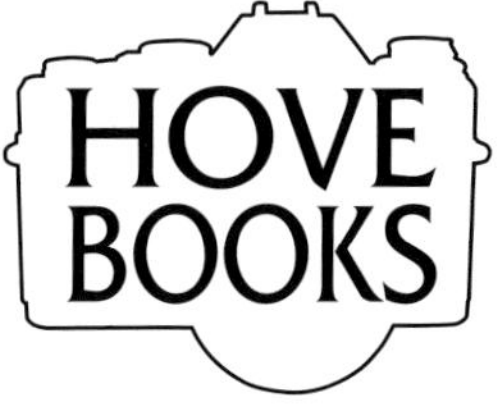
HOVE
BOOKS

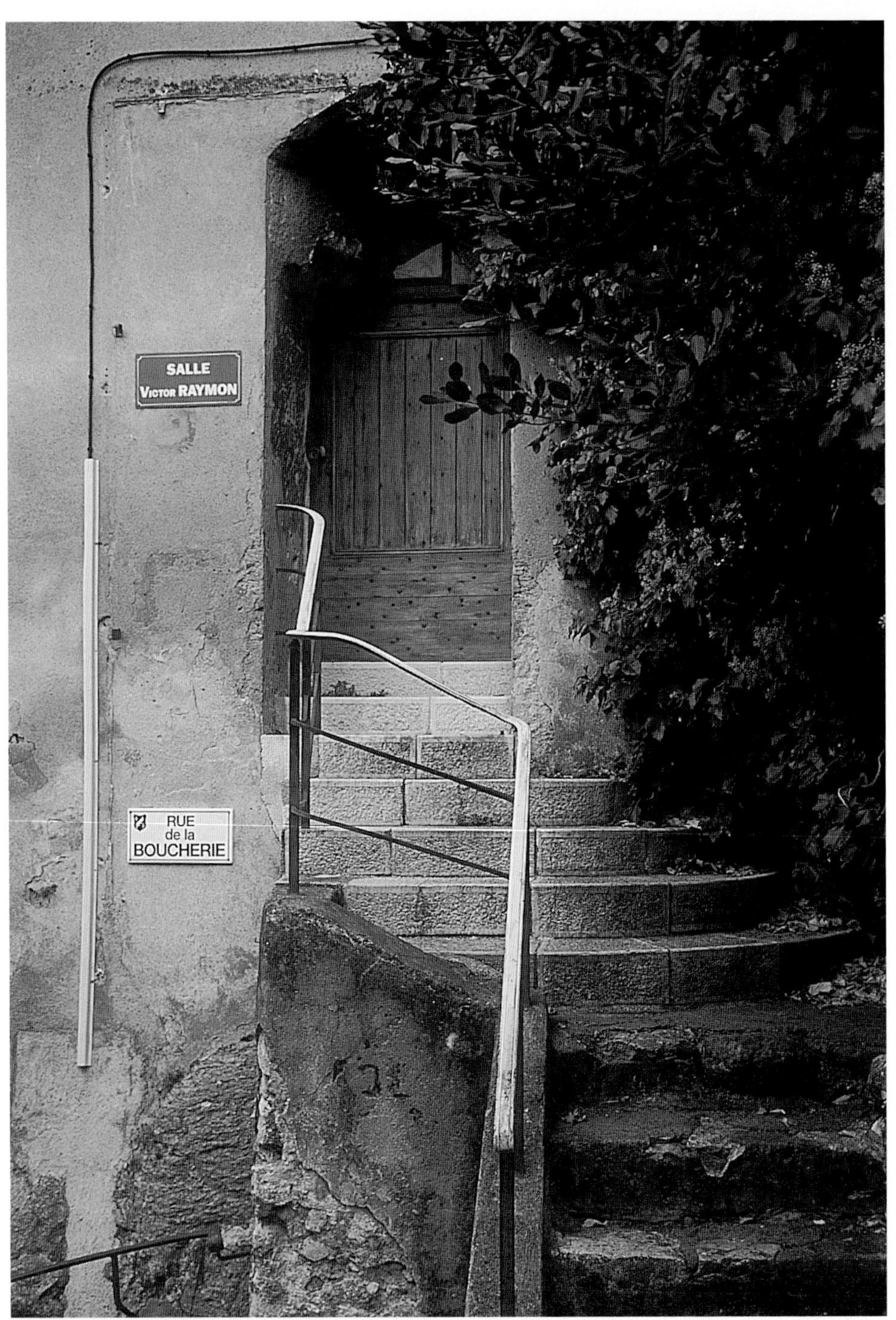
SALLE
Victor RAYMON
RUE
de la
BOUCHERIE

Richard Hünecke

Leica LEICA M6 TTL

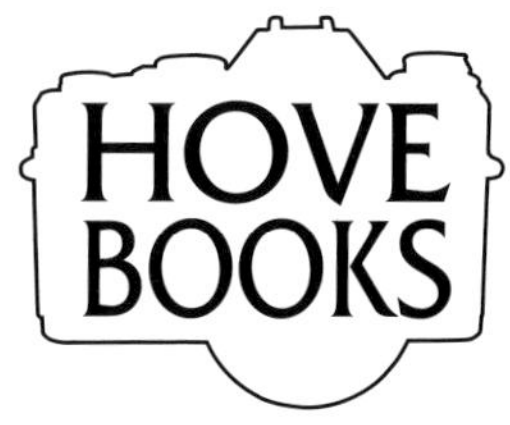

Leica M6 TTL
First English Edition 2000

First German Edition By Laterna Magica, Munich, 1999

British Library Cataloguing in Publication Data
A catalogue record for this book is available from the British Library

ISBN 1-897802-13-7

Translation Hayley Ohlig

Editor Dennis Laney

Typesetting *Facing Pages*, Southwick

Printed by Mladinska Printing House, Slovenia

The author and publisher wish to thank Leica AG Cameras for the illustrations on pages 7,12, 24, 33, 57, 59, 59, 61, 94, 96, 98, 100 (2), 113, 116, 117, 121 (2), 122, 125, 126, 129, 131, 132 and for their permission to use their registered Trade Marks. The following Trade Marks occur in the book:-

Leica ®
LEICA®
ELMAR®
ELMARIT®
SUMMARON®
SUMMICRON®
SUMMILUX®
NOCTILUX®
TELYT®
LEICAVIT®
TELEVIT®
VISOFLEX®
PRADOVIT®

All other photos are by the author except where indicated.

All enquiries to the Publisher:
Hove Books Ltd
30 The Industrial Estate
Henfield Road
Small Dole
West Sussex
BN5 9XR, U.K.
Fax: 01273 494992

U.S.A. to:
The Saunders Group
21 Jet View Drive
Rochester
N.Y. 14624-4996
Fax: (716) 328-5078

Contents

Introduction

The Timeless Leica

One always tenderly remembers one's first love for life. In the same way, the affection for the camera that accompanied me along the path to a higher level of photographic achievement endures with me. I cannot otherwise explain the feeling that comes over me when I return to the Leica M3 after a prolonged absence forced on me by my professional obligations. The same applies to my Leica M6. I readily admit that I

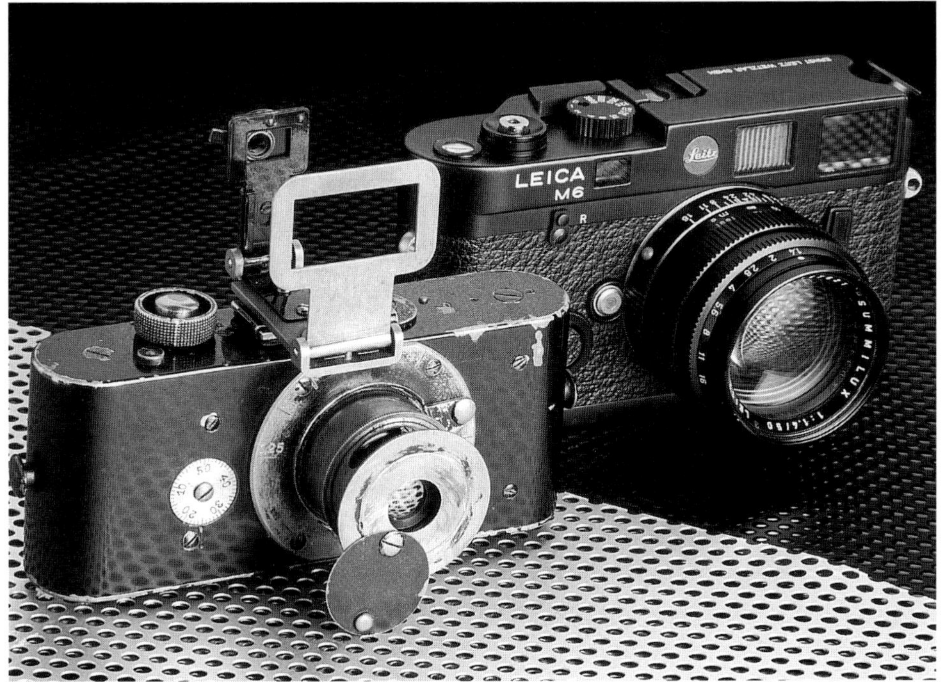

The original Leica was built in 1913, the Leica M6 behind it in 1989. Unmistakable and remarkable is the fact that the basic shape of the original Leica has survived through many camera-generations and is still appropriate. The Leica M6 TTL, now in 2000, continues this uninterrupted tradition.

entertain these feelings for an inanimate, but endearing lump of glass, steel, brass, chrome and aluminium. Henri Cartier-Bresson, France's leading photographer, said "photography with a Leica can be likened to a long, passionate kiss, but also to the crack of a whip, or a session on the psychiatrist's couch." Jim Rakete says of the M6 "it is the most well-mannered camera, and offers the highest level of job satisfaction thanks to its discreet operating sound." I can only agree.

This book of mine about the Leica M6 TTL is much like a declaration of undying love on my part towards a camera that has accompanied me everywhere I went for nigh on forty years. It is by no means just an old object of fond nostalgia, but rather a high-precision tool with a touch of cult mystique. But surely, you will say, my confession of an almost forty-year love affair is not entirely true as the M6 only appeared in 1984, and the M6 TTL only a few months ago, or is it? The Leica M6 TTL is the most recent manifestation of the M-Leica which first appeared as the M3 in 1954, but it does, of course, boast many features and refinements that were not available, or possible, with the original M3. The important point is that its basic design, layout and handling are the same as those of the M3.

The main differences between the M6 and the M3 are as follows. The viewfinder of the M3 was optimised for the 50mm focal length whereas that of the M6 and M6 TTL is a variable wide-angle finder with two settings at 28mm and 35mm. The M6 can accept a motor drive. But the M6 TTL and the M3, and all the models in between, have the same heart, albeit much refined over the intervening four decades. This is the unique coupled rangefinder and the equally unique precise focal plane shutter with its rubberised cloth blinds. Thanks to this shutter the M6 TTL is the uncontested "Whispering Queen."

The evolution from the basic single-lens reflex in the early days of 35mm photography to the microprocessor-controlled auto-focus, auto-everything cameras of today proves that neither super electronics nor the most exotic glasses and sophisticated lens design mark the future compatibility or development potential of a camera system. Future compatibility and development potential of a camera system depend on the interchangeable lens mount and the degrees of freedom it offers for future improvements. If they have already been fully exploited the only option for the next generation of cameras is a new bayonet mount. An example of such a radical switch was the change from the M42 screw mount to the K-bayonet. But even the forward-thinking design of the K-bayonet had trouble moving into the era of AF-multi-auto functions. Cameras and lenses whose system bayonets were not suitable for making the leap into the high-tech era can now be found in the collectors' window of the photo store.

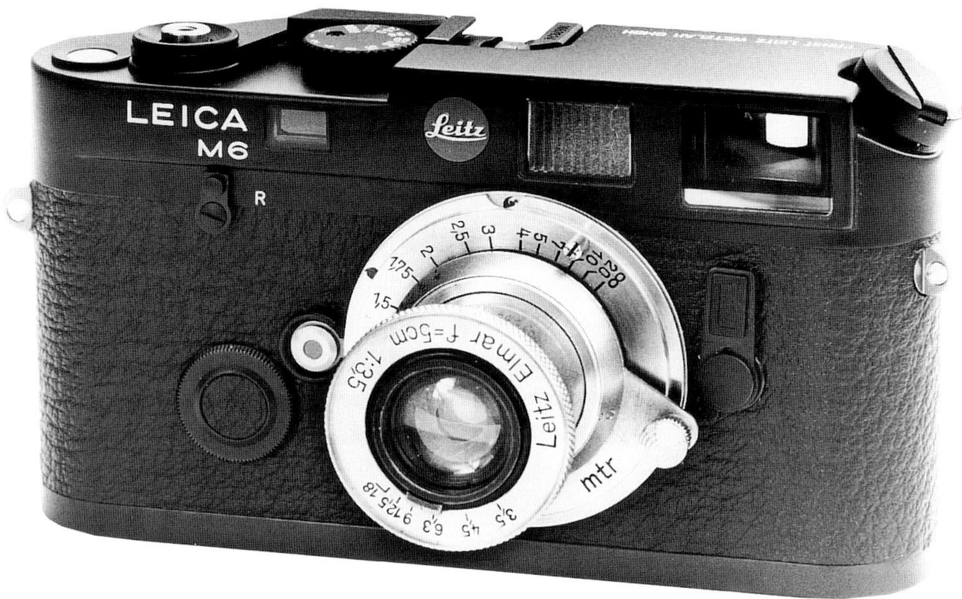

The 1937-vintage Elmar 50mm f/3.5 on the Leica M6 - the M 39/M-bayonet adapter ring 14097 makes it possible. It allows the legendary Elmar to be mounted on the Leica M6 TTL and it can be used with all its functions.

The Leica M photographer knows nothing of this kind of problem. Any differences between the bayonet of the M3 from 1954 and that of the M6 TTL of 2000 is undetectable. Lenses such as the Summicron 50mm f/2 or any other lens in the first M-series fit onto the M6 TTL as well as any M-series lens made in 2000! There are few cameras that can boast such a 46-year history of uninterrupted compatibility and continuity. But that is not all. By using the screw/bayonet adapter ring 14097 for focal lengths between 21mm and 50mm, or 14098 for 90mm, or 14099 for 135mm, you can use any Leica lens with a 39mm screw mount on your M6 TTL. Even these old lenses integrate reliably with its exposure meter and both of its exposure metering systems. Thus you have nearly sixty-years worth of lens production available! Had Oskar Barnack lived to see this he could truly have congratulated himself on a really first class design. There is but one problem in the use of the old screw lenses: the screw/bayonet adapter rings were discontinued many years ago so you will have to rely on the second-hand dealers.

All M-lenses produced to date fit mechanically onto the Leica M6 TTL and function with the expected degree of precision with its rangefinder. The only casualty of development is the camera's exposure meter: The Hologon-M 15mm f/4, Super-Angulon 21mm f/4 and 21mm f/3.4, and Elmarit-M 28mm f/2.8 with serial numbers below 2,314,921 protrude so far into the camera body that they interfere with the silicon photocell located in the upper left corner behind the bayonet and so produce incorrect meter readings. But anyone working professionally with the M6 TTL will have a hand-held meter in their bag because sometimes an incident-light exposure meter reading will give a better result than a TTL reading.

These days we are constantly confronted with the dilemma that something "in" today as the latest state-of-the-art product could be absolutely "out" tomorrow. As a result, items that maintain their value become more and more important. A Leica has lasting value. This includes the Leica M6 TTL even though it "only" offers simple dynamic exposure metering through the lens with an LED display in the viewfinder. Taking a hand-held shot of the Coliseum in Rome just to prove you were there is something anyone can do with any fully automatic compact camera. But subtly capturing the lives of the local people in an arresting manner, using imagination to convert the interaction between shapes, light and colours in the scene into an impressive image is generally beyond the scope of preprogrammed unthinking electronic camera electronics. Of much greater importance is the ability to select shutter speed and aperture quickly, confidently and, above all, without interference from homogenised program modes in order to create lighting conditions optimised for the subject and creative concept while selecting a plane of focus within the subject to convert the photographic idea into an image on film.

Painting and literature, music and architecture, indeed, all art forms have their famous works. Even photography has them. Only Leica succeeded in being both a legend and a reality. Oskar Barnack had been working on the development of cine cameras at the Ernst Leitz Optical Works in Wetzlar since 1911. In order to experiment with exposure on motion picture film he needed a small camera, so he built himself one. He recognised that this exposure testing camera could be the basis for realising his dream of "small negative, large picture" to avoid having to lug around a heavy, large format plate camera. That 1913/1914 camera with its fixed exposure time of 1/40 second became the original Leica from which the Leica I was developed in 1924. It pioneered modern 35mm photography. The subsequent Leica II, Leica III and their variants could finally stand up against the large format cameras of the time.

Today, the Leica I is not only a legendary figure in the story of 35mm photography, here and there one can still find a Leica I in use. It, along with its successors with interchangeable lenses with their screw mount, represent, then as well as now, high precision, reliability and durability. Leica earned its unequalled reputation on the strength of ever more seemingly impossible feats. The Leica M3 in 1954 personified absolute perfection of the 35mm rangefinder camera and lifted the reputation and fame of the Leica to new heights. TTL metering for ambient and flash illumination and the rangefinder optimised for the focal length range 28mm or 35mm to 135mm found on the two variations of the M6 TTL fulfil the needs voiced by serious photographers for years. If one did not already know that a plateau, originally seen as a final step in a cycle of development, was simply an intermediate resting place, one might consider the M6 TTL as the final chapter in the saga of "35mm cameras with interchangeable lenses." The Leica M6 TTL is the only camera of its type anywhere in the world. If it remains so, we will wait to see. All of this undoubtedly creates the fascination I still feel, even after forty years, when I take up my M6 or my M3.

It is true that for a Leica M6 TTL with the classic trio of lenses, 35mm, 50mm and 90mm, one has to empty one's bank account. This same amount of cash could be used to procure two current, high-tech SLR's from the Far East, or the top-of-the-line model with a few lenses. One might debate the merits of the two different "capital investments" until the cows come home, but discovering the differences in practice is fascinating! Fascination with the M6 TTL, along with its timelessness and absolute precision do not take better pictures all on their own. The brain behind the camera which formulates the idea for the picture is an indispensable part of the system. The joy of the Leica is that it provides the most direct connnection with that brain, compared with any other 35mm camera. I obtained my first Leica M3 in 1960. Despite various encounters with sand dunes and breaking waves in Sylt and Cote d'Argent, it still works as accurately as it did forty years ago. The equally aged four-element Hektor 135mm, f/4.5 produces impressive image quality that can compare favourable with modern lenses. I still use its removable optical head on my bellows unit for product shots with magnification ratios down to 1:1.

Designers at Leica A.G. use slightly different concepts to create lenses for the M6 TTL. These are fast maximum apertures and maximum imaging quality, even when wide open. The legendary Hektor 135mm, f/4.5, once *the* lens for close-up work to 1:1 magnification ratio, the original Summicron 50mm, f/2, and the modern classics of the M-series, with the Apo and ASPH classes, all feature the same unique timelessness of the small, but high-class M-system. May it remain thus for a long time to come, even as an alternative to the electronic-automatic homogeniser in photography.

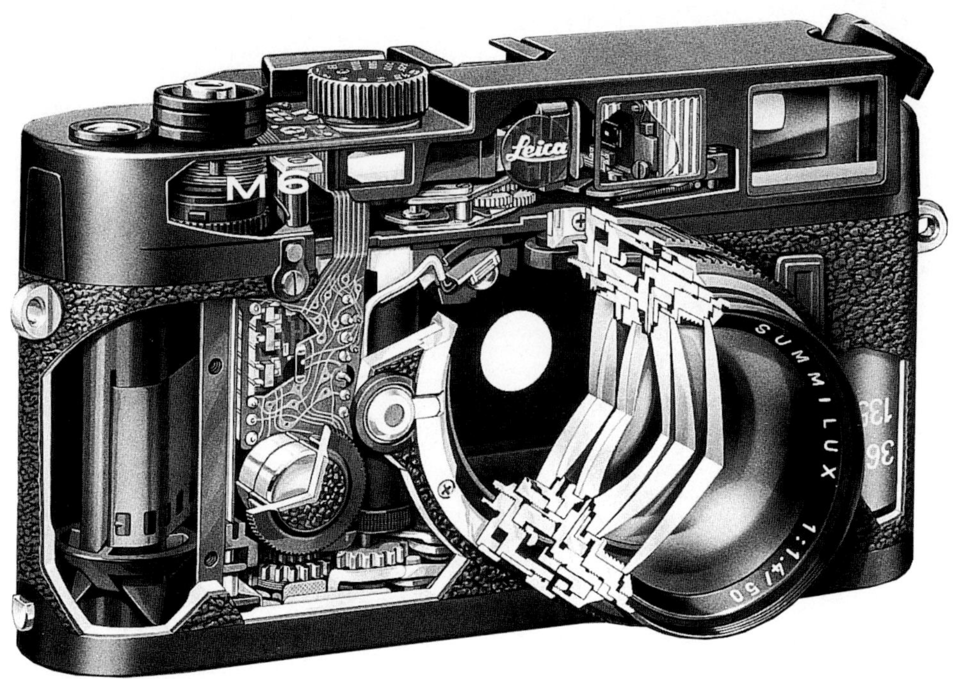

Every last millimetre of space inside the Leica M6 TTL is used to house high-precision mechanics, together with the exposure metering system for ambient and flash illumination developed specifically for it.

The Leica M6 TTL is a true M-series camera like all its predecessors from the M2 to the M6, improved and enhanced with several additions. The legend lives on to the joy of all those who were, are and will be purely fascinated by photography.

Chapter 1

M6—The Whispering Queen

"The Leica M6 cannot be improved upon!" is a statement attributed to Luigi Colani, leading designer of ergonomically satisfying consumer goods. Whether one accepts this statement or not,75 years ago Oskar Barnack had grasped the truth of a concept that was later to become familiar in the design world as "form follows function", and gave his first Leica a unique, timeless shape. Put a Leica I or III, or an M6 from 1984 beside the M6 TTL and the same shape and profile will be evident in all three cameras from 1925, 1933, and 1998: the slim housing with not quite semi-circular transitions from the front to rear sides, the lens located slightly to the left, the placement for the advance lever, shutter speed and rewind knob, the rangefinder eyepiece on the far left outside, the arrangement of the three viewfinder windows. This array of windows is becoming increasingly distinct from the practically uniform, angular to smooth humps, characteristic of today's reflex cameras. The heart of the Leica M-system is hidden behind this elegant exterior: the rangefinder for setting the lens focus and the viewfinder, giving an image unrivalled in brightness, outlined by brilliant frames.

The development from the Leica III to the Leica M3 of 1954, then to the M6 of 1984 made the camera only slightly bigger: from almost 134mm wide, 67mm high and 30mm deep to about 139mm wide, 77mm high and 34mm deep. Furthermore, a full 2mm of that extra depth is taken up by the hinged back flap which the Leica III lacked. The penalty for the additional TTL flash control of the Leica M6 TTL is an extra 2.5mm in height in order to create space for the newly designed electronics to measure ambient and flash illumination. Given its features, the Leica M6 TTL cannot be a lightweight: with the chromed Summicron 50mm f/2, it tips the scale at 940g.

Oskar Barnack did not record how many hours he spent shaving his first Leica down to its ergonomic profile. Even the slightly larger M6 TTL maintains these ideal proportions. The perfect alignment of controls to fingers is a testament to the masterpiece of ergonomics Oskar Barnack created with the Leica I over 70 years ago. Someone who has never held a Leica before instinctively hooks his thumb behind the subtle protrusion of the advance lever, rests the M6 on the little finger of the clenched hand, presses the camera using the two middle fingers onto the ball of the hand and rests the index finger right on the release as if there was no more natural position in the world. One has to try this grip on the M6 TTL to fully understand how securely one can hold it with just the one hand, while still giving the thumb enough freedom for the three short movements that make the M6 TTL ready for the next shot. The position in which the left has to support the M6 TTL depends on the lens used: it holds the small Summicron-M 35mm f/2 ASPH differently than the Apo-Telyt-M

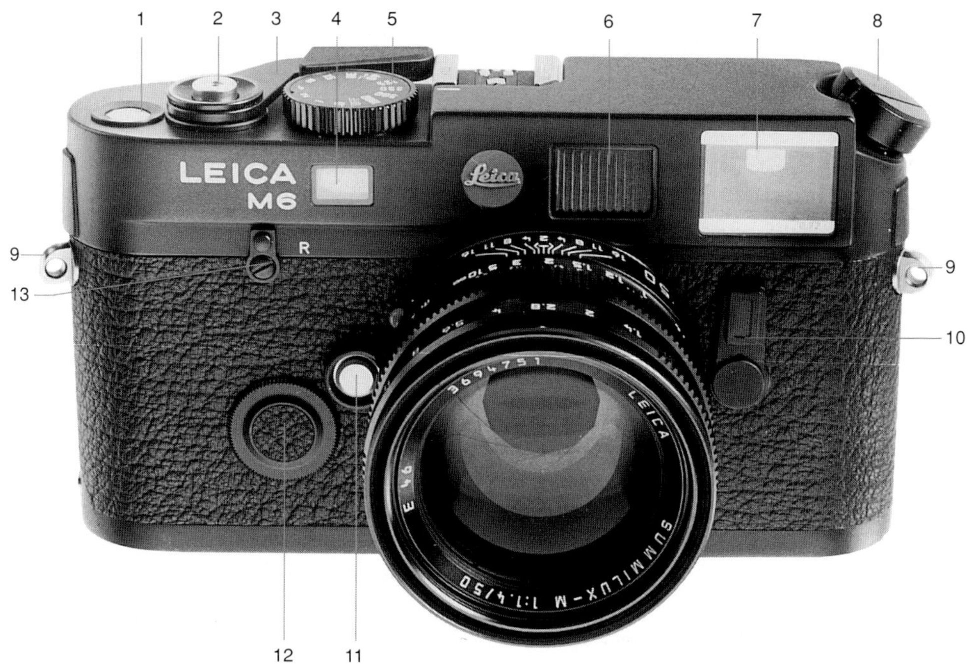

1—Frame counter
2—Shutter release with thread for cable release
3—Rapid-advance lever
4—Rangefinder window
5—Shutter speed dial
6—Window for illuminating the format frames projected into the viewfinder
7—Viewfinder window with mirror strips at the top and bottom edges
8—Flip-up rewind crank
9—Eyelet for neck-strap
10—Selector for viewfinder frames
11—Lens release button
12—Battery compartment
13—Lever to allow the film to be rewound

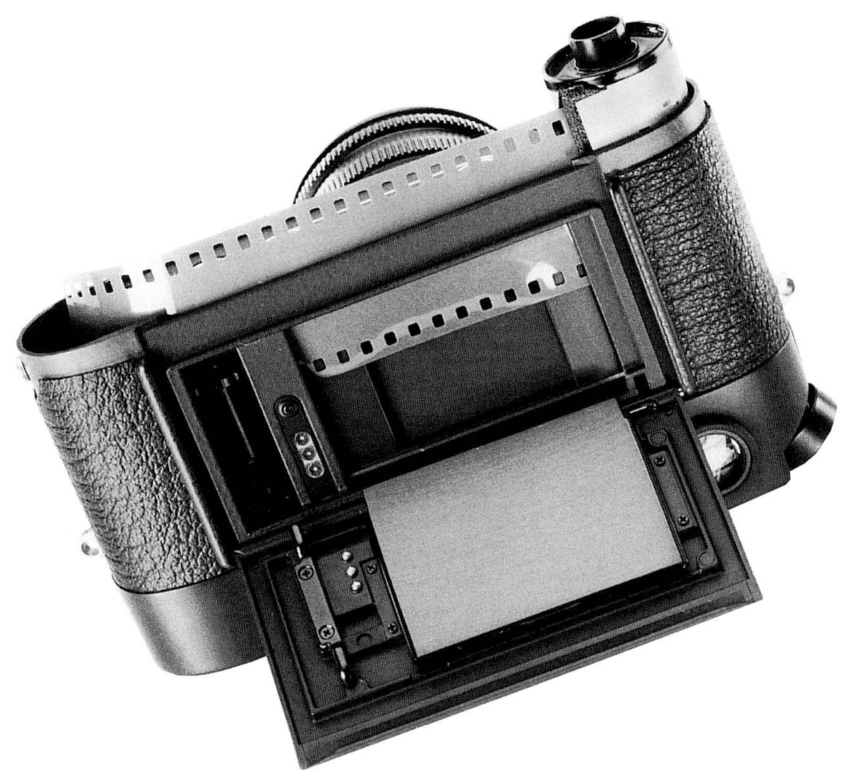

This is how you load film into the Leica M6 TTL. Slide the cassette and film into the slit, close the back flap, attach the bottom plate and swing the rapid-advance lever twice—done.

135mm f/3.4. One can learn these grips much quicker than the push-button controls of a high-tech reflex camera. Oskar Barnack's Leica I remains a timeless masterpiece.

Three Jobs Before the First Shot

Anyone switching from a reflex camera to a Leica M6 TTL had better forget all the rules learned through personal interaction with high-tech reflex cameras. Photography with the M6 TTL is pure photography, concentrated on three finger movements. The thumb takes care of film transport and cocking the shutter, using one lever which could not be better designed; the index finder controls the shutter speed and the shutter release, while two fingers on the left hand suffice to focus and set the aperture. These levers, buttons and rings move with typical Leica positive, dampened feel, making the fingertip control a great experience.

The first "wow" experience of retraining comes with loading the film into the M6 TTL. After removing the base plate—it is still removed and mounted in the same way as Oskar Barnack's Leica I—a section of the back, not the whole thing, opens up. The open section is large enough to uncover the picture window, film guide and the sprocket wheel. Leica designers still maintain that the completely enclosed camera body provides superior stability for which the Leica is renowned. The small flap in the back does not reduce this stability in any way. The extremely rigid camera body guarantees that the basis for the rangefinder system, the distance between the bayonet and the film plane, and the zero position of the rangefinder and lens, are maintained, no matter what demands are made on the camera. Whereas with a reflex camera in which the viewfinder image corresponds to the film plane, and hence you can determine any change in the lens/film distance by a change in the position of the plane of focus in the viewfinder image (or in the split-screen focusing aid) one has to focus the M6 TTL indirectly.

By turning the focusing ring on an M-lens the two partial images of the subject seen in the rangefinder can be made to coincide with each other. You can then rely on the fact that, at this setting of the M-lens focusing ring, the subject plane will be in focus on the film plane. The rangefinder will maintain its accuracy, as long as the camera does not suffer a severe shock, such as by being dropped.

Does one really need a larger opening than the small 7.5 x 3.5cm opening in the back-plate of the camera to load the film cassette and feed the 10cm-long film leader between the camera back and the shutter unit? All one has to do is check three things: the film has to be parallel to the film guides on the film gate, the sprockets must engage into at least one side—but much better both sides—of the transport drum and the film leader has to stick at least 1.5cm into the take-up spool. When you have checked these three points, you can tension the film slightly using the advance lever, close the back flap and lock the bottom plate in place. Practice the loading procedure with an outdated film from the rummage box. Hold the M6 TTL with the lens facing you, then turn it upside down for this operation. The movements you will practice during the next ten minutes will become second nature by the third film at the latest. Now try it on the move: turn the M6 TTL so that it hangs around your neck on a normal length strap with the bottom plate facing up and the lens resting against your body. If you are not walking too quickly, the M6 TTL will remain in this position and you can remove the bottom plate and tuck it into a pocket. The exposed, and obviously rewound, film drops out of the camera into the palm of your hand for storage in another pocket, where the new film, relieved of its packaging and in easy reach, can also be found. Push it into the M6 TTL with the movements you practised on your coffee table. I will admit that this sounds a bit like finger acrobatics—but try it before you complain. Some high-tech reflex cameras, thanks to the limited space left after the electronics have been fitted in, only accept the film cassette if it is cunningly tilted slightly, which has been known to destroy many a fingernail.

Before you attempt your first shot, advance two frames by taking dummy shots in order to move the pre-exposed film past the film gate and thus place the first unexposed frame behind the shutter. High-tech reflex cameras take up to three or four dummy shots to arrive at the same place. Anyone who goes in for that sort of thing can use a pocket calculator to figure out how many films it takes for those two wasted frames to pay for the differential between a high-tech camera and an M6 TTL. It is a few thousand. The Leica M6 TTL will survive them without any trouble. Leicas have been sent to the factory for service whose shutter speeds and rangefinders were only slightly out compared to nominal settings after 350,000 shots or more. Whether high-tech reflex cameras can boast the same performance is not yet known—they have not been around

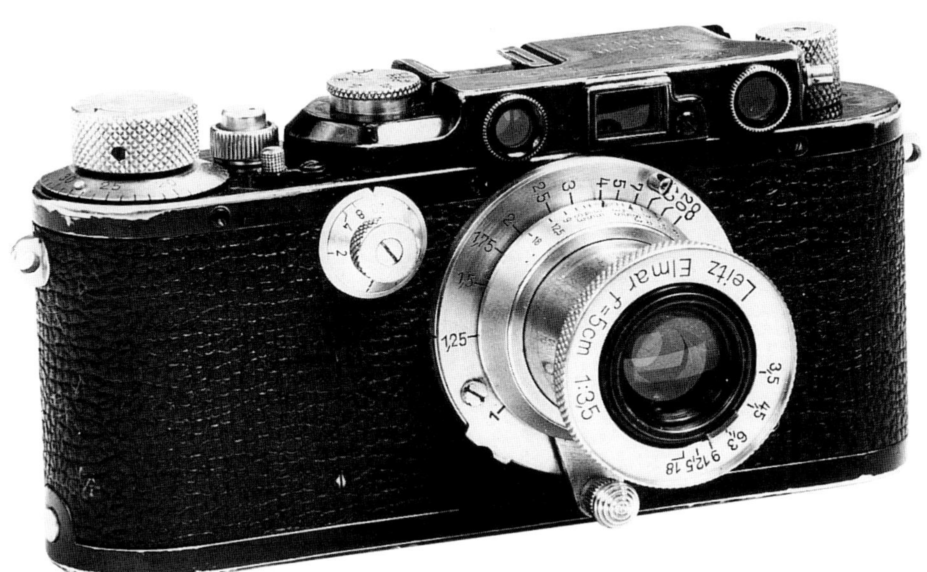

A 1928 Leica, later rebuilt to become a Leica IIIa. The outline of its housing and the arrangement of viewfinder, lens and operating controls are already as they appear—albeit improved and even more ergonomic—on the Leica M6 TTL—timeless Leica!

long enough for a significant number to survive such a shooting marathon.

The M6 TTL Does Need Some Power

After the two dummy shots, the frame counter shows “0” The M6 TTL is ready for the first shot as its mechanical shutter control mechanism does not require electricity. The two batteries in the compartment next to the lens release button are only required for the metering electronics and TTL flash control. If the LEDs in the viewfinder do not light up when you lightly depress the shutter release, it could be for one of three reasons. The shutter speed dial is set to “OFF” and so the metering system is disconnected from the battery. Or you have not advanced the film to

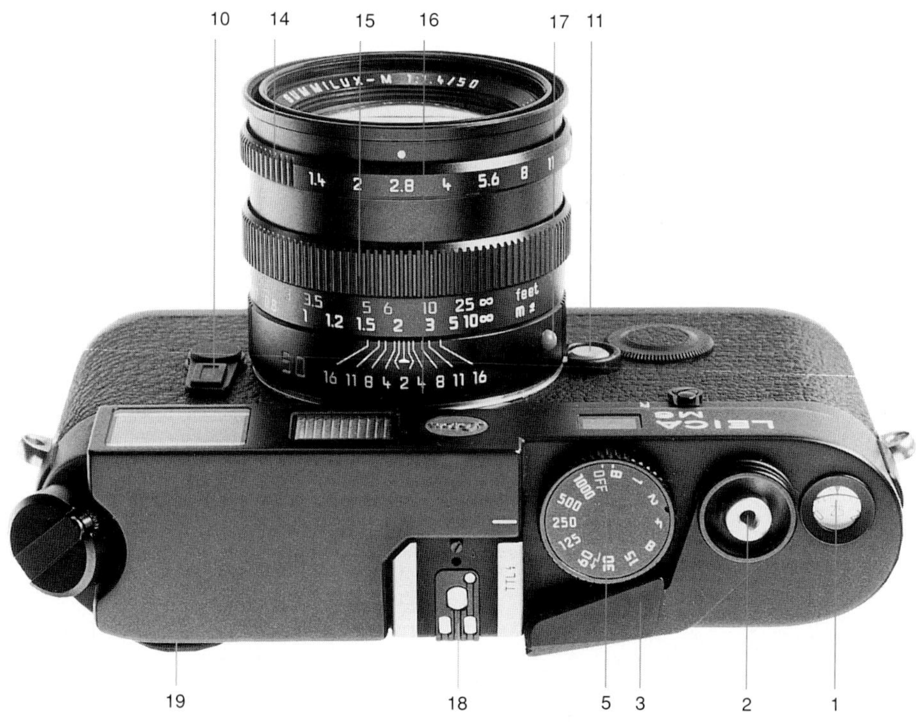

1—Frame counter
2—Shutter release with thread for cable release
3—Rapid-advance lever
5—Shutter speed dial
10—Selector for viewfinder frames
11—Lens release button
14—Aperture ring
15—Distance ring
16—Depth of field scale
17—Index mark for lens mount
18—Hot shoe with centre and control contacts
19—Eyepiece

the next frame so the white metering spot on the first shutter blind is not in the silicon photocell's line of view: the system is turned off. The third possibility is that the two EPX 76/G13 silver-oxide button cells or the CR 1/3N lithium batteries are still in the camera's box. If the left-hand arrow LED is flashing, it is warning you about the futility of taking a picture because the lens cap is still on the front of the lens. If the right-hand LED is flashing, it is telling you that the battery is already so weak that it needs to be replaced.

Factory-fresh batteries should, according to Leica technicians, last for 2900 meterings. If one assumes one shot per metering, this would correspond to about 80 36-exposure films. I cannot attest to whether or not this number can be achieved in practice as I lost count, once after 1245 shots and once after 2065. At first glance, 80 films do not sound like much, particularly since some photo studios chase 10 films a day through the M6 TTL. How many of those 360 shots are actually used at some point is another topic, and one which we will not discuss here. If one shoots about one film per week, a fresh set of batteries should last a year and a half, two films a week makes their life about 10 months. One should splash out on new batteries for the M6 TTL at least every year and a half, as one never knows how depleted a set of batteries really is. After such a period of use, or a longer one, silver-oxide or lithium batteries suddenly stop supplying power. With the Leica M6 TTL this is no cause for alarm: it works even without batteries, only the exposure metering and flash-triggering operations do not work. Since one would rather not do without either of these functions, one should always have a spare set of batteries in one's pocket, particularly if the LEDs in the viewfinder seem to be a bit darker than usual. The alternative to a spare set of batteries on extended trips though the wilderness is having a selenium exposure meter handy. It does not need batteries and is indestructible, as long as one does not try to drown it or leave it in the glove compartment to rust for weeks on end. My more than 35 year-old Gossen Sixtomat displays the same reading as a new, electricity-dependent unit with a silicon photocell. Because of its design, a selenium exposure meter has a very wide angle of view and does not exhibit any centre-weighted characteristics, you should shoot a test series to see what you are metering. You should experiment with both subject metering—from the camera to the subject—as well as incident metering—metering from the subject towards the camera with the diffusion screen in front of the cell.

The Leica M6 TTL does not have sensors to read the DX-code off a film cartridge. You have to set the ISO value manually on the dial on the back of the camera. The Leica designers might have been able to cram the requisite six contacts to read the DX-code into the appropriate area, which is already full with the shutter mechanism, but setting the film speed via the DX-code only makes sense in a professional camera if you can override it manually and have the ability to enter correction values to optimise the exposure metering system for specific light and subject conditions. Such technology, which would have to be integrated with the metering system, would only make sense if it was linked to an electronically controlled shutter—and then the M6 TTL would not be an M6 any more! Remember the fate of the Leica M5, whose metering system was well designed but took up far more space than that of the M6 because of the state of technology at the time. This made the M5 much larger and heavier than the M3 or M4. After only four years and a run of only 31,000 cameras, the production was halted. Now it is a coveted and expensive collector's item—and still an excellent camera!

The Leica M6 TTL's exposure meter can be programmed for film speeds from ISO 6/9° to ISO 6400/39° via the ISO-selector on the back on the camera. Three gold-plated contacts transmit the ISO value to the metering circuitry. A further correction control is not available—and why should there be one: if one wants more or less sensitivity, simply select an appropriately higher or lower ISO-value. Exposure bracketing to produce a perfectly exposed image can be achieved by using the aperture ring. Older M-series lenses only offer full-stop apertures, while newer models offer half-stop settings as well. The throw between click-stops on the M-lenses is long enough for the ring to be set between full increments for a finer degree of control while bracketing. More details on this subject can be found in the next chapter.

Now, at last, the first shot! Press the shutter release until you find the first contact point, then press further—and hear a quiet, elegantly muffled "click": the Leica M6 TTL does not draw attention to itself when a picture is taken—that noise you heard was the shutter! Whether it is set to 1/1000 sec. or 1 sec., it is always that quiet. It does not intrude in the silence of a large cathedral or in the tension-filled pause in the dialogue in Act III. This "whisper-shutter" is the only sound when shooting with the M6—and it is barely perceptible! The sound of the advance lever can be likened to a pocket watch. "Whispering Queen" is a title that no camera available now or even in the foreseeable future will be able to take away from the Leica M6. Mount a Leica Winder-M instead of the bottom plate on the M6 and it is still noticeably quieter than any motorised reflex camera.

The M6 TTL Viewfinder

A reflex camera user who looks into the Leica M6 TTL viewfinder for the first time will immediately notice

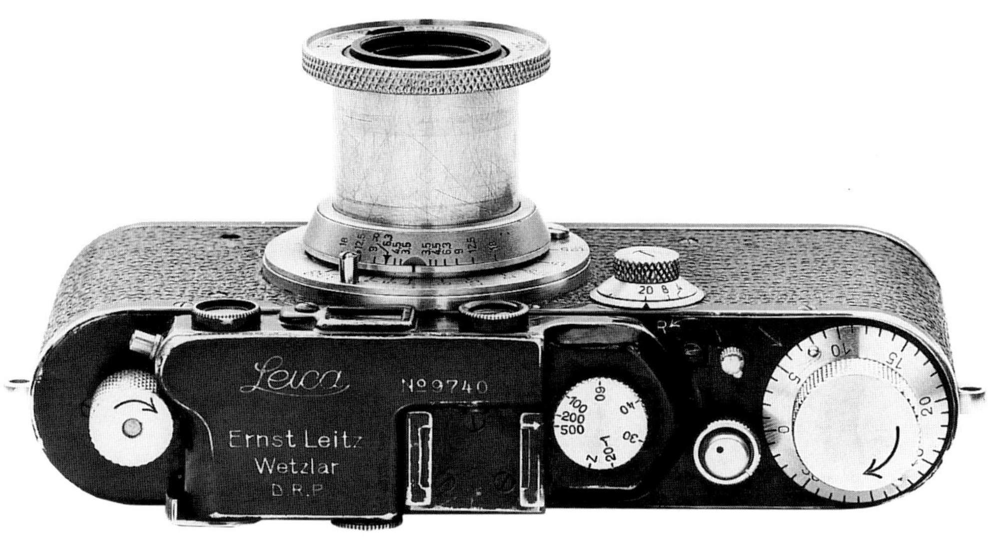

Timeless Leica: even from this perspective, the similarities between the Leica M6 TTL and this over 60-year-old Leica I/III are impossible to miss.

two things: the viewfinder image is amazingly bright, clear and brilliant and does not have any of the more or less visible markings seen in that of a reflex camera. And: the M6 TTL's finder always shows the same section of the subject area, regardless of the lens mounted on the bayonet, and it is in focus from front to back. One function the Leica M6 TTL's finder cannot perform: one cannot see the plane of focus in the image nor can one analyse the depth of field corresponding to the selected aperture.

You are now faced with a decision that is a function of your personal focal length preferences, and hence your individual method of capturing subjects, scenes and ideas on film: the choice of viewfinder magnification. A far greater benefit of the Leica M6 TTL than the TTL flash exposure control function is, in my opinion, the ability to choose between a 0.72x and 0.85x viewfinder magnification! The Leica M6 TTL with a 0.72x magnification exhibits the traditional wide-angle perspective of the Leica M4-P where the image boundaries for 28, 35, 50, 75, 90 and 135mm lenses are reflected into the viewfinder. This viewfinder image is slightly larger than the frame for a 28mm lens. A viewfinder with a 0.85x magnification has an approximately 18% larger subject rendition, similar to the Leica M2, where the image boundaries for 35, 50, 75, 90 and 135mm are reflected in. The

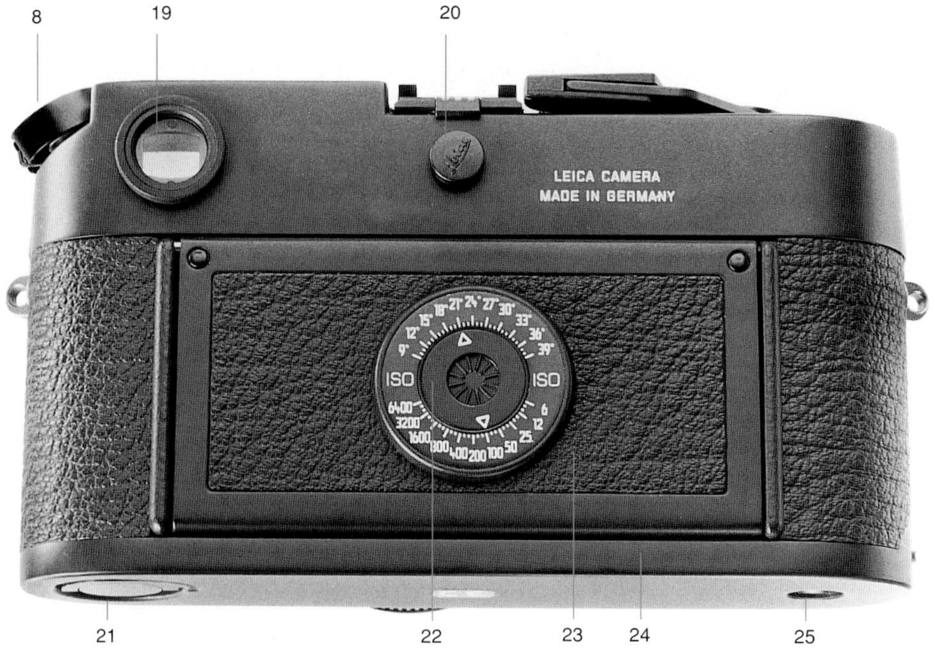

8—Flip-up rewind crank
19—Eyepiece
20—Sync. socket protected by a cover
21—Catch to release the base plate
22—ISO-dial for setting the film sensitivity for the exposure meter
23—Rear flap
24—Removable base plate
25—Tripod socket A 1/4 (1/4")

M6/0.85x is therefore of interest for those photographers who tend to work with longer focal lengths rather than with wide-angles. One can select an image composition more easily in a subject that is magnified by 18%. The effective measuring base of the range-finder, increased by the same factor from 49.9mm to 58.9mm, also increases its already legendary accuracy. Focal lengths from 75mm and longer benefit the most from this.

The M6/0.72x subject strengths lie more in close-up and personal shots with short focal lengths. You therefore have to embark on a trip of photographic self-discovery to decide if you prefer shooting with wide-angles or lean more towards longer focal lengths. Having both an M6/0.72x and an M6/0.85x in your camera bag would mean you do not have to make a decision—but please consult your financial advisor first! If you, like me, intend to have 30 years of

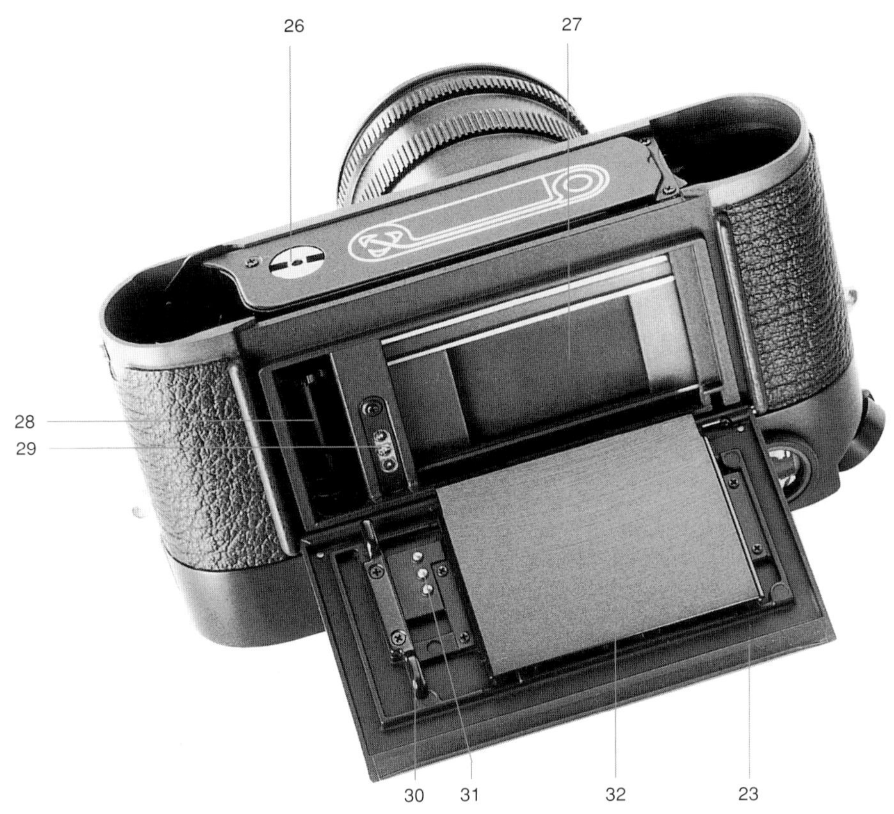

23—Rear flap
26—Coupling for Leica Winder-M
27—Rubberised-cloth shutter
28—Sprocketed film transport drum
29—Contacts corresponding to 31, transmit ISO value to the exposure meter
30—Film guides
31—Contacts for the ISO setting dial
32—Film pressure plate

success with your M6 TTL, a second one will only strain your budget by an additional £5 per month.

The M6 TTL viewfinder shows a bit more subject than the frame for its shortest focal lengths, both in the 0.72x and 0.85x versions. One can therefore see unwanted cars or people entering the image in time to avoid taking the shot. The viewfinder on the M6 with a magnification ratio of 0.85x shows slightly less than the image area of a 28mm lens. With a bit of practice, one can estimate the image area of a 28mm lens if time does not permit mounting the 28mm finder on the camera.

The various frames reflected into the viewfinder, depending on the mounted lens, are very accurate outlines of the corresponding sections of the subject area that will be cast on the film by the appropriate lens. If one is shooting from the same position, the perspective does not change with different lenses, the proportions between the various subject

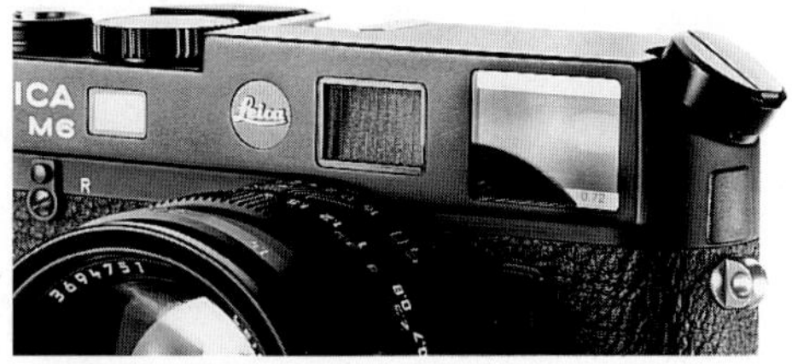

The three windows of the Leica M6 TTL. On the left is the rangefinder window, in the middle over the lens is the window to illuminate the viewfinder frames, and the large window on the right is for the viewfinder. On the silvered strip at the base of the viewfinder window is inscribed 0,72x or 0,85x to indicate the camera model.

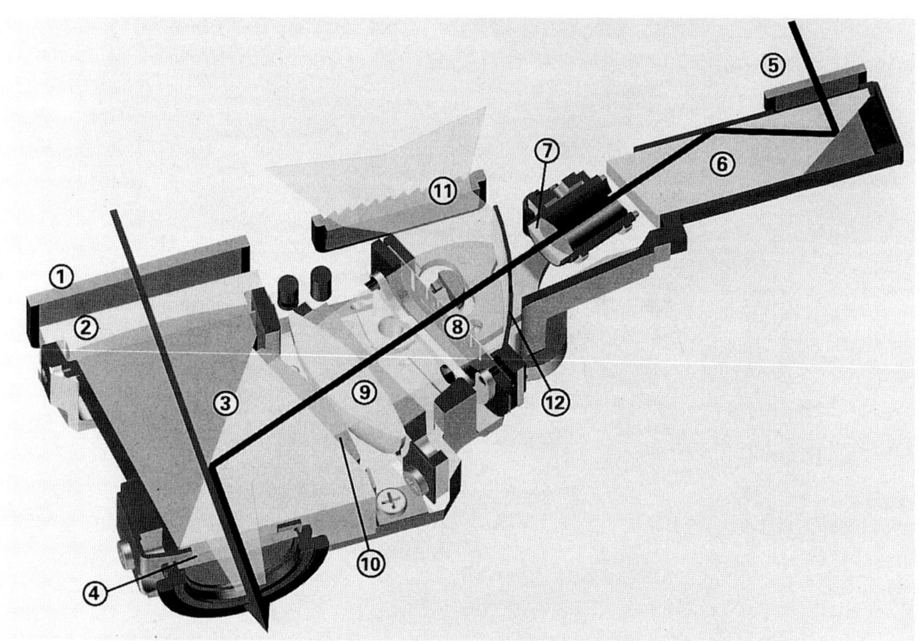

The hidden life of the Leica M-cameras' viewfinder system, a mechanical-optical masterpiece, consisting of 104 high-precision mechanical and optical components, more complex than the viewfinder of a reflex camera.

A viewfinder optic (1) consisting of a flat lens with a negative refraction index (2) and splitting prism (3). eyepiece (4), rangefinder window (5). pentaprism inverts the light coming from (5) to produce an image that is right-side-up and left-right correct (6). swivelling measuring optic (7). viewfinder frame masks (8). optical system (9, 10) that takes the rangefinder image from (7) and the viewfinder frames via the prism (3) into the eyepiece (4). window to illuminate the viewfinder frames (11). concave mirror (12) that redirects the light coming through window (11) onto the projection frames (8).

planes remains the same. But each section of a subject area taken with a longer or shorter focal length has its own appeal—and this is an important lesson in image creation. The proportions between elements in a subject only change if one changes one's vantage point without changing focal length.

The viewfinder of the Leica M6 TTL is the last word in mechanical and optical design in camera manufacture. Had Oskar Barnack's successors not developed it between 1950 and 1954, it probably would not have had a chance of being designed today. Its 104 individual parts, its optical system consisting of four lens elements and two prisms, as well as the two 0.06mm and 0.08mm thin masks for the reflected frames, resist all attempts at automated assembly. Only careful manual labour allows all these parts to be fashioned into a mechanical-optical masterpiece. The precision of the rangefinder is the sum of the precision of its component parts: unlike the image of the subject that is visible by looking straight into the large viewfinder window, the small boundary details captured by the rangefinder have to travel a longer distance through the refraction prisms and hence appear slightly smaller in the viewfinder image. An intermediate optic magnifies this detail image to the same size as the viewfinder image (the minute size difference between the two images could have a negative effect on achieving critical sharpness for some subjects).

Two 0.06 and 0.08mm thin masks take care of reflecting the frames for the M6/0.72x viewfinder focal lengths of 28, 35, 50, 75, 90 and 135mm. The frames appear in pairs: 50 + 75mm, 28 + 90mm, 35 + 135mm. In the M6 with 0.85x magnification, the pairs are 35 + 135mm and 50 + 75mm while the 90mm frame appears on its own. This system is not confusing, even for someone who is holding the M6 for the first time: the larger of the two frames always corresponds to the shorter focal length, while the smaller one represents the longer focal length. You are always aware of which lens is mounted on the camera because you know your equipment and can tell with the tips of your fingers which lens it is. Also, most lenses can be seen in the bottom right-hand corner of the viewfinder.

Small detents in the bayonet ring of the lens control the selection of the image frames. You can use the image frame selector to choose which frame is reflected into the viewfinder, independently of the lens currently in use. This is a useful tool for determining which lens will provide the best result for the current subject without having to mount them all in turn. The frame for the 135mm lens is, however, very small, even in the M6 with a magnification of 0.85x. In order to judge the subtle details of a distant subject accurately, a bit of concentration and even imagination is required. The small image in the viewfinder does not have the same telephoto characteristics evident with reflex cameras. But believe me: an alert eye and an engaged imagination will allow you to capture the subject just as effectively with the M6 and a 135mm lens as you could with the 135 on a Leica R3, R6 or R8. After almost 40 years of shooting with the Leica M3 and M6 and almost 20 years with the Leica R3 and R6, I know what I'm talking about. Use of a 135mm lens is simplified greatly with the Elmarit-M 135mm f/2.8 with its viewfinder spectacles—but it is no longer available: the new APO Telyt-M 135mm f/3.4 replaces it also does the Tele-Elmar-M 135mm f/4.

The official name for the aforementioned spectacles is "viewfinder attachment." It magnifies the viewfinder image 1.5 times. Depending on the magnification factor of the M6 TTL's viewfinder itself, 0.72x or

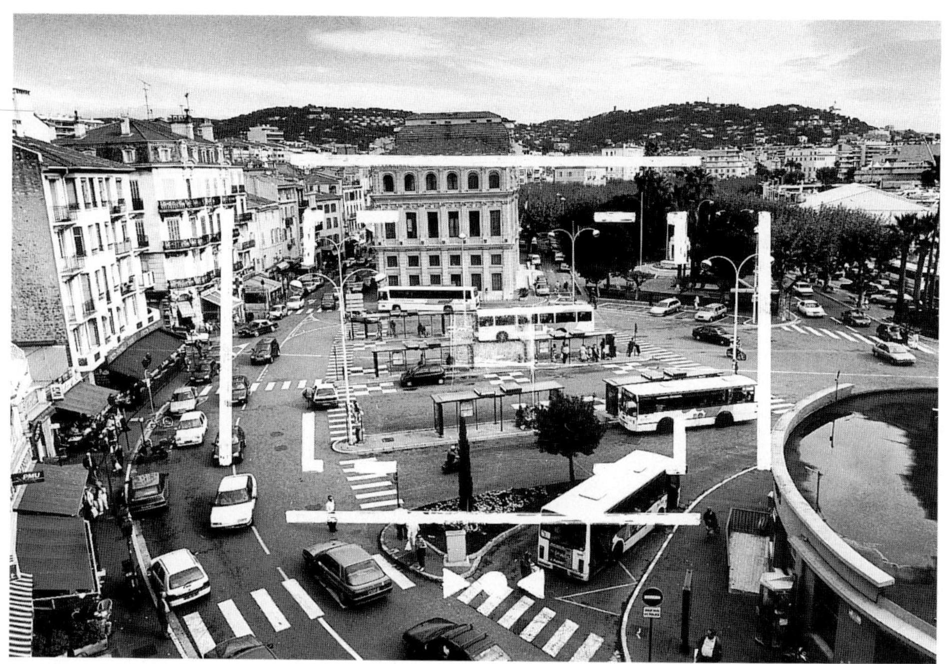

50 mm + 75 mm

When a lens is locked onto the M6, a lever causes the correct projected frame to appear in the viewfinder. In the M6 with the 0.72x viewfinder magnification, there are always two projection frames that appear simultaneously: 50mm + 70mm, 28mm + 90mm, 35mm + 135mm. The somewhat brighter field of the rangefinder appears in the centre of the projection frame. At the lower edge of the viewfinder image, the LED's for the exposure metering seem to "float." One can use the projection frame selector to project any desired frames into the viewfinder image regardless of which lens.is fitted.

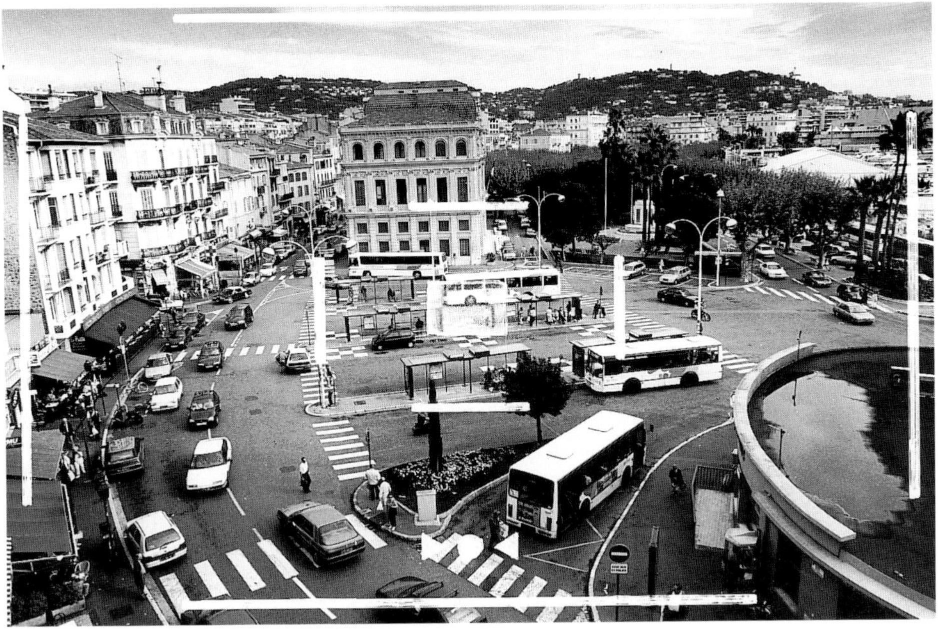

28 mm + 90 mm

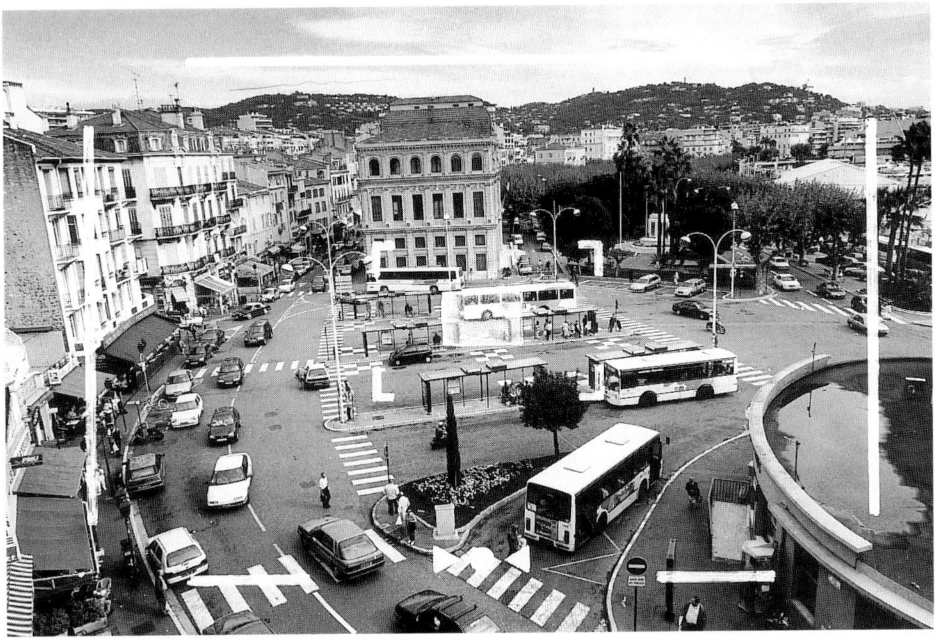

35 mm + 135 mm

0.85x, the result is that the image which appears in the 90mm frame paired with the 135mm frame is magnified by a factor of 1.08 or 1.28. The Elmarit-M 135mm f/2.8 is, however, heavier and, thanks to the spectacles, larger than the APO-Telyt-M 135mm f/3.4. But anyone who likes working with the 135mm should grab this last chance to get a viewfinder magnifier and buy an Elmarit 135mm f/2.8. This lens could soon become a sought-after item.

The viewfinder of the Leica M6 TTL is not plagued by the blackout created by the moving mirror in a reflex camera. One can therefore keep an eye on the image right up until the moment of exposure to avoid capturing unwanted trespassers in the image. Also, the viewfinder image in the M6 TTL 0.72x is so much larger than the 28mm frame that you can even see intruders before they enter the frame. The same holds true for the 35mm frame in the M6 TTL 0.85x. If you are shooting with flash, you can see the scene "frozen" by its illumination. The viewfinder in a reflex camera cannot show this for you because it is dark at the moment the flash fires.

Small Tricks with the Viewfinder Frames

The reflected frames that appear in the viewfinder according to the lens or the frame selection lever are more than just white lines that correspond to the image projected onto the film. There are a few tricks concealed in the sets of lines. One rule of imaging geometry states that a lens will project a slightly smaller section of the subject onto the film at its closest focusing point than it will when focused at infinity—an eye right at the keyhole sees more of the interior of the room than an eye 30cm away from said keyhole. This "image shrinkage" is negligible with short focal lengths. With a 50mm lens, the loss is about 12%, whilst with a 135mm lens focused at 150cm, the loss rises to a significant 20%. This is where the first trick of the reflected frames comes in. The inside of the white lines corresponds to the image that will appear on a framed slide when the lens is at its closest focusing point. The outside edges of the lines correspond to the subject area captured at a distance of two metres. The closer the lens is focused to infinity, the larger the subject area outside the white lines that will be captured on film—at infinity, about three line-breadths more than the indicated area. This condition guarantees that in the worst case, the entire image contained within the lines will appear on the film.

I must say that in my extensive experience with the Leica M3 and M6, I never gave a thought to the three-line-breadth increase in the image area at infinity and still managed to capture exactly what I wanted on film. The viewfinder image on most reflex cameras shows less than what actually appears on film.

Since the optical axis of the lens and image is located a few centimetres diagonally below the viewfinder, the Leica M6 displays a degree of viewfinder parallax: the lens sees a slightly different, somewhat lower and to the left, section of the subject than you see when you look through the viewfinder. Basic rangefinder cameras use a smaller viewfinder frame to compensate for image shrinkage and parallax. But the Leica M-cameras can do better: a sensor monitoring the focusing cam on the lens mount also controls the position of the reflected frame in the viewfinder, as well as in the rangefinder, along the top-left to bottom-right diagonal. The viewfinder parallax is so well corrected that you can make use of the entire frame when the lens is focused at its minimum distance. You can test the function of the parallax adjustment by mounting the M6 on a tripod and focusing from infinity to close-up and back again. Or you can remove the lens from the M6, look into the viewfinder and carefully press against the sensor with your fingertip. A spring pushes the sensor to the front to the close-up position—the reflected frame therefore moves from bottom-right to top-left when pressure is applied to the sensor.

The central window of frosted glass illuminates the image frames. The large window is the viewfinder. The mirrored stripes at the upper and lower edges ensure that one can read the LED displays clearly under all lighting conditions. The projection lens of the rangefinder, moves in response to movement in the focusing helicoid, and “sees” the subject through the little window on the outside.

A magnification ratio of 0.72x or 0.85x exists over the entire viewfinder image of the one or other Leica M6 TTL models. The image area visible outside the M6/0.72x 28mm frame is smaller than the image area of the Elmarit-M 24mm f/2.8 ASPH. If time does not allow the mounting of the the 24mm finder, one can learn to guess the image area of the 24mm with a bit of practice. More reliable results are achieved using the special bright-line finder. If you don’t need the accessory shoe for a small flash unit, the 24mm viewfinder can stay there permanently. It does not interfere with the use of the rangefinder.

In the M6/0.85x viewfinder, the image you see surrounding the 35mm frame is only slightly smaller than the image area of a 28mm lens. You could therefore estimate the image composition for the 28mm lens in the viewfinder without running too big a risk of cutting off some important elements at the edge of the frame.

There is another feature of the Leica M6 TTL rangefinder. You can grab a reflex camera wherever and however you want—except by the front element of the lens and the eyepiece. If you are equally reckless with the M6, you will quickly have a plentiful selection of fingerprints on the three viewfinder windows. They are not terribly distracting on the central window. Fingerprints on the viewfinder and rangefinder windows obscure the viewfinder image and interfere with the distance metering. So train your fingers not to stray on the windows and to stay away from them when focusing!

You may think these are not be the best parameters for fast-action photography. The speedwith which one can react with a Leica M-camera has been proven by the amazing shots taken by both famous and unknown photographers over the past 45 years. You will have this routine with the M6 mastered much faster than a basic course in computers. Thanks to its hump-, bump- and wrinkle-free shape, the Leica M6 lies so securely in your hand that you can risk hand-held shots that you would avoid with a reflex camera.

The Leica M6 TTL with a higher viewfinder magnification of 0.85x has the following projection frames: 50mm + 75mm, 90mm, 35mm + 135mm. Since the image area for a 28mm lens is larger than the entire viewfinder image, there is no frame for a 28m.

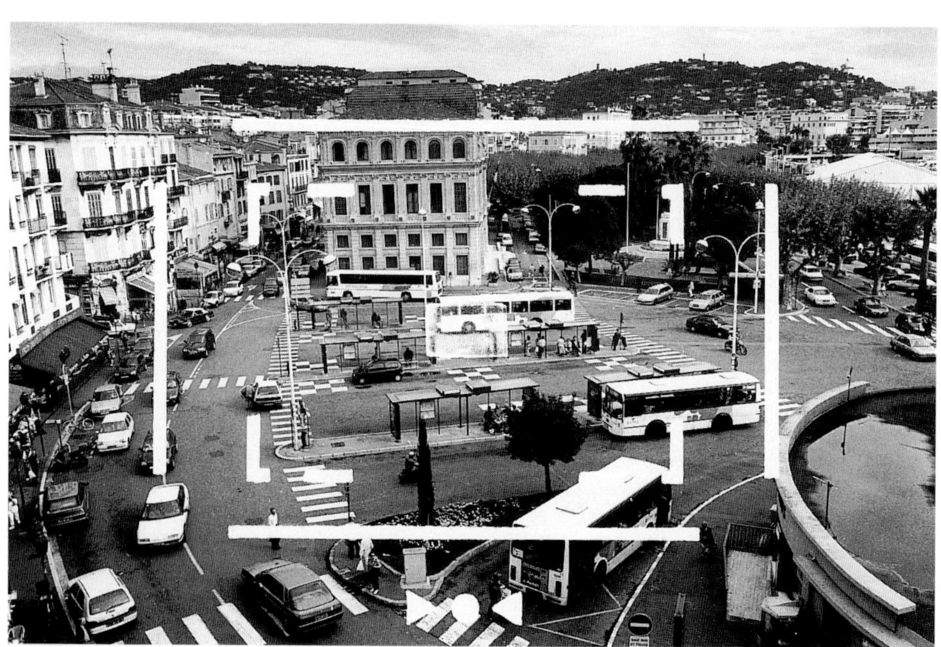

50 mm + 75 mm

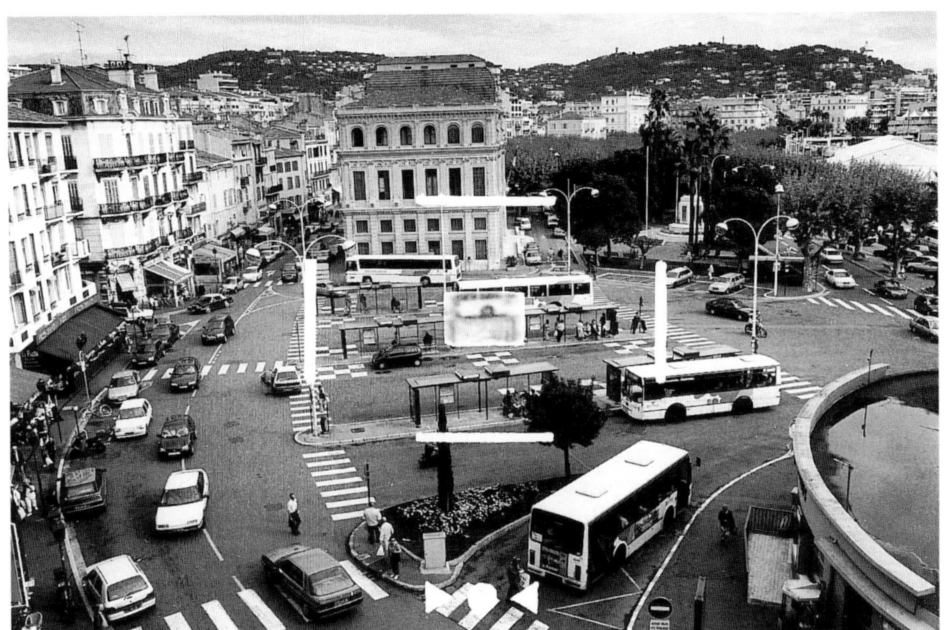

90 mm

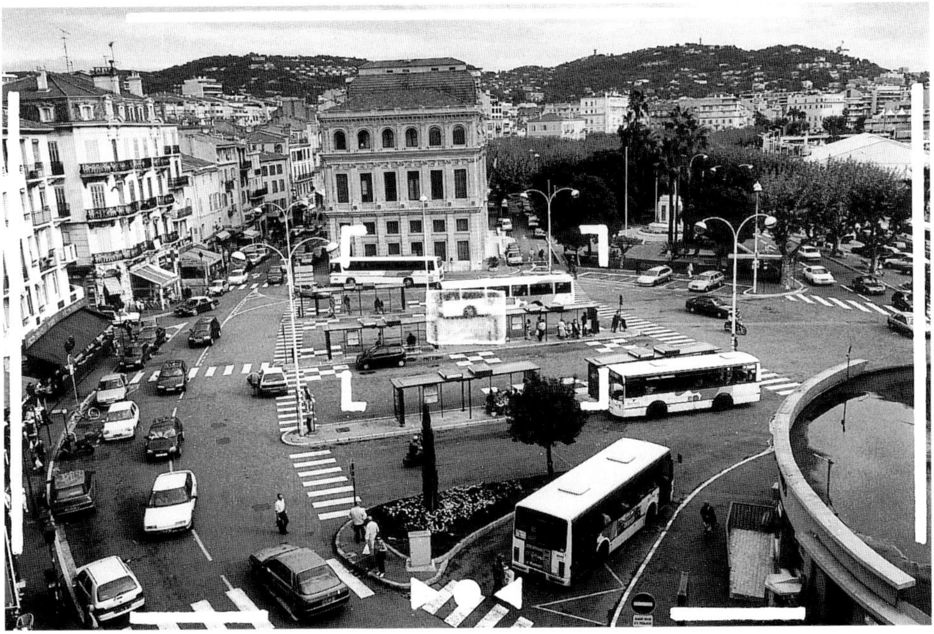

35 mm + 135 mm

Leica M6-TTL = Long-base Rangefinder

Mechanical-optical rangefinders work on the principle of triangulation. Their effectiveness and accuracy depend on the length of the measuring base. The Leica M6 TTL rangefinder works on this principle and follows the same rules. Two measuring optics, one of which is movable, look forward towards the subject and the distance between them determines the measuring base. On the Leica M6 TTL, the mechanical measuring base, the distance between the centre of the large viewfinder window and the rangefinder window, is 69.25mm. With a 0.72x magnification ratio, the optical (=effective) measuring base is 49.9mm long. On the 0.85x sister model, the metering base is 58.9mm long. The movable measuring optic is hidden behind the small rangefinder window, while the other one is made up of the elements in the large viewfinder. A combination prism/lens element system reflects the image of the small subject area created by the movable measuring optic into the bright metering field in the centre of the viewfinder.

If the two measuring optics aimed at the subject are as parallel as railway tracks, the two axes do not intersect and the two images appear coincident with each other so only a single image is apparent in the measuring field, then the lens is focused at infinity. This is an unquantifiable infinity and only has a theoretical relevance to our interest in photographic distance metering. the subject will not really be at the far edge of the universe. The point of infinite focus for a particular lens is significantly closer, usually at a distance that can be covered by foot.

With the APO-Telyt-M 135mm f/3.4, the Summicron-M 90mm f/2, the Summicron-M 50mm f/2.0 and the Super-Angulon-M 21mm f/3.4, I have noticed repeatedly that the edges of objects further away than 1000m appear directly on top of each other in the viewfinder. A mere 1mm (!) rotation of the focusing ring towards the close-focus end makes the wall of the house located so far away display clearly evident double images.

Turning the focusing ring from infinity to close-up causes the barrel of the optical head, or a projecting bar attached to it in the case of longer focal length lenses, to withdraw into the outer lens barrel. The rangefinder's spring-loaded sensor follows its movement exactly and thereby turns the measuring optics from their default setting at infinity. When the image from the rangefinder of a line, an edge or a contour in the subject, coincides exactly with the corresponding part of the subject image in the viewfinder, then the lens will be precisely focused on that feature. Any features in the subject which are out of focus will be seen as a double image. The precise transmission of the focusing movement on the lens, via the sensor to the

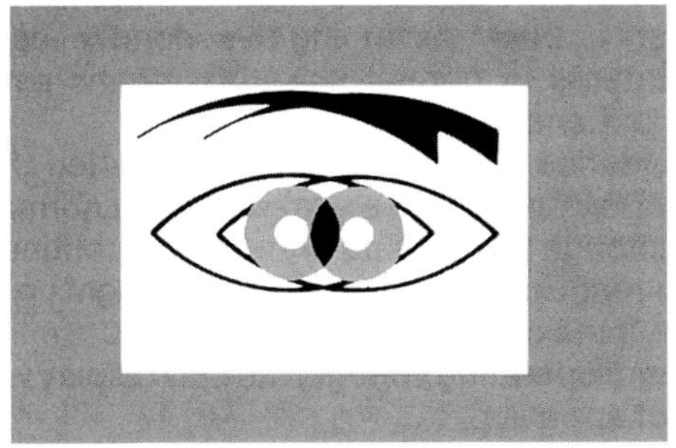

Out of focus

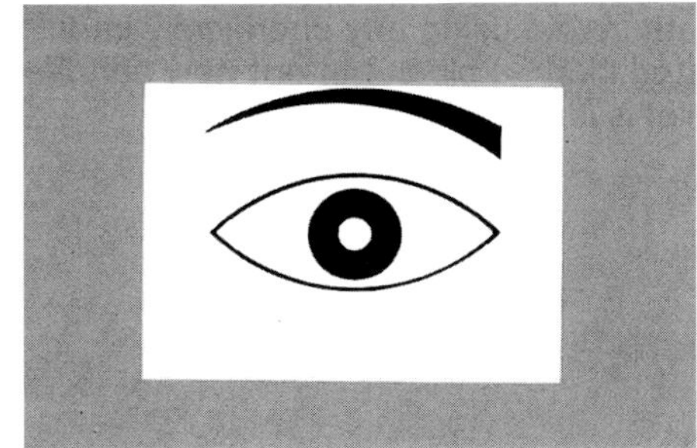

In Focus

Focusing using the coincidence method:
Using the M-lens's focusing ring, one causes the double-image of the part of the subject on which one wishes to focus to merge into a single image.

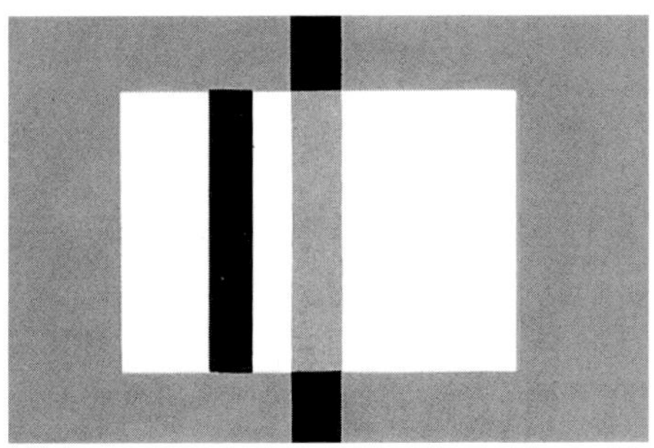

Out of focus

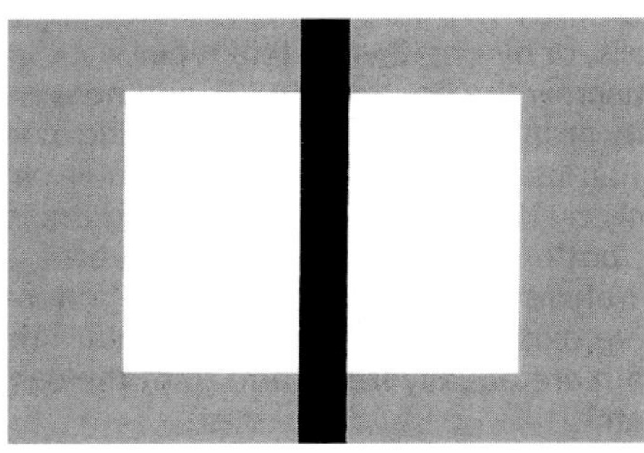

In focus

Focusing using the split-image method:
When the distance setting is incorrect, the lines passing through the rangefinder image from top to bottom will be "cut off" at the upper and lower edges of the metering field and will appear shifted. Turning the lens's focusing ring until the lines match up means that the lens is focused on that line.

turning measuring optics will guarantee that the subject details whose double image you united into one are in focus.

Uniting the double-images visible in the rangefinder into one image, coincidence-type, is one method for focusing the lens. The other is similar to the split-image method used on reflex cameras and is useful when focusing on subjects with vertical lines or narrow subjects such as flower stalks. When focusing, check the upper and lower edges of the measuring field's crisp outline. If the line passes through the viewfinder and measuring field without bends or interruptions, the subject is in focus. This split-image method is just as fast and accurate as the coincidence method. Since one can combine the two methods, the Leica M6 TTL rangefinder will only ever meet two subjects it cannot handle. These are completely smooth, structureless, contrastless and shadowless surfaces, and lines running parallel to the upper and lower edges of the measuring field, such as Venetian blinds.

On the other hand, the images in the rangefinder field are so precise that one can focus on edges that intersect with the measuring field at an angle of as little as 30°. In my 39 years of photography with the Leica M3 and M6, I encountered about twenty or thirty subjects with these kinds of rangefinding problems. A scratch in the finish, a crack in the sandstone, the head of a screw were usually enough of a reference for the rangefinder.

A subject located at "infinity" will exhibit noticeable double edges with a slight turn of the focus ring. At the other extreme, one can focus quite easily on, say, typewriter text at a distance of about one meter thanks to the brightness and brilliance of the viewfinder. This is true, regardless of the focal length of the lens, for any M-lens as the viewfinder magnification ratio is constant. We practising photographers will be forever indebted to the Leica designers who endowed the M6 rangefinder with its practically eternal precision. My first Leica M3 and its Summicron 50mm f/2—no "M" then since the "R" was a few years in the future—were made in 1960. They have survived all the tortures of sandstorms in the dunes of Sylt and salt spray in the Atlantic breakers. In mounting the 39-year-old Summicron onto the 1999 Leica M6, and mounting the 1999 Noctilux-M 50mm f/1 onto the 1960 Leica M3, I did not notice the slightest loss of accuracy in either of the old/new combinations. Will we be able to say the same of present-day high-tech AF reflex cameras in 25 years?

Which One is More Precise?

The Leica M6 TTL rangefinder or a reflex camera with a split-image indicator, or autofocus? The precision of the mechanical-optical rangefinder is a function of the length of its measuring base. The Leica M6 TTL 0.72x effective optical measuring base is 49.9mm, while its companion model, the M6/0.85x, is 10mm longer at 59.8mm. These values are determined by the 69.25mm distance between the measuring optics multiplied by the viewfinder magnification. These measuring base lengths are true for all M-series lenses, with the following exception: the 1.5x magnifying viewfinder attachment that came with the now discontinued Elmarit-M 135mm f/2.8 increases the effective measuring base to 74mm for the Leica M6/0.72x and 88mm for the M6/0.85x and thereby markedly increases the measuring accuracy.

The effective measuring base for the split-image indicator in a reflex camera is a function of the geometric-optical relationship of focal length, the unimpaired size of the lens's opening at maximum aperture (lenses in which the focusing operation is performed at maximum aperture are the most prevalent) and the diameter of the indicator on the focusing screen. The diameter of the indicator is always a compromise. In order to take full advantage of the large diameter of a fast lens, the indicator would have to be much larger than normal—and would have an adverse effect on subject composition and focus control on the ground glass. A larger indicator, on the other hand, would be partially dark behind a slower lens with a smaller internal opening. The result is that most split-field indicators have a diameter between four and six millimetres. Their effective measuring base is also determined by the focal length of the lens and the viewfinder eyepiece. The interaction of these factors means that the effective measuring base of a reflex camera is roughly proportional to the square of the focal length of the lens. Small differences in the calibration of the viewfinder eyepiece in different camera models lead to negligible differences in the measuring bases of different cameras with the same focal length lenses. The values in the table can thus only be average values:

At a focal length of about 115mm, the effective measuring base is the same as the M6/0.72x, while at about 120mm the metering base is longer than that of the M6/0.85x. For shorter focal lengths, it is smaller and the M6 has the clear advantage, whereas the reflex camera has the advantage with longer focal lengths. With the "spectacles" Elmarit-M 135mm f/2.8, the M6/0.72x and M6/0.85x have the advantage over reflex cameras with a 135mm lens

The autofocus system of a 35mm reflex camera, and the distance between its metering beams, is also dependent on the maximum opening of the lens. In addition, the light has to pass through the partially reflective reflex mirror, the metering field boundaries, and the image splitters before reaching the approximately

Effective Measuring Base for Split-image Indicator in a Reflex Camera

Focal length mm	Effective base length mm
21	1.63
28	2.78
50	9.82
90	29.20
135	65.70

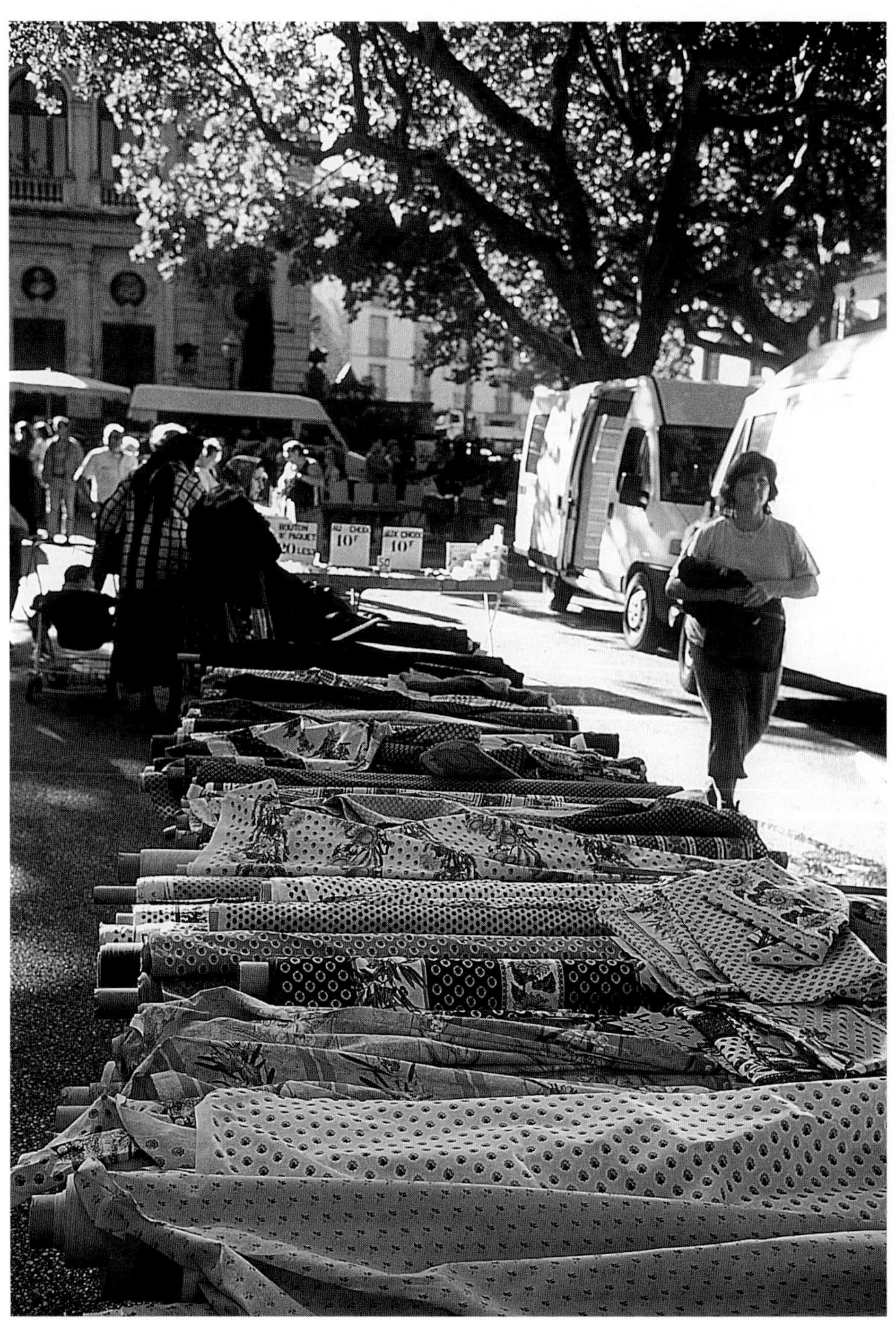
10F
10F
50

5mm-long AF sensors. One can assume that the measuring base for autofocus 35mm reflex cameras is not significantly different from that of a non-AF 35mm SLR. In terms of the measuring base alone, the Leica M6 TTL offers a higher degree of accuracy, particularly with fast lenses with focal lengths below 120mm, than AF reflex cameras since the latter only use a portion of the lens opening for distance metering.

The M6 TTL viewfinder with its reflected image frames, even under poor lighting conditions, is also noticeably brighter than the viewfinder of a reflex camera, even with a f/1.2 lens on the bayonet. The M6 TTL therefore offers excellent definition of detail in available-light photography with fast lenses, when darkness is almost complete, and precise focus is the top priority! Absolute focus was and remains the domain of the Leica M-cameras: at a distance of 3m, the Summilux-M 75mm f/1.4 at an aperture of f/1.4 offers a depth of focus from 2.93 to 3.07m—narrow enough for an expressive portrait and perhaps too narrow to determine exactly the position of the plane of focus under low light on a ground glass screen. The Leica M6 TTL rangefinder does not have this problem!

Short focal length and close distance—this makes the Provençal bolts of material appear large in front of the background which indicates the context. Summicron-M 35mm f/2.

The unique precision of the M6 TTL rangefinder does not help if one cannot see the details in the viewfinder clearly. The split-image method, however, allows even those with somewhat poor vision to focus accurately. Thanks to the wonderful design of the viewfinder, calibrated to –0.5 dioptres, photographers wearing glasses can still see the entire viewfinder image. A narrow rubber baffle around the eyepiece protects the lenses from scratches. Someone who only wears glasses in certain situations can screw accessory correction lenses onto the eyepiece. These are available from +3.0 to –3.0 dioptres in half-dioptre increments. They also have a rubber baffle to prevent scratches.

Some writers insist that one of the disadvantages of an autofocus camera is also present in the Leica M6: namely that focusing is always tied to the centre of the viewfinder image. If one would like to position the main subject elsewhere than in the middle of the frame to create better image composition, one has to use focus lock on the AF reflex camera. However, if the user does not have full and perfect control over his or her finger, the camera could well refocus on the wrong detail after the camera has been moved to compose the picture. The Leica M6, on the other hand, maintains a selected focus setting until you focus on a different target by adjusting the lens.

A constant stream of critics insist that the Leica designers should have turned the M3's unique rangefinder into a true-image viewfinder for the M6 over 25 years ago. Such a viewfinder would show the image captured by the currently mounted lens on a viewfinder image whose size remained constant, much like the zoom-viewfinder found on some compact cameras. But what these critics fail to do is provide a method for changing the viewfinder's optics to suit the current lens via the existing bayonet, which cannot be changed, such that the exact image area of the lens is shown on the entire viewfinder while maintaining the rangefinder's accuracy. The top three criteria which designers had to follow in the development of the Leica from the M3 to M4 and M5 to the M6 alone form insurmountable obstacles to the development of a zoom-type range-finder: the "new model" cannot be larger or heavier, must maintain the age-old ergonomic feel and cannot become more complicated or noisier! It has to be as easy to use, as robust, as reliable and as precise as the "old" one!

Any designer assigned the task of developing a zoom-rangefinder under these conditions would, after careful consideration, turn the computer off and go fishing. The chances of catching the big one are much better out there. There is a world of difference between complaining and doing. If you feel a twinge of regret the next time you look through the M6 TTL viewfinder, wondering if you spent your money wisely, remember that you have one big advantage over the designer: you don't have any trouble with the rangefinder. Maybe the Leica M5 did not enjoy a long life because it did not adhere to the prerequisites?

How Professional is the Leica M6 TTL?

Given the variety of 35mm reflex cameras that are advertised to the public as "pro" and "pro-system," one cannot avoid this question, regardless of whether one covets the M6/0.72x or M6/0.85x. The fact that the Leica M6, with or without TTL, or the M2 to M5 are absolutely professional cameras is not disputed—even the Eskimos know that by now. At some point or other they no doubt encountered a researcher, reporter or geologist using a Leica-M. This is already the first step in proving professional equipment—real shooting under any and all conditions: the Leica M6 and its lenses can survive temperatures as low as –20° C without any special handling. However, you should then load the M6 with lithium batteries rather than silver-oxide ones. At low temperatures even a lithium battery is somewhat reluctant to share its energy, but the silver-oxides are much more reticent. The slower reaction times of the metering system are also true of any electronic function. Those who wish to use their M6 TTL and its lenses in colder conditions, can and should have their equipment adjusted at the factory. These are characteristics of a professional camera system. All sensitive components contained in the Leica M6 TTL are enclosed by a cast metal housing whose very shape provides stability. The flange focal distance, the distance between the bayonet and the film plane, is maintained even under the most adverse conditions. The hardened chrome camera bayonet can survive thousands of lens mountings—even further proof of a professional camera system.

The pro who is not over-careful with his equipment will appreciate this: there are no levers, posts or bumps sticking out the back of Leica M-lenses: one can stand an M-lens up on its bayonet! Should hurried, rough handling create scratches in the bayonet flanges, they won't affect the secure mount of the lens on the M6.

The Leica M6 TTL rubberised-blind focal-plane shutter, with its 40+ years of production, is the quintessence of precision. It is not the fastest focal-plane shutter in the world, but it is by far the quietest and the one that gives rise to the least vibration—a very important factor in the professional credentials of the M6 TTL! In a reflex camera, the combination of shutter, mirror and aperture blades combine to generate the equivalent of a drum beat in the stillness of a cathedral.

The Leica M6 is fast in its own way: not in the speed of its shutter but in the speed of its reactions: a 1/4000sec. fast shutter speed is tempered by the time elapsed between pressing the release and the actual shot. It takes between 100 and 180 milliseconds to meter the exposure, set the aperture and/or shutter speed, automatically focus the lens, close the aperture and flip the reflex mirror up. If the photographer wants to capture an optimal shot of fast-paced action, he or she has to press the trigger that much earlier. Even the Leica M6 TTL has its shutter release time-parallax. It is only 10 to 12 milliseconds short as its trigger releases the shutter directly. The M6 is at least 10 times faster than a reflex camera; it offers "just-in-time" photography. Professional photographers love cameras that react quickly.

A simple experiment will show you how fast you are with the M6. Hang an object about the same weight as the Noctilux-M 50mm f/1 on a dark string close to a light background. Mark the vertical null position with a clear black line. Now pull the pendulum one meter to the side, let it swing freely and then try to take a picture from about two to three metres of the Noctilux or whatever object you chose when it hits the null position. In the interests of a fast shutter speed, use a high-speed b&w film which you can develop according to your proven methods. A good loupe will show from the negatives by how much you missed the mark, how much earlier or later you have to fire to capture the string on the line. I don't know if one can shorten the 1/30s it takes for a message from the grey cells to reach the fingers with training. I think it's possible—the M6 will then react even faster.

The Leica M6 displays information regarding the shutter speed, aperture and distance setting using mechanical elements. A glance into the viewfinder says it all, no additional button-pushing required. Touching the release while looking into the viewfinder will also tell you if the selected data are still adequate for the current situation. Carried in the right hand, with the fingers around the end of the camera and the thumb on the release, you can take indirectly aimed shots, just like James Bond does through his jacket pocket. Your degree of success is, naturally, better with a wide-angle lens than with a 135mm telephoto. You have to guess the distance and select the exposure values in advance. A slightly closed aperture takes care of additional depth of field. For a 35mm lens, the following holds: the width of the subject that can be captured in the horizontal format is about the same as the distance to the subject—this should be guessed as accurately as possible. The height of the captured image is, given the scale of the small format film, about two-thirds of the width of the subject. For vertical shots: the subject can be as tall as the distance to it but only two-thirds of the distance wide. Aiming at the centre of the subject from the wrist is simply a question of practice. Since one carries the M6 TTL in such a manner for these palm shots that the thumb is on the release, the advance lever is between the thumb and the palm so that the thumb can quickly and easily advance the camera to the next frame.

There are two essential prerequisites for this style of photography: practice, practice, practice to get the subject in the centre of the frame, and use colour or b&w negative films rather than slide films because one can still trim and straighten the shot in the darkroom. Here is yet another advantage of the M6 TTL on the professional scale: thanks to the rangefinder's 69.25mm long measuring base, the only spot available for the eyepiece is the outermost left end of the housing—a great spot for practical purposes. In the horizontal format, the camera can be held up to the right eye, giving the nose lots of room to stick out to the left of the camera. Vertically, the nose can be located to the upper right or bottom left of the housing. There is always enough room between the photographer's head and the camera to advance the film without having to remove the camera from the eye.

All these professional qualities of the Leica M6 TTL do not answer the question as to whether such a rangefinder principle can still be accorded the term "professional" when faced with the completely different and, in a few respects, far more versatile reflex system. The only response, after careful examination of all facets, has to be yes! This rangefinder is the whispering alternative to the albeit high-quality but noisy aperture and reflex mirror system. The M6 is the unobtrusive, barely audible camera that is simply a necessity to record events from close-up without intruding. If you find yourself complaining that you cannot hear the subject of a television interview for all the clicking and banging of motorised reflex cameras, when the flash illumination completely annihilates the image, then you will know what intrusive photography is. One has to ask oneself: have these reporters never heard of the Leica M6 and its high-speed lenses? They should be required for such situations! What is apparently true in some states in the United States: if one is allowed to take pictures in court at all, then it can only be with Leica M-cameras! If that is not a testament to the professional nature of the Leica M6 then what is?

A Word About the Quality of the M6 TTL

The testing of equipment and reporting the results is a favourite pastime in magazines and newspapers. The results are not very positive for us users. If one tests one camera and one or two lenses out of a yearly production run of ten to one hundred thousand pieces, the result is only a "snapshot." If the test report is favourable, the product is given an A+ while the quality control officer's desk at the manufacturer may be littered with dozens of units that have been returned because of a flaw that had not come to light during the course of a relatively short test because the problem only manifests itself after a period of prolonged use. If this were not the case, recall notices for products such as cars would not be a daily occurrence, despite millions invested in exhaustive testing before the first production model rolled off the assembly line. There will always be the chance anywhere that humans work, or machines are programmed, that errors will creep in and not be noticed for a while. Should the result of such an error fall into the hands of the magazine tester, the product will have a negative image, even though the problem was short-lived. Trying to assess the long-term quality of production models in a one-time test is unrealistic. In-house testing, according to statistically determined quality-control procedures, have to take care of that. Testing each unit of a production run is only possible for very limited runs. Even the tightest quality-control net cannot ensure long, trouble-free service, cannot offer greater precision and reliability. These qualities and the acceptable tolerances have to be part of the design, from the very first

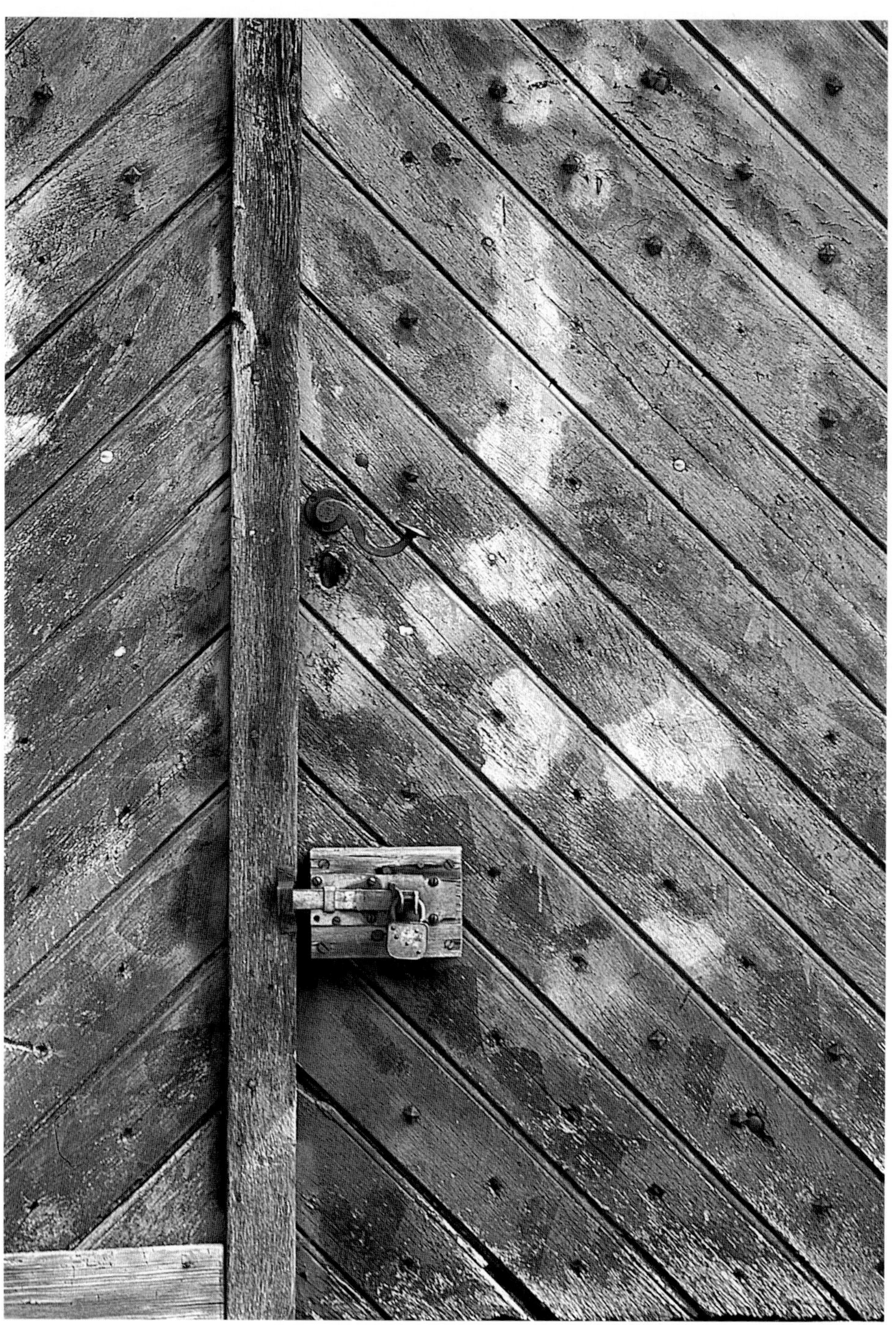

drawing, and then be built into the camera and lens.

Defining the quality of the Leica and its lenses would be a textbook for the highest achievable standards in mechanics and optics. The focal plane shutter, designed in the early fifties, cannot show any wear after 100,000 exposures—it fulfils this requirement splendidly. 100,000 shots, using one 36-exposure film per week, would take 53 years! With one film a day one would hit 100,000 in eight years. Only those who chase 8 films a day through the M6 can achieve 100,000 in one year. To say that the M6 shutter is only warming up after such a marathon is a bit exaggerated, but not completely untrue. Leica cameras whose shutter has been fired over 350,000 times have been sent to the factory and found to be operating within acceptable tolerances. Besides, anyone who values his or her M6 TTL will afford it an inspection after 100,000 shots. If use is sporadic, maybe even once or twice in between.

The Leica and its lenses are designed for reliable operation between +60°C and –20°C. Those who wish to shoot for even a short time at lower temperatures should have the camera adjusted at the factory. One cannot expect the usual quick reactions from the batteries for the exposure meter and its electronics at such low temperatures. At temperatures above +50°C, the photographer and the film will give up long before the mechanics in the camera. The question whether the camera can be adjusted to work at higher temperatures is only of theoretical interest.

Allowing sunlight to hit the exposed front element of the lens can burn a hole in the shutter blinds. This burn-hole risk has existed since the advent of rubberised cloth shutter blinds. Some deny it, but the warning is still valid. I was out walking on October 15th, 1961, in the noonday sun and obtained a prizewinning burn-hole in the blinds of my M3. The repair cost a whopping DM 42.80—today it would be much, much more expensive. The sun-induced burn-hole is therefore a reality, albeit a rare one. You should avoid allowing the sun to strike an unprotected lens.

The Leica M-bayonet can easily survive ten-thousand lens mountings and dismountings. The tiny scratches in the bayonet ring caused by dust do not affect the flange focal distance at all as they are negligible in the massive bayonet mount. Overtaxing the system by bringing the camera and lens into hard contact with their surroundings should be avoided however.

A longer focal length is better for flat subjects.
Elmarit-M 135mm f/2.8.

The Leica quality control system is charged with ensuring that all tolerances, data and performance specifications are met by camera and lens. Should the measured values of the units, taken at random from the production line, vary from those prescribed, the entire production line is halted until the cause can be found. The ability to do this is the direct result of not having thousands of units produced each day on a variety of conveyor belts. The Leica M6 TTL—and R8—are built in small runs using a large degree of manual labour.

A very specialised area of the Leica quality control process is the calibration of the rangefinder for the various lens focal lengths. In theory, this should not be a problem. A lens focused on an object at infinity will be at a distance from the film plane equivalent to its focal length. To focus on a nearer object it must be moved further away from the film plane. For example, a 90mm lens with a closest focusing distance of 1m will move forward 10.6mm when changing focus from infinity to 1m. Lenses of longer focal length will need to travel further, and those of shorter focal length not so much. The moving measuring optic in the rangefinder covers a certain angle of movement between the infinity position and when it is directed at an object 1m away. This angle will be the same regardless of the focal length of the lens fitted to the camera. The angle is adjusted by the spring-loaded mechanical sensor in the bayonet mouth which is moved in or out by the cam in the M-lens. This quantifiable distance must be the same as that traversed by the mechanical sensor on the M lens, which is operated by the focusing movement. The control device on each lens therefore has to be designed so that the sensor arm covers the requisite distance from the infinity position to close-focus while the lens is being focused. In the case of the 90mm lens referred to above the cam moves only about one third of the 10.6mm moved by the lens head.

In practice, even Leica's high-precision manufacturing process has to include tolerances. It could possibly produce one unit at a time that met absolute zero tolerances. But not in a small series and even less when several individual components such as lens, camera and rangefinder are assembled into one system. There will be lenses, therefore, whose focal length is shorter or longer than the nominal focal length. But the rangefinder travels an unchanging distance from infinity to close-focus. The optical engineers therefore match the lens's control device precisely to its effective focal length. This explains why the small brass ring on Leica M-series lenses sometimes looks a bit uneven. Save yourself the trouble of writing a bitter letter concerning quality control: you would simply be pointing out one of the characteristics of the Leica hand-made mystique. An unobtrusive testament to this is a small, two-digit number beside distance scale on an M-lens. It stands for the unavoidable, minimal deviation of the stated focal length from the actual one and the corresponding customisation of the control device. When rangefinder cameras were the norm in camera stores, it is said that proprietors were rather unimpressed with the customisation of control and focal length. After all, the photographer usually shoots at f/5.6 or even f/11 and any focusing errors will disappear in the generous depth of field. However, the maximum aperture of a Leica lens is a true working aperture. In order to use the razor-thin plane of focus obtained so expensively in a fast lens, the control device has to be calibrated exactly to the lens's actual focal length!

Equally high requirements are demanded of the Leica M-lens's helicoids. Leica technicians employ either brass with brass or brass with a special aluminium alloy. The mating surfaces are then ground so precisely that excellent pair-tolerances are achieved. Such matched pairs can only accept a very thin layer of special grease that maintains its consistency and lubrication over a wide range of temperatures. It is no doubt a malicious rumour that some lens manufacturers use a bit more grease to make up for helicoid pairs that do not quite fit each other well enough. This may work until the grease displaces itself under the heat of a tropical sun and causes play in the whole assembly. Leica lenses cannot offer you that diversion, even after ten hot summers.

This should close the chapter on the quality and professionalism of the Leica M6 TTL. Both terms are inseparable from this camera. What other justification can one find for such a significant outlay of cash to obtain such precision and to satisfy to one's heart's desire, particularly in today's society of instant gratification? You can, after all, create impressive pictures with cameras that do not require you to empty your bank account. My answer, after almost 40 years of living with, and in some cases off, the Leica M3/M6 is short and clear: everything! Everything, over and above the mere practical aspects, that manifests itself in the unqualified, unlimited, blind faith in the tool that is the Leica M6. You may consider my answer very personal and unique and regard it skeptically. But I am sure of one thing: yours will be just the same in ten years time when asked the question of what use you had and still expect to have of your high-precision Leica M6 TTL.

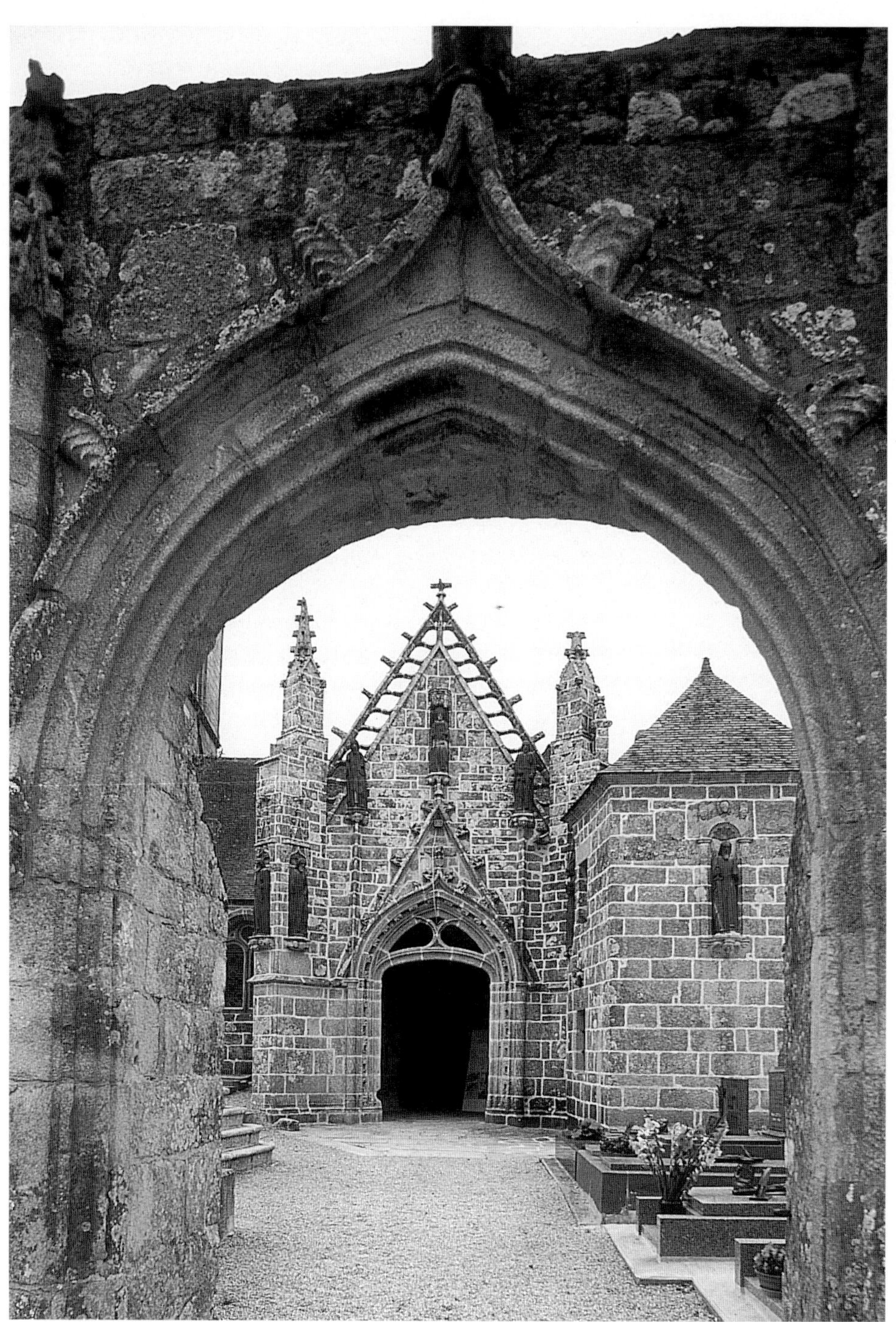

Chapter 2

Leica M6 TTL – Selective Exposure Metering

The provision in a camera of fully automatic exposure metering and a range of subject programs does not alter the fact that good negatives and slides, that can be enlarged easily and show all the subject detail and colour, can only result from the balanced interplay between the light striking the subject and the film sensitivity on the one hand, and an appropriate shutter speed and aperture on the other; in other words, the exposure value. If one of the factors on one side of this equation is changed, then one or both on the other side also has to change accordingly in order to maintain the exposure balance. This holds true in all respects for the multiprogram modes in a high-tech reflex camera: even it can only select any one of a multitude of shutter speed/aperture combinations, based on the exposure value determined from the subject illumination and the film speed.

Bright, diffuse light captures all the details of this Breton architecture on film without any intrusive contrasts. The short focal length creates the through- and overview. Elmarit-M 28mm f/2.8.

Anyone who doubts this should take a multiprogram reflex camera and a hand-held exposure meter to a delicately lit subject. Then put the camera through all its exposure modes and make notes of the shutter speed/aperture combinations it displays in the viewfinder. Then compare them to the data given by the hand-held exposure meter and note all the combinations its calculator-dial offers as corresponding to the reading. Provided the subject illumination did not change during this exercise, you will notice the following: the shutter speed selected in aperture-priority mode, the aperture selected in shutter-priority mode, the shutter speed/aperture combinations displayed in any of the exposure modes, will all correspond exactly to the combinations given by the hand-held meter, and thus to the same exposure value! Any slight differences in metering could be the result of different angles of view, or different weighting of the centre of the image compared to its edges, but these differences are immaterial for this discussion.

The basis of photography can be stated as follows: subject illumination and film speeds are factors that cannot be changed at the moment of the shot. The readily changed variables are the aperture and shutter speed. Two questions result: "how do I meter something?" and "How do I translate the meter reading into an appropriate shutter speed/aperture combination based on the subject and my creative idea?"

The first question is mostly technical in nature, but it does move into the realm of creative photography in the case of extreme lighting conditions. Dividing the metered result is also mainly a technical undertaking: it is also a significant part of the photographer's creative process in turning ideas into pictures.

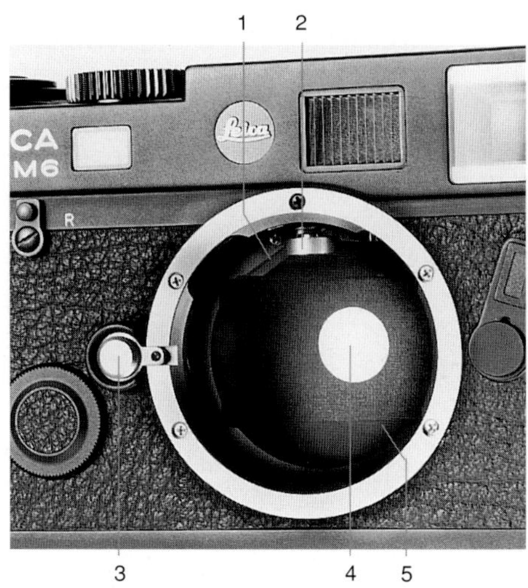

Unchanged for 45 years: the Leica M-bayonet

1. *The silicon photocell for the M6 TTL's exposure meter is hidden behind this to guard against stray light.*
2. *Rangefinder sensor for the helicoid in the M-lens*
3. *Lens lock*
4. *White metering spot, 12mm in diameter (= 13% of the film format) on the first shutter blind. If the silicon-photocell cannot see it, the exposure metering system is off.*
5. *The silicon photocell for TTL flash exposure control is located behind this ledge.*

From Exposure Value to Exposure Appropriate for the Subject

The exposure value is always the base to which you have to adjust the shutter speed and aperture. Structures and colours in the body of the image reflect varying amounts of light back in the direction of the camera. The lens transmits the colours and illumination of the subject onto the film. The brightness of the middle of the subject strikes the 12mm diameter metering disc in the middle of the first shutter blind. Its 113.1 square millimetres are about 13 percent of the 864 square millimetres of the 35mm image area. The metering disc reflects the light striking it onto the silicon photodiode located above and to the left of the bayonet. This, in turn, transmits this brightness as an electronic signal to the M6's metering system. In order for it to correctly evaluate the information and prompt the correct display in the viewfinder, it needs a reference base.

Scientists used the reaction of film to light to come up with the "normal" photographic subject. What it looks like, they didn't say, but it reflects 18% of the light striking it back towards the camera. This reflective quality is the international calibration level for exposure metering systems and is called "neutral grey." How light—or dark—18% grey is can be seen on a grey card. The grey card is the artificial subject used by professional and amateur photographers as a metering base in high-contrast or unusual lighting situations. The grey card is also helpful if one wishes to meter a certain element of the subject from relatively close-up but cannot get close to it. A grey card held about 50cm in front of the lens replaces the unreachable subject detail. It has to face the same way as the subject and cannot have any shadows on it.

The sensitivity of our films is calibrated to this neutral grey. Thanks to accommodating tolerances, they now accept 5% or 6% deviations from this 18% value. In this tolerance around the 18% mark are: tanned skin, wet white sand, dark blue sky, red shingles and a silk dress like it, spring-fresh green grass and leaves, moderate brown fur and feathers

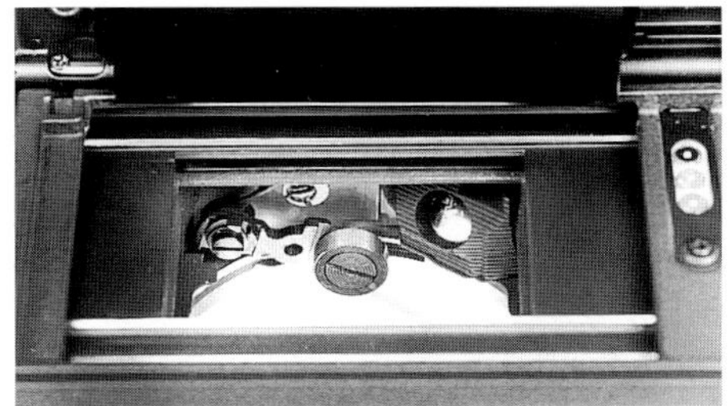

The view from behind through the opened back flap in the M6 TTL. In the centre is the strong sensor lever for the rangefinder, beside it is the bright "eye" of the silicon photocell and on the far right, already out of the depth of field, are the three contacts that connect the camera's electronics to the ISO-dial on the back plate.

and oranges. Should the metering sensor "see" parts of the subject that correspond in brightness or colour to any of these things, the resultant exposure value will ensure that the subject will be captured accurately on the film. Lightly pressing the release causes arrow-shaped and/or dot LED's to appear in the viewfinder. The exposure values metered at this moment are not stored while the release is held at this point! The exposure values are therefore only accurate for the section of the subject that is in the middle of the frame at that moment and using the arrow and dot to select shutter speed and aperture will only be for that spot.

But our range of subjects is not confined to the small tolerance around 18% grey. It stretches from brilliant white at about 95% to black velvet with a mere 0.5% reflection of light. Freshly turned soil is about 5%, light-blue spring sky about 55%, dark tree bark about 10%, dry white sand around 50%, freshly chopped birch logs offer about 38% light reflection—these are but a few examples of the reflection values of our subjects. The M6 TTL exposure metering system calculates the subject illumination using the set film speed to determine the exposure value, and it is this that you have to divide into shutter speed and aperture to create an exposure on the film that is appropriate for the subject.

Black is Black and White is White

Two factors are responsible for the sometimes large differential between physically correct and subject-appropriate exposure: the M6 TTL silicon photocell, like the exposure meter of any other camera, "sees" even the most colourful subject as a series of light-to-dark shades of grey. On top of that, the metering system cannot tell if it is looking at a poorly illuminated light surface or a brightly lit dark one. The M6 TTL compares this impression of grey with its calibrated 18% grey value. Based on the way it has been calibrated, it will react It can only react as follows: with illumination brighter than 18% grey, it will select an exposure value to reduce this subject to neutral grey, while darker subjects will be brightened to this level using exposure values that are too low. The actual shutter speed/aperture combination you select using the dot and arrow is immaterial: the cream-coloured convertible will be just as grey as if it had just survived a 6,000km rally through a lava field, while the old-timer steam locomotive will seem to have been dragged through a bleach-bath.

Both exposures are physically correct but are not appropriate for the subject. Both subjects will only appear correctly on the film if you help them out. As a result, you have to deviate from the physically correct exposure and give the bright subjects more exposure and the dark ones less. For the cream-coloured cabriolet, use the shutter speed dial and/or aperture ring to move the exposure indicator in the viewfinder so that the right arrow lights up at the "0" point as well. This indicates an overexposure of half a stop. Turn the dial further until the "0" point disappears and you have a full stop overexposure. You can capture the cream-white with the desired brilliance on the film. Since you cannot guess this point exactly, open the aperture another stop for a third shot.

Since the Leica M6's shutter speed dial has to click in at the engraved markings, one can only achieve a subtle exposure bracketing using the aperture ring. This does mean one has to sacrifice the desired depth of field—but only by a maximum of a half-stop. This will have no noticeable effect on the image. To increase the exposure by a full stop, you can of course use the shutter speed dial.

On the other hand, a matt black basalt statue, say,will only come into its own in the picture if you correct the physically accurate exposure metering, using the shutter speed and/or aperture dial, onto the side of underexposure. If the left arrow and the "0" point appear, the exposure will be darkened by half a stop. This should make the statue look better in the picture. Maybe an even shorter exposure would do better—you simply have to try by turning the aperture ring another half-stop to the left. As soon as the "0" point disappears, the image is underexposed by a bit more than a full stop.

You can close in on the appropriate exposure for the subject by bracketing. After taking a shot at the metered "0" point, turn the aperture ring in half-stop increments to the left or right without looking at the LED's. If you would rather bracket the exposure using the shutter speed dial, remember that the ring must click in at its engraved markings.

To achieve the physically correct exposure, you simply have to turn the aperture ring or shutter speed dial in the direction indicated by the arrow in the viewfinder. Even the best metering system cannot replace the time-honoured professional method of bracketing the exposure of a scene that differs greatly from a normal subject, whether it be a little or a great deal, depending on the situation. You should adjust the exposure to capture the bright or the dark important elements in the subject, but you will just have to accept the rest of the subject in the manner it appears on the film. How far one can, should or may deviate from the metered exposure without seriously affecting the rest of the subject cannot be calculated. Your concept of the image, your mood, your experience have to be taken into account. However, you can count on it that your neighbour will consider an image thus created as being incorrectly exposed. He would prefer it brighter or darker—taste and mood can be argued about interminably.

Regular use of exposure bracketing is not a waste of film, but rather applied experience, because the Leica M6 TTL precise exposure metering system assumes that all subjects reflect around 18% grey. Exposure bracketing allows one to familiarise oneself with the film, gain valuable experience about the interaction between light, exposure and the reaction of the film, and how all these components combine to create an image. Those who constantly switch from film to film will only learn these things with great difficulty.

No hard and fast rules exist concerning the amount of exposure correction a certain subject requires. But experience offers guidelines for certain situations: landscapes under a high, bright sky, architecture in side or back light, portraits with strong side light, subjects in fog, snowscapes, beach scenes, shots at dusk. A large amount of bright sky or strong side light over architecture and landscapes can require corrections up to two-and-a-half aperture or shutter speed stops, depending on the situation, if one still wants detail in the shadows. Effective back-lit moods, without completely filling in the shadows can perhaps only be obtained with a one-stop over exposure. You simply have to experiment to find out if the matt-black leather seats in the convertible, or the gate weathered to a dark-brown patina, will appear correctly with a one-stop under exposure, or only after one-and-a-half.

Black-on-black subjects in which one still wishes to see subtle nuances defy all recommendations, except this one: starting from exposure data metered from the subject, under-expose in half-stop increments. Directly metered black will always appear too light on film, and a correction to the plus side would simply be a waste of film. For scenes without too much contrast in front of a large, light background, opening the aperture by half or a full stop can be optimal, while the same scene in front of a dark background would require closing the aperture by half or a full stop. Scenes in fog or on snow often need over exposures from 1 to 3 stops.

These recommendations derived from experience are only "correct" if the white metering dot on the first shutter blind of the M6 TTL is overwhelmed by the described brightness conditions. Its size of 13% of the film format, and 13% to 23% percent of the projected frame size, means that the M6 TTL offers spot metering. If the shadow cast by the gate post falls across the hood of the cream-white convertible and then through the metering cell, the exposure meter will not produce the exposure required for the hood of the car. That is why the phrase "up to" appears in the correction recommendations and that means don't be satisfied with just one shot in capturing lighting conditions but rather shoot a small series, particularly if you are using slide film.

From Contrast to Compromise

The appeal of a subject is found in its details, in its contours and in its colours. The contrast in brightness in many subjects is often enough to exceed even the most accommodating contrast range in a film. More than four stops between light and dark, in other words a contrast of 1:32, is more than one should ask of the best colour negative film if one wants detail in the highlights and shadows. Colour slide film will just about manage 6 stops, or a contrast range of 1:64. If the slide is to be printed, however, one should not make full use of this contrast range.

The cream-white cabriolet with the matt-black leather seats in front of a dark-brown lava wall under a bright, spring sky, or the age and dung-darkened farm cart standing in a field of snow, will confound even the most accommodating film with their contrast ranges of 1:250 and more. The same is true of the black-and-yellow striped bumblebee in the light-pink flower bloom under a bright sun. If you use the side of the cabriolet or the traces of the cart as the target for the exposure meter, then the metered result will be a matter of chance as to how the light and dark areas are distributed on the metering cell. With its area of 13% of the image size, it is regarded as a spot meter, but at an area of 13 to 23% of the frame size in the viewfinder, it is still large enough for a mixed metering: in addition to the cream-white door of the cabriolet, it could see a bit of matt-black leather, dark wall or super-bright sky, or with the cart it might see a bit of snow caught in the dark-brown traces. This brings two factors into the exposure game, which both have, at best, an uneasy relationship. These are the photographer's creative idea and his or her acceptance of compromise in converting that idea into a picture.

Should the farmer's cart appear almost as a silhouette in front of a field of glittering snow, then the chance-metering might just provide the right result. If the snow itself had been used, it would appear dramatically shaded and structured, with strong highlights if the sun had illuminated it with a bit of back light. In other conditions it could look like flour that was left exposed beside a cement factory for the better part of a week. The same is true of the cabriolet beside the dark lava wall. If one adjusts the exposure with a one-stop larger aperture on the cream-white hood, the matt-black leather could appear too "heavy" in the image. Exposure values generated from the seats themselves would be too generous for the paint—it will look like heavily diluted vanilla ice-cream. If the contrast difference between the paint, the dark wall and the black seats is more that five stops, despite lightening the image, then you have to make a decision either to adjust the the optimal image for the black leather, and therefore against the paint, or in favour of the paint when you will have to compromise and accept the way the leather looks in the picture. The bright sky and the wall behind the car do not enter into these compromise decisions. One must accept them the way the correct treatment of other elements of the subject force them to appear in the image.

The perfectly accurate rangefinder system of the M6 TTL is complemented by the, almost, perfectly accurate metering system. The two metering points do not have to be the same! With an automatic reflex camera, while one's finger is resting on the sensitive point of the release just before the moment of releasing the shutter, the camera is busy metering the centre of the frame. In order to meter on a point other than the centre of the image, one has to use the exposure lock button. If one forgets this feature of the release-synchronous metering of a reflex camera, the metered spring sky will ruin any hope of a springtime mood in the image. With the Leica M6 TTL, meter readings away from the centre of the image are routine. Would you be better off with a large area, centre-weighted average metering system rather than the one described? The system itself offers the answer. Multi-zone metering, with or without weighting the central area, zone metering, separated centre and edge metering are all methods developed from experience to free the reflex camera from the danger of creating horrible images when faced with subjects that vary greatly from the "normal". How successful this system is, is something anyone who has shot with an auto-reflex camera can tell you. Replacing a living, breathing, sentient photographer with electronics is just not that easy. Unthinking spot metering of the tennis player's white shirt will produce just as inappropriate an exposure as the unfeeling centre-weighted average metering of a marketplace with a great deal of bright sky in the image. Incorrect metering can be generated by any metering system!

The Leica M6 TTL Exposure Metering System

Lenses for the Leica M6 do not have, and do not need an automatic aperture. Turning the aperture ring closes the diaphragm to the desired opening right away. This means that the camera is metering the light reflected from the subject through the correct diaphragm opening. The silicon photocell measures the light emanating from the subject after it passes though the working aperture and is reflected off the metering dot on the first shutter blind. The metered value is then transmitted as an electronic signal to the exposure calculator. This unit then determines an exposure appropriate to the subject, based on this transmitted value as well as the film speed selected on the ISO dial on the back of the camera. If the exposure value is higher than the one currently determined by the selected aperture and shutter speed, a left-pointing arrow appears in the viewfinder indicating that the shutter speed dial and/or aperture ring should be turned in this direction until the arrow disappears and the dot lights up. Should the metered exposure value be lower than the shutter speed/aperture combination, the arrow points to the right and you have to turn the shutter speed dial and/or aperture ring in that direction until the arrow disappears and the dot shows up.

In the narrow alleys of the old quarter of Biot, the short focal length is the standard lens. Elmarit-M 28mm f/2.8.

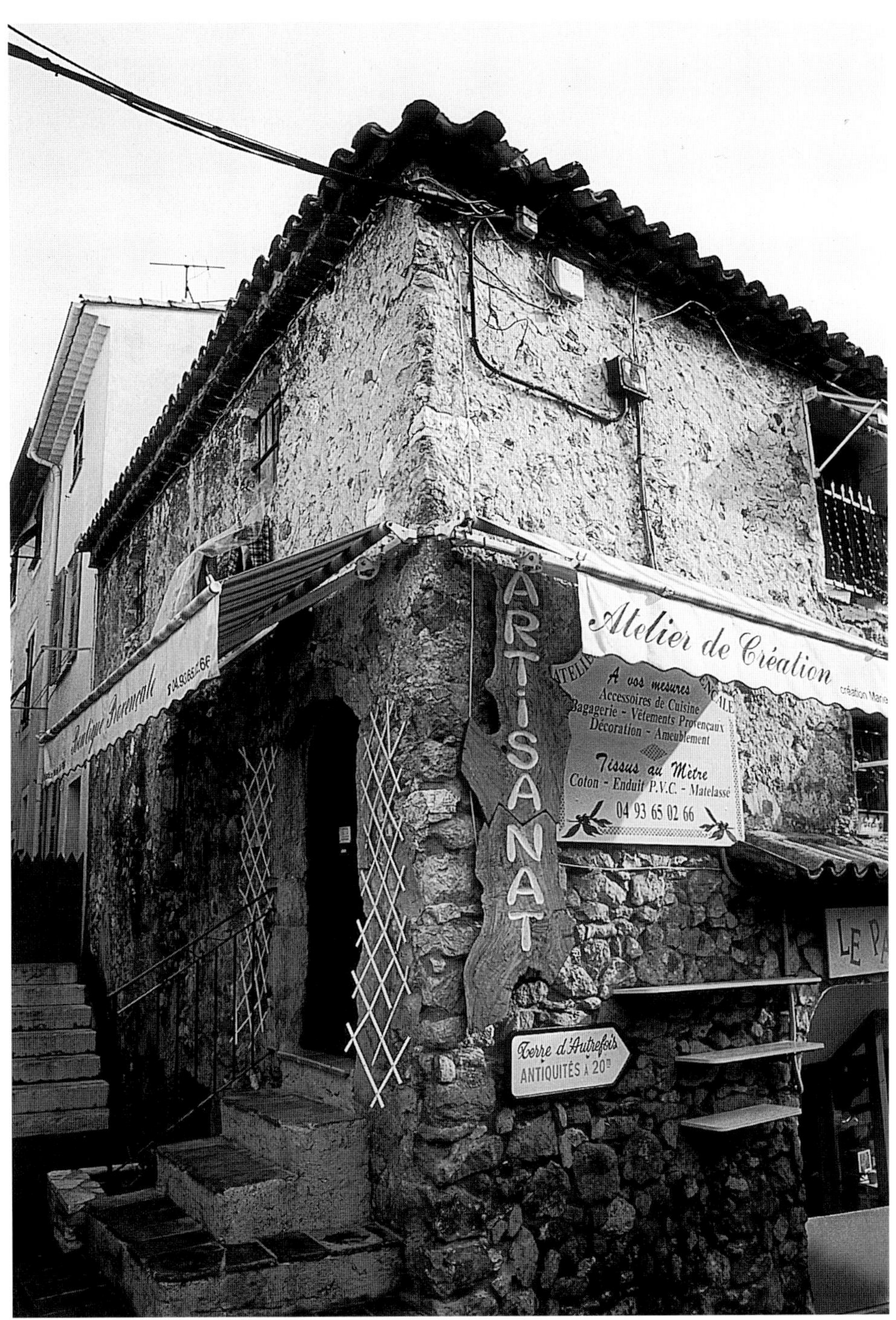
Atelier de Création
ARTISANAT
A vos mesures
Accessoires de Cuisine
Bagagerie - Vêtements Provençaux
Décoration - Ameublement
Tissus au Mètre
Coton - Enduit P.V.C. - Matelassé
04 93 65 02 66
Terre d'Autrefois
ANTIQUITÉS À 20m

Some lenses from the early days of the Leica M-system, such as my 1960-vintage Summicron 90mm f/2, which have baroque-style rings and do not sport an "M" in their name, have an aperture system that is the opposite of today's lenses: one has to turn the ring in the opposite direction to that indicated by the arrow in order to make the arrow disappear. This does not in any way affect the precision and accuracy of selecting an appropriate shutter speed/aperture combination. If the left arrow LED blinks with a small aperture, the subject illumination has fallen below the lower boundary of the range of the metering system. You have to open the aperture or increase the light on the subject so that the meter can produce a reliable result.

The following example typifies of the character of the Leica M6 TTL exposure metering system. A correct exposure, according to the metering system, will be produced using a Summilux 75mm f/1.4 at an aperture of f/4 and shutter speed 1/125 sec. In order to reduce the depth of field to increase the impact of the image, increase the aperture to f/1.4 and adjust the shutter speed to 1/1000 sec. in order to maintain the same exposure value. The right arrow will appear in the viewfinder even though only the dot should appear—both shutter speed/aperture combinations correspond to an exposure value of 11. The reason is that the numbers engraved on the lens aperture ring are calculated using the relationship between the focal length of the lens and the diaphragm opening. The actual working aperture and the true light transmission of the optical system are not taken into consideration at all. The fact that super-fast lenses exhibit noticeable vignetting is not part of the calculation at all. All of these facts combined lead to a loss of light compared to the engraved aperture when a lens is opened wide. Since the TTL meters directly though the actual aperture, a slight under exposure will result and the right arrow will appear when using an aperture of f/1.4—or f/1 with the Noctilux 50mm f/1—while keeping the relationship the same.

On the other hand, closing the lens by half a stop from its maximum aperture will not change the exposure display. This minimal reaction on the part of the LED-display corresponds to the difference in the exposure between the lens being wide open or closed by a half-stop being barely visible.

Using the Leica M6 TTL LED-display system is so easy and quickly understood that one does not have to describe it in greater detail. With some multiprogram reflex cameras, one practically has to have the instruction manual with its example settings in one's pocket at all times in order to avoid any mistakes. Whether the subjects will always wait while you flip through the book is another matter.

The White Dot and the MeteringField

The wonderfully simple exposure metering system of the Leica M6 TTL requires your imagination in only one respect: the exposure metering area is not marked in the viewfinder. Leica designers could have gone to a great deal of difficulty in displaying this information in the focal-length-independent viewfinder of the M6 TTL and projected a correspondingly larger or smaller metering area along with the format frames. Or the eight different sizes of metering circle could have been engraved somehow onto a screen where they would always be visible. Both solutions would have greatly reduced the clarity of the viewfinder and subject control. So they did without these displays and instead gave the Leica photographer this guide: the 12mm large metering circle corresponds to 13% to 23% of the subject area that is marked by the format frame corresponding to the mounted lens. Translated according to the viewfinder magnification and angle of view, the diameter of the metering field, centred on the rangefinder field, takes up about two-thirds of the short side of the format frame. This sounds complicated, but a bit of practice is all that one needs to be able to gauge the size of the metering circle accurately. This is true for both models of the M6 TTL, the 0.72x and the 0.85x.

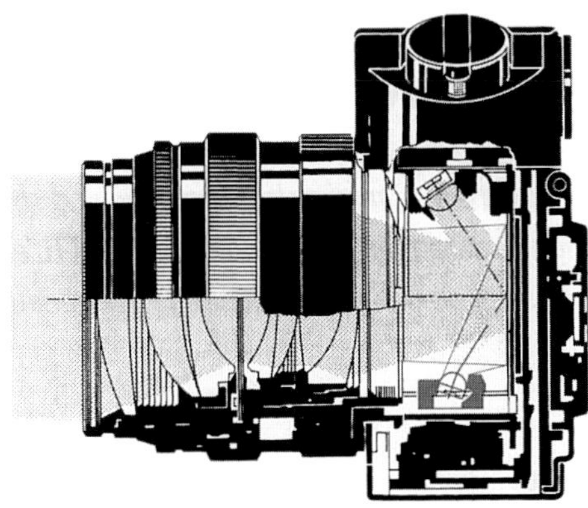

Light paths in the Leica M6 TTL:

The silicon photocell located behind the camera bayonet measures the subject illumination bouncing off the 12mm white metering spot on the first shutter blind. The aperture selected on the M-lens is considered directly in the metered result.
The photocell on the floor of the M6 TTL measures the illumination of a flash-lit subject using the light reflected directly off the film in TTL flash control mode.

The format frames themselves also offer reference points for estimating the size of the metering circle. With the Elmarit-M 21mm f/2.8 ASPH and the 24mm f/2.8 ASPH, these references are only indirect as their image size is larger than the viewfinder image. Use the frame selection lever to project the format frame for the 50mm lens into the viewfinder, only its corners protrude beyond the area of the metering circle for the 21mm and 24mm lenses while the metering circle sticks out over the long-sides a little. (The Super-Angulon-M 21mm f/4 and the Super-Angulon M 21mm f/3.4 are not compatible with the TTL exposure metering system.because of their construction).

Select the 75mm format frame with the Elmarit-M 28mm f/2.8. Its corners are outside the metering circle while its top and bottom edges do not quite contain it. The 90mm frame offers the same guidelines for 35mm lenses.

Use the 135mm format frame with a 50mm lens and you will also have a good idea about which parts of the subject are contained within the metering area. When using 90mm and 135mm focal lengths, even the Elmarit 135mm f/2.8 with the viewfinder attachment, one can consider the rangefinder metering area as the centre of the exposure metering cell without running the risk of making a serious error.

Storing all this information concerning metering areas and format frames in one's brain can seem a daunting task at first, but a bit of practice proves the opposite. My idea of crib notes in the form of sketches on the back of the M6 met with limited success. Often I only remembered them after I had taken the shot. Maybe you will have better luck with it. For years now I have only used the rangefinder image as a reference and have not suffered any grave consequences. One obviously has to examine the surrounding area for extreme light or dark parts that could violate the 18% rule and result in an incorrect reading. One should then offer the exposure meter a different target. You can meter distance and exposure on two completely different areas with the M6 without having the two readings interfere with each other. One can suffer incorrect meterings with any metering system. Photography is still an undertaking for the brain behind the camera in spite of any automated system. If one relegates important decisions to another intelligence, one should not be surprised if the result, while not incorrect, is not what one expected.

My method of using format frames as a reference for the size of the metering cell is obviously not wonderfully accurate. Even more generous is the method of using the rangefinder image with a bit more

The diameter of the 12mm white spot on the first shutter blind corresponds to about two-thirds of the short side of the frame for the current lens. No projected frame appears for the Elmarit-M 21mm f/2.8 ASPH as it would be larger than the viewfinder. Use the frame selector to project the frame for the 50mm lens into the viewfinder as it covers about 80 percent of the area of the metering spot.

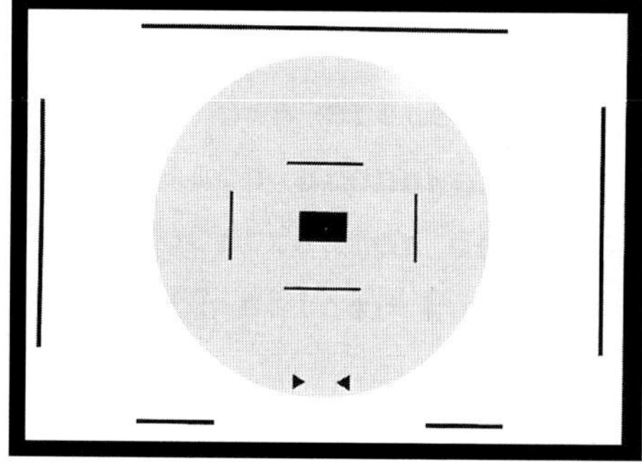

21 mm

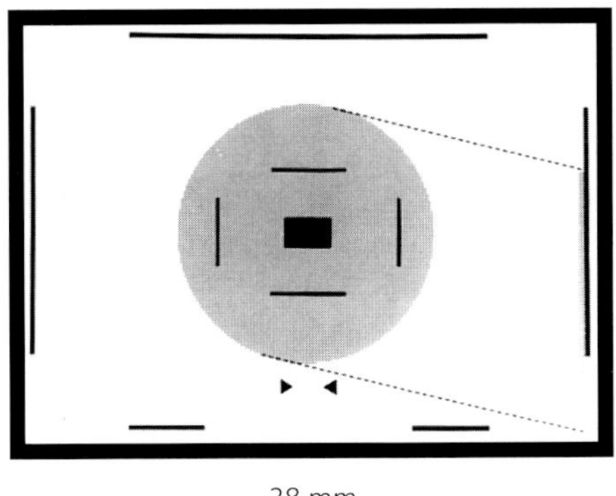

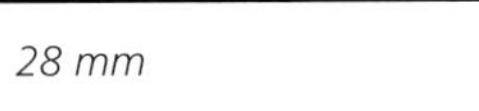

28 mm

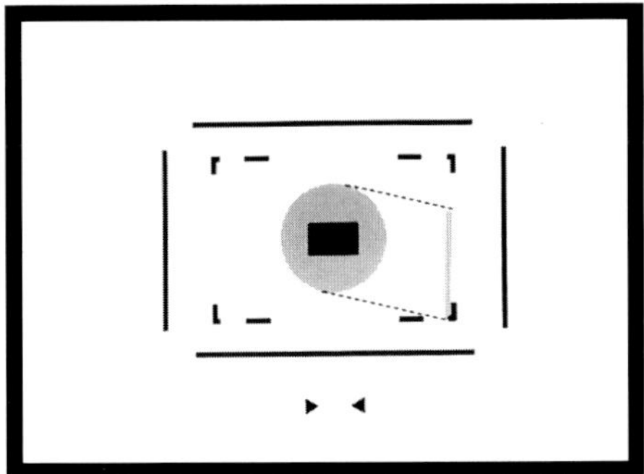

75 mm

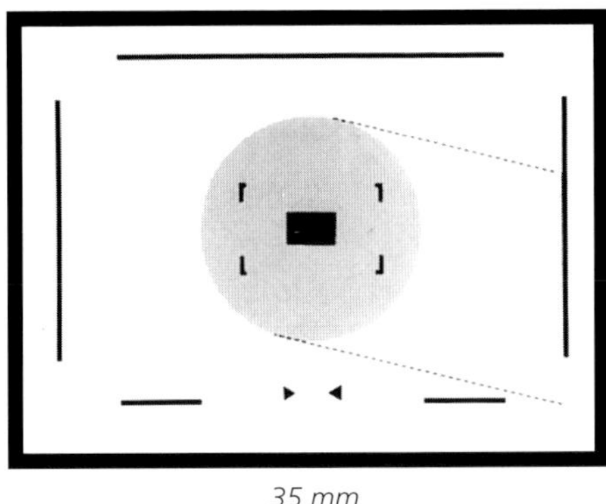

35 mm

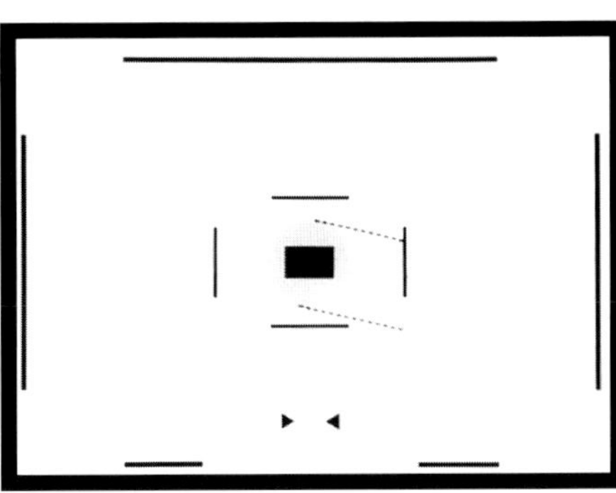

90 mm

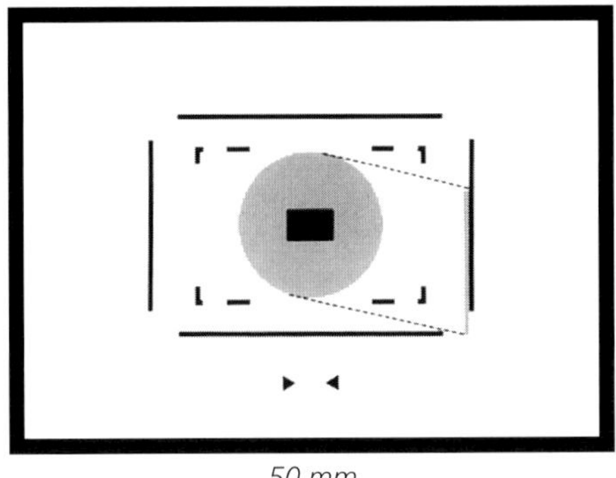

50 mm

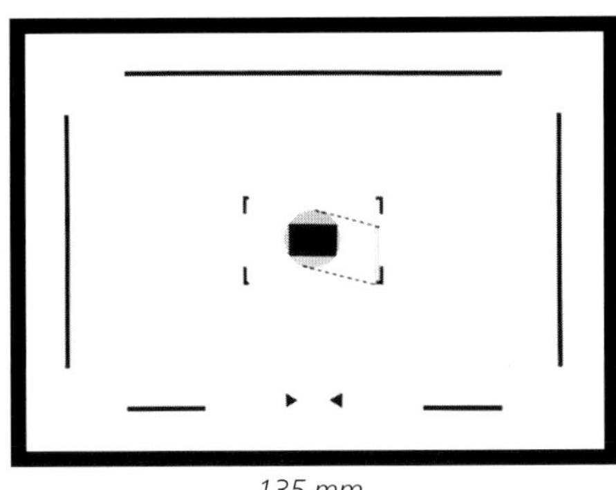

135 mm

around it as a guide. How much less accurate my methods are than estimating two-thirds of the short side of the corresponding format frame, I will gladly leave to your judgement. Whether you estimate it this way or that way, this is not the be-all and end-all. The most important element is that you find your own method of using the exposure metering system of the M6 TTL and stick with this self-discovered and accurate system until it becomes as much second nature as the manner in which you tie your shoes every day.

One could easily spend an evening debating whether a metering cell comprising 13% of the image area or 13 to 23% of the format frame projected into the viewfinder corresponding to the current lens can still be considered spot metering. One can! "Spot" is not defined based on a certain metering angle depending on the film format. "Spot," unlike centre-weighted average metering, means that the subject illumination is measured off a small, clearly defined area. But there is no hard and fast rule about the metering angle. This angle is the result of the photographer's experience and desires, of diverse theories, of the intentions of the camera designer and perhaps his experience as well. Whether or not all camera designers know as much about photography as they would lead us to believe is not a certainty, particularly given some of the "simplifications" with which high-tech reflex cameras are endowed.

So the metering angle alone does not determine the degree of "professionalism" of a metering system. There are average metering reflex cameras that enjoy an excellent reputation among professional photographers as they can adjust the metered result at any time to fit the subject and their needs. After all, a photographer who cannot deviate from the result determined by a narrow-angled meter does not have much imagination at all. A meter system that allows customisation is much more valuable than one which boasts a defined metering angle. The Leica M6 TTL allows the photographer all the freedom that he or she needs and deserves!

The Metering Sensitivity of the M6 TTL

The Leica team had to dig deep into their box of tricks to develop a metering system as precise and perfect as that in the M6 TTL because of the steep angle at which the silicon photocell has to read the light reflected off the white metering area. This device is 100% "Made in Germany"—nothing comparable comes out of the Far East.

The metering range of the Leica M6 TTL exposure meter stretches from 0.063 cd/m2 to 125,000 cd/m2 at an aperture of f/1. This results in a working range from -1EV to 20EV or from f/1 and 2sec. (shutter speed dial set to "B") to 1/1000sec. at f/32 at ISO 100/21°. Should the subject

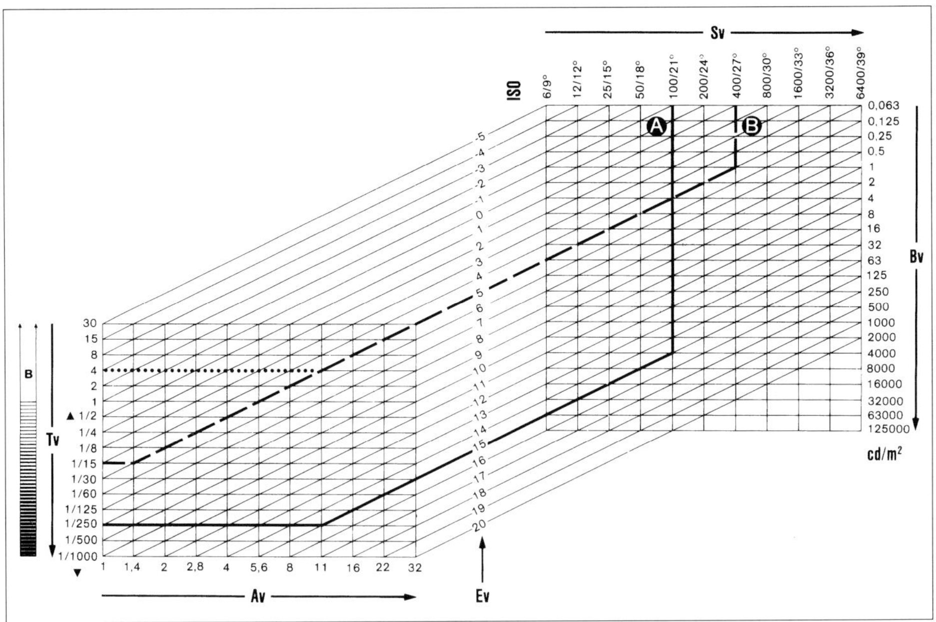

Diagram of the metering sensitivity of the Leica M6 TTL.
The subject illumination as measured by the metering system, between 0.063 and 125,000 cd/m², combined with the ISO-value of the film sensitivity, produces the exposure value. It can be divided into various shutter speed/aperture combinations.

Example A: brilliant sunshine has a brightness of about 4000cd/m² which, combined with an ISO 100/21° film, produces an exposure value of 15 for combinations between 1/30s at f/32 and 1/1000s at f/5.6.

Example B: candlelight, about 1cd/m², combined with an ISO 400/27° film, produces an exposure value of only 5, equivalent to a shutter speed of 1/15s at f/1.4 or 4s at f/11 which you cannot set on the M6's shutter speed dial, but have to control using a cable release and a stopwatch.

illumination fall below the lower metering boundary when using small apertures, the left-arrow LED flashes in the viewfinder.

If you remove your finger from the shutter release after selecting the shutter speed and aperture, the LEDs stay on for about 12 seconds longer. This time span is long enough to correct the shutter speed or aperture. If you press the release when the subject illumination is below the lower boundary, and the light level increases during the 12 seconds that the exposure meter remains active, the flashing LED in the viewfinder changes to constant. A filter matches the sensitivity of the silicon photocell to that of the eye.

Careful examination of the white dot on the first shutter blind could

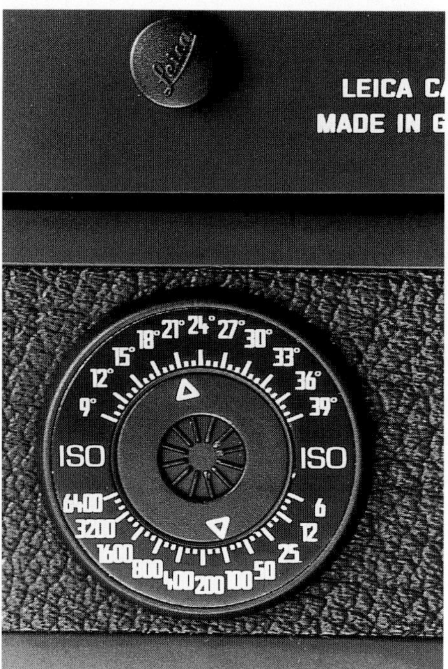

The Leica M6 TTL ISO dial, with its top setting of ISO 6400/39°, gives the user the option of pushing even the fastest colour films an additional two stops.

lead one to believe that the white paint is applied inconsistently or poorly—but that would be wrong: one cannot apply paint with a smooth finish onto a weave that has to roll up and unroll again very rapidly as this "coat of paint" would reduce the suppleness of the rubberised material. The durability of the white dot made of ageless and colourfast metal-oxide paint is tested to withstand 100,000 shutter movements.

Exposure Value Splitting à la M6 TTL

Dividing the exposure in the Leica M6—as in all modern reflex cameras as well—is based on the same principles as those used by Oskar Barnack in his first Leica in 1924 and by the inventor of the Kine-Exakta, the predecessor of all 35mm reflex cameras: a focal plane shutter directly in front of the film and an aperture in the lens. The following holds for any camera technology: just as one can divide a pizza into two equal halves, one can also divide it into one larger and one smaller piece, one can divide the exposure value equally into shutter speed and aperture or allocate a larger portion of it to shutter or aperture. Then the remaining light-controlling element has to be satisfied with whatever is left if the image is to be exposed correctly: one cannot add anything to or remove anything from the established exposure value. The numerous combinations of shutter speed and aperture for any given exposure value give the creative freedom available to the photographer to capture his ideas and the subject on film.

The focal plane shutter in the Leica M6 TTL and the aperture in the lens are, on one hand, light-reducing devices, while on the other they are are image creating tools. If you allow an automated system to divide the exposure value into shutter speed and aperture or do it all by yourself is a moot point in theory only. If you assign this task to an impersonal computer, you should not be surprised if the—generally—correctly exposed image is missing a certain something.

The Focal Plane Shutter of the Leica M6 TTL

Without a doubt, it is not the newest kid on the block. But it sprints across the film gate with the same qualities it boasted 45 years ago and which have made it famous and a living legend: unsurpassed precision, reliability, durability, vibration-free and practically noiseless. The two blinds made of thin, light-tight rubberised material travel from left to right (if the camera is held in shooting position).over the film gate The blinds and their drawing tapes are wound onto relatively thick spring-loaded drums. These provide adequate space for springs that are larger than they need to be so that they are not played out after the shutter traverses the 36mm-wide film gate, but rather always operate in their peak performance band. They can therefore perform well over 100,000 sprints without any problem at all and you can leave a cocked shutter lying around for months on end without having to worry about it. Larger diameter spring-loaded drums turn more slowly for any given shutter speed than would thinner ones. This has a very positive effect on life span and resistance to wear. Also the noise of a mechanical system seems to increase with the cube of the speed of its motion. A halving of the operating speed would therefore reduce the noise to one eighth! This is thus one of the reasons why the Leica M6 TTL shutter works so wonderfully smoothly and quietly. Another reason is the fact that the rubberised cloth shutter blinds move much more quietly than the blades and their attendant levers of metal focal-plane shutters. Large spring-loaded drums offer a longer braking path for the shutter blinds than the few millimetres over which a metal shutter blind has to be stopped from high speed to a standstill. Something that can use a longer braking path to stop from a slower speed can do so more quietly and with less vibration.

The shutter speed, or exposure time, is the result of a constant speed of travel of the shutter blinds over the film gate and the size of the gap between them. You set the

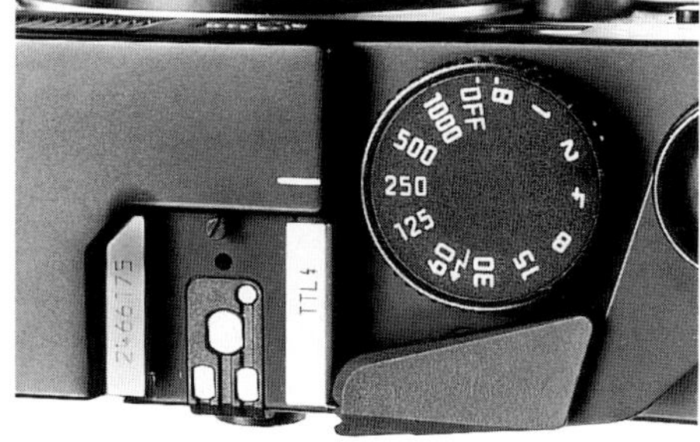

The larger shutter speed dial of the Leica M6 TTL is now even easier to control with an index finger sliding along the edge of the housing. In the "off" position, the metering system is turned off.

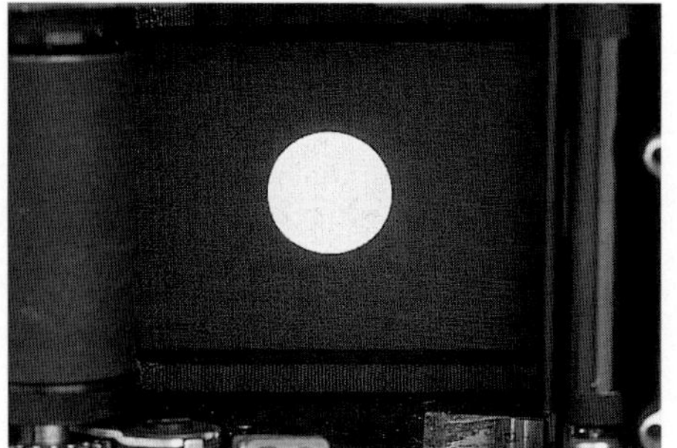
1

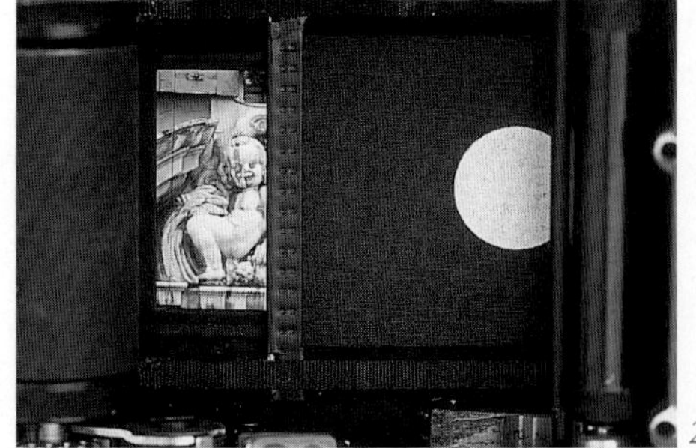
2

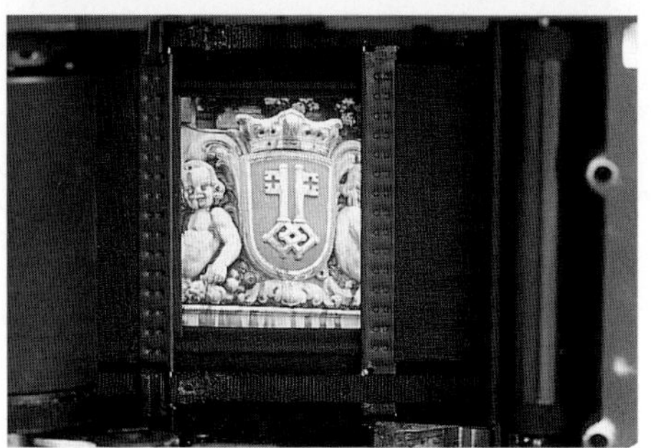
3

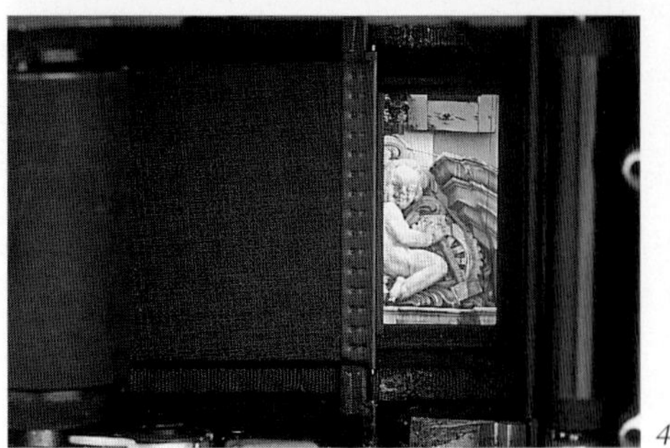
4

1: The Leica M6 TTL focal plane shutter consists of two blinds made of rubberised material that lie directly in front of the film gate. The first one bears the white dot for the exposure metering system.
2: When the release is depressed, the first blind starts moving across the film gate.
3: After a brief delay, which corresponds to the shutter speed selected on the shutter speed dial, the second blind follows the first. The actual shutter speed or exposure time corresponds to the width of the gap between the two blinds and the speed at which they move.
4: The first blind disappears behind the far edge of the film gate and the second is approaching and ends the exposure.

Leica M6, Visoflex II, Bellows unit, Hektor 135mm f/4.5.

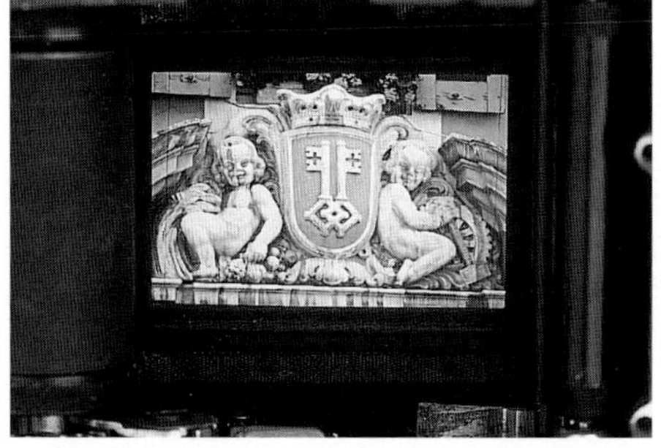

A flash can only illuminate the film format evenly and consistently if the first shutter blind has cleared the film gate and the second has not yet started.

Leica M6, Visoflex II, Bellows unit, Hektor 135mm f/4.5.

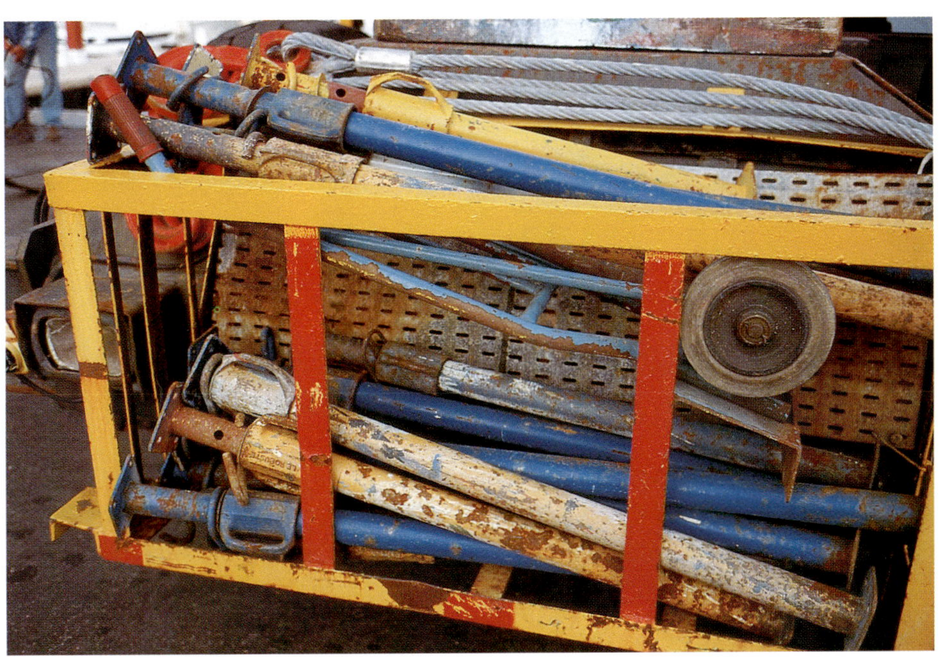

Colour, not quite fresh and a bit worn off, glows brightly under a lightly clouded sky and with a slight under exposure. Summicron-M 50mm f/2.

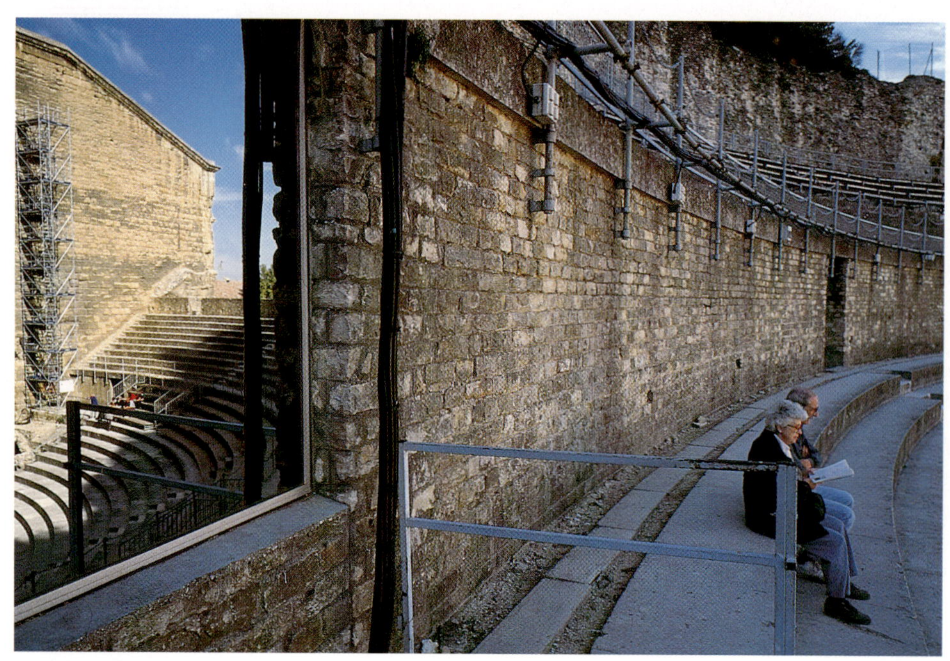

Reality and reflection in the upper rows of the Roman amphitheatre in Orange.
Elmarit-M 21mm f/2.8 ASPH.

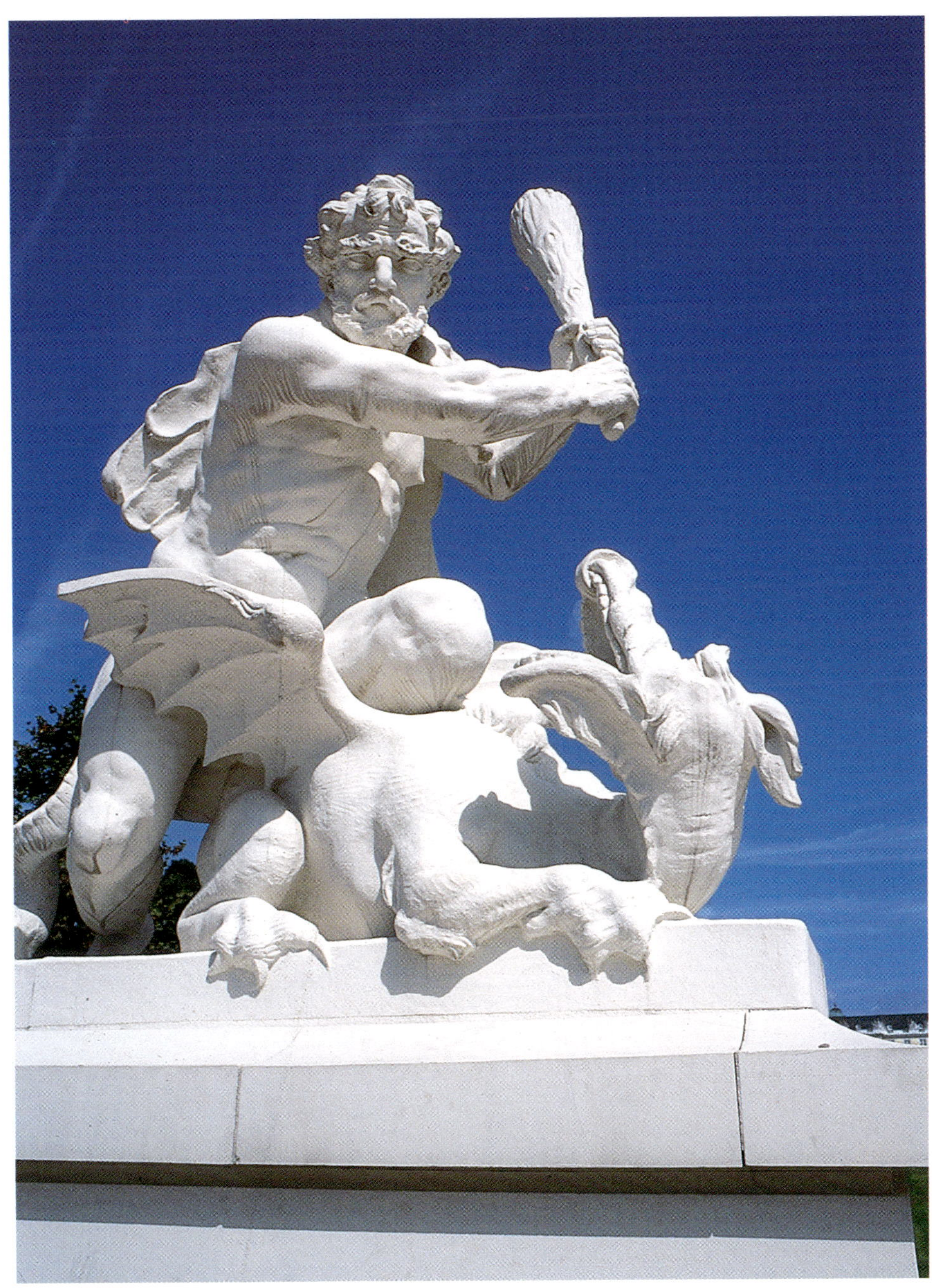

One should, in theory, shoot monuments such as this with a longer focal length, but with the super-wide-angle directed steeply upwards, the sky turns into an infinite background. Elmarit-M 24mm f/2.8 ASPH.

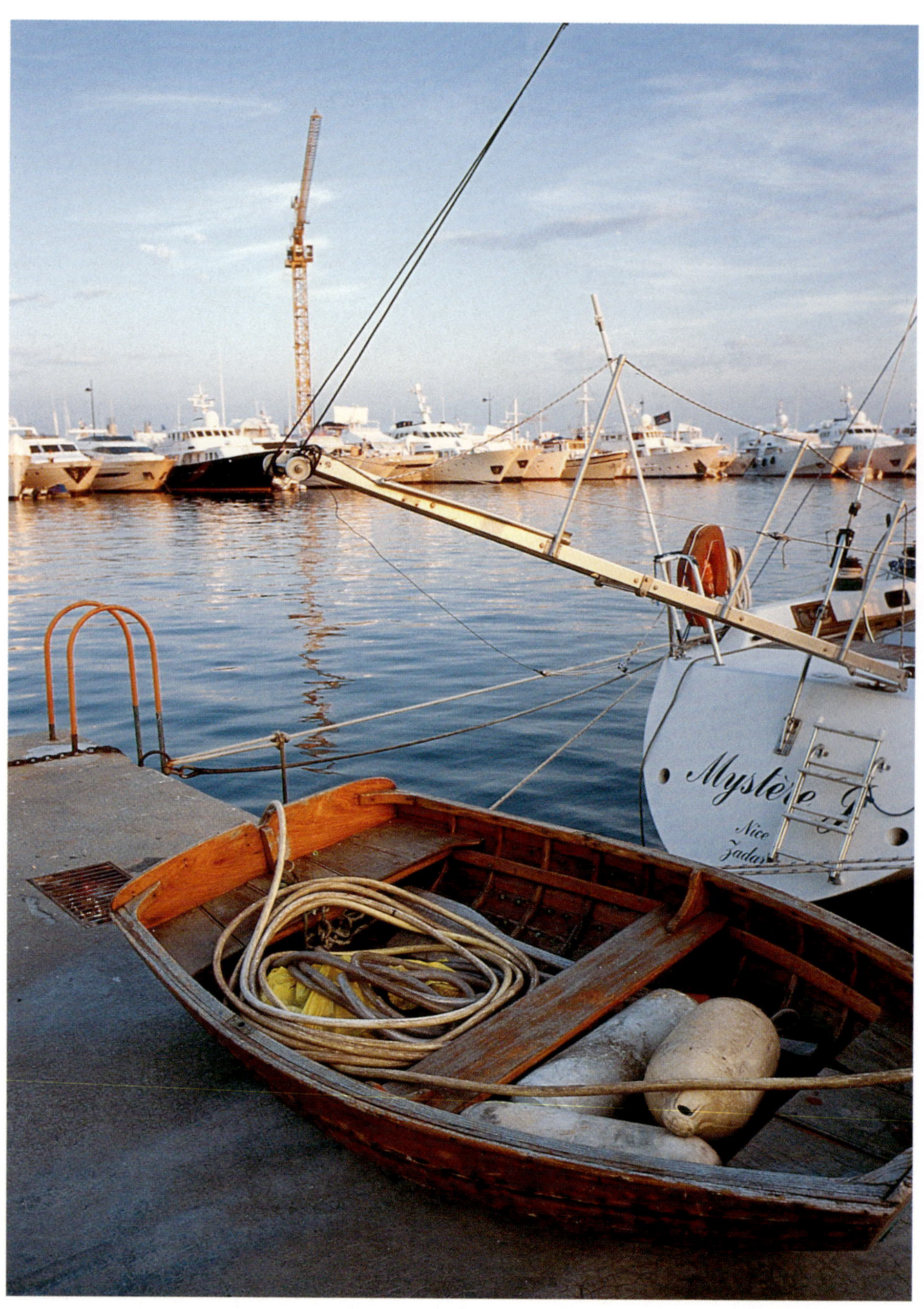

Moments before sunset, the light is fascinating but already so weak that only maximum aperture will provide a safe shutter speed. this is no problem with the Elmarit-M 21mm f/2.8 ASPH.

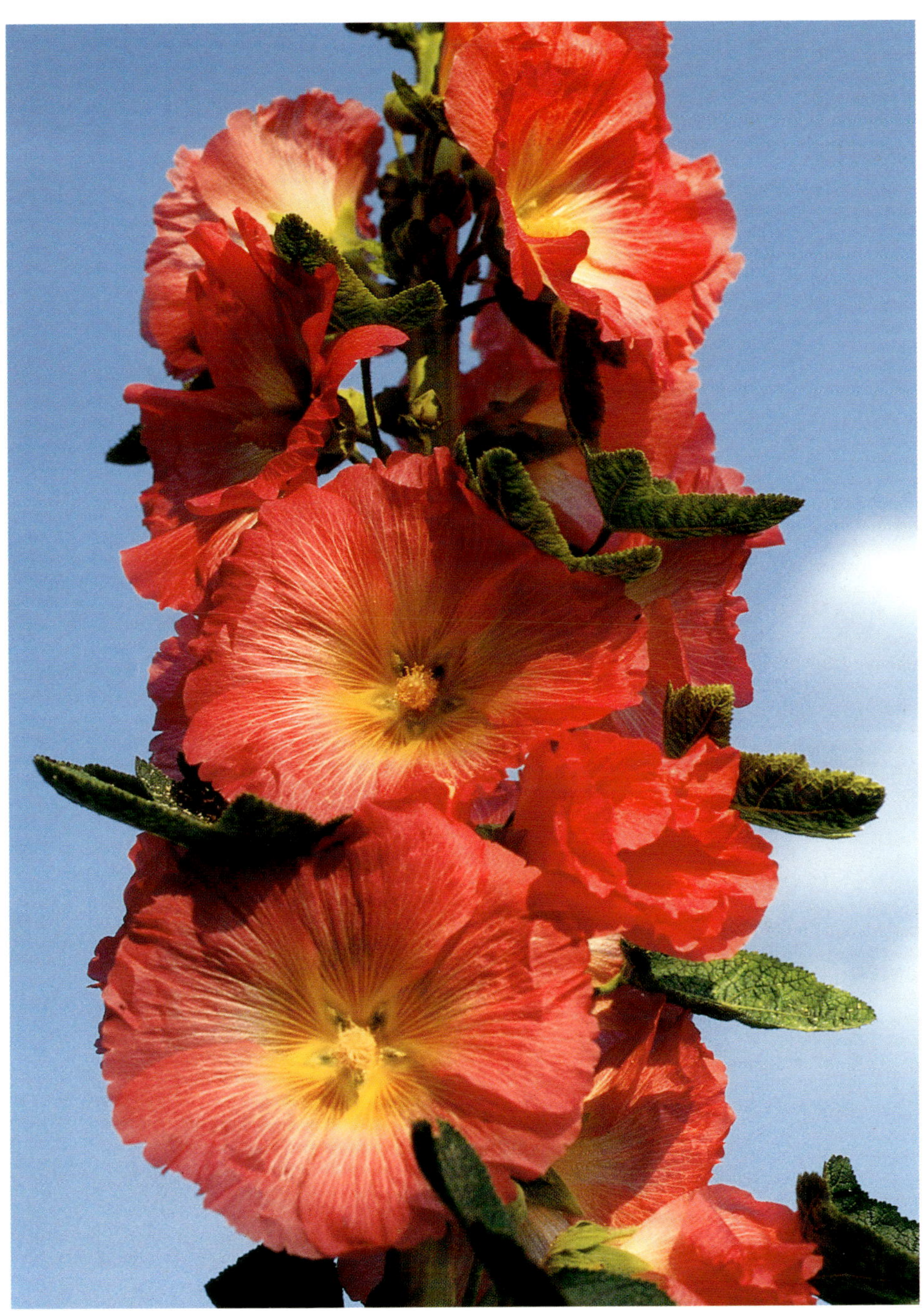

The 90mm lenses for the M6 can be focused down to 1m—close enough for this 3m high bloom. A slight under exposure made the colours more saturated in the image. Summicron-M 90mm f/2.

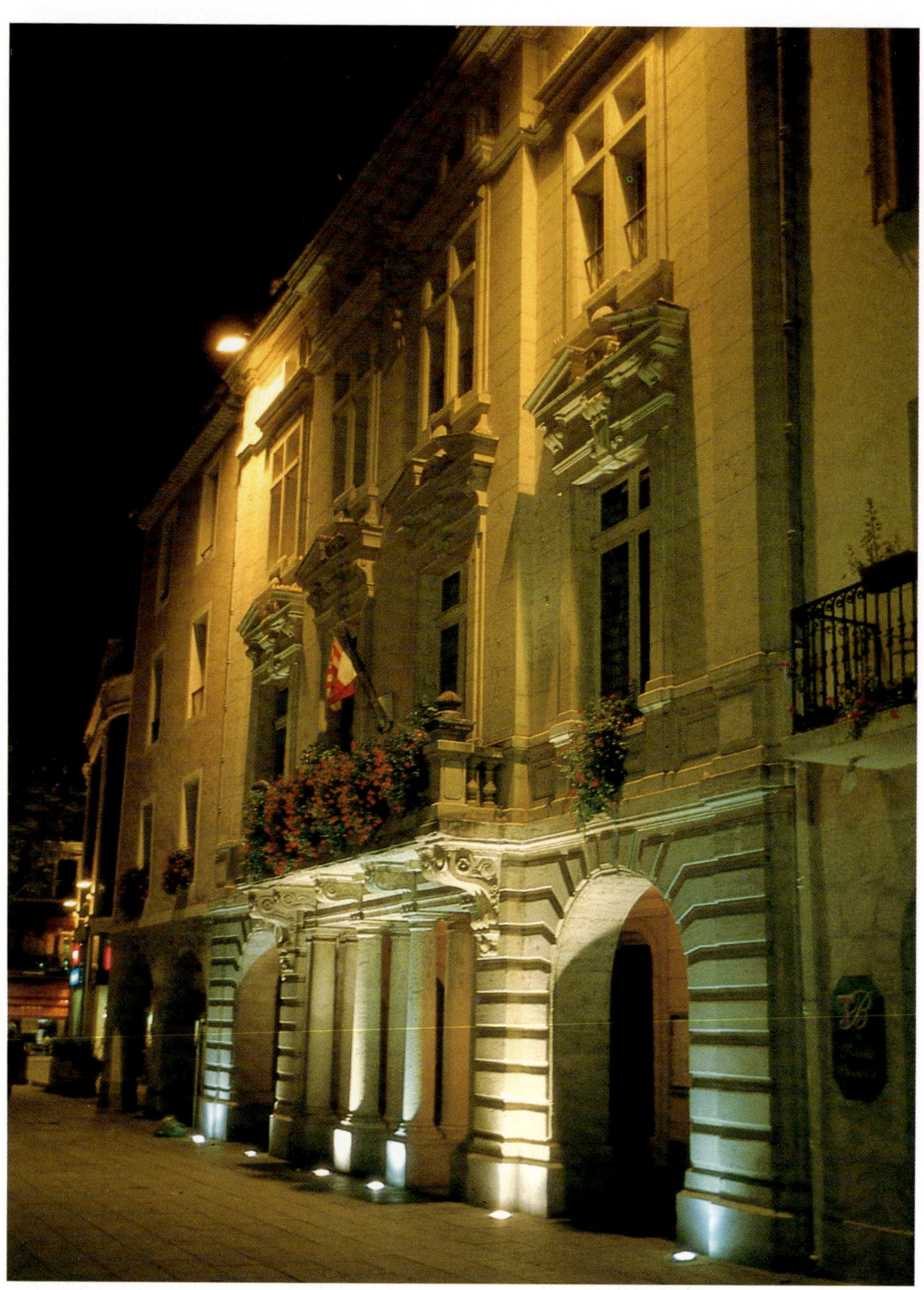

If you have not brought a tripod, the only way to capture this effectively lit facade would be to take your chance with maximum aperture at 1/8s. With the M6 TTL and its lenses this is no problem at all. Elmarit-M 28mm f/2.8.

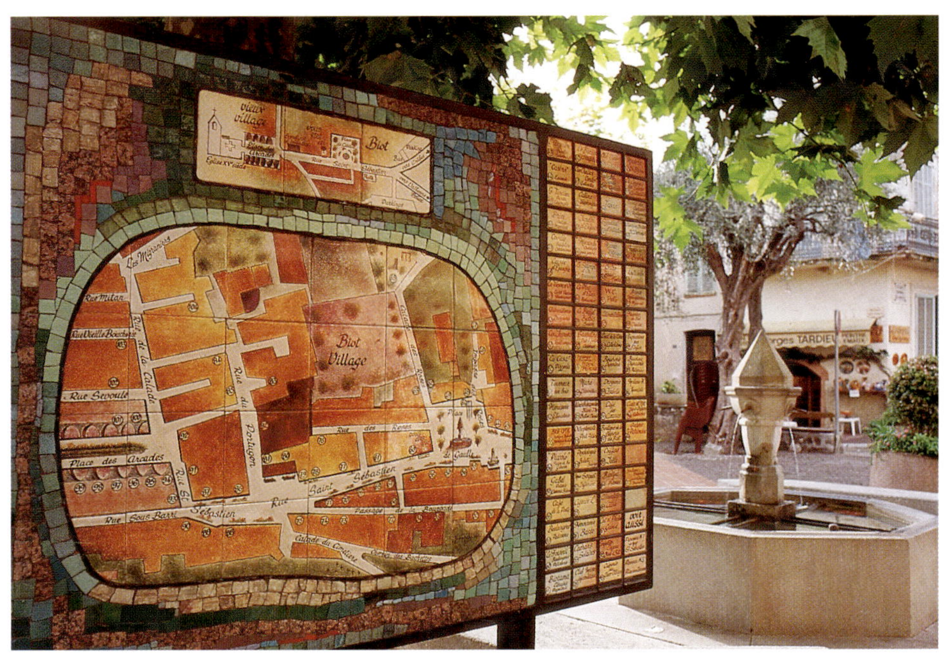

A tile map of Biot in Provence, made by artists living there. The super-wide angle of view allows one to capture a bit of the ambience as well. Elmarit-M 24mm f/2.8 ASPH.

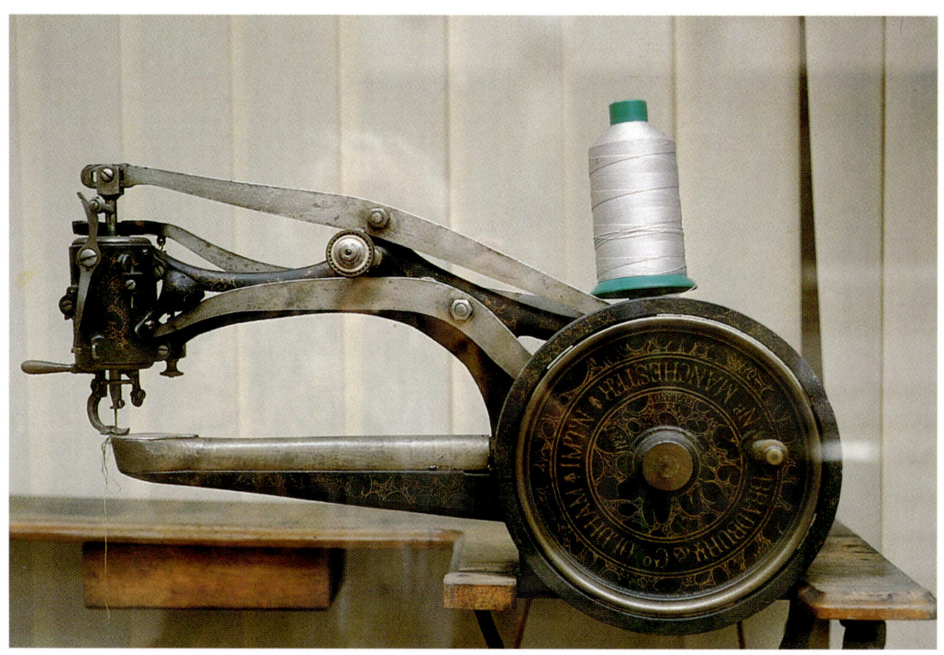

A classic machine, like the M6, the Sattler sewing machine was taken at maximum aperture through the showcase window. Summicron-M 90mm f/2.

width of the gap directly by using the shutter speed dial. If you have the M6 at your eye in order to select a shutter speed appropriate to the aperture using the LED display, all you have to do is push your fingertip along the rim of the shutter speed dial, projecting slightly back of the edge of the housing, from click-stop to click-stop. Since the shutter speed setting is electronically connected to the exposure metering system, the dial must click into an engraved setting. Intermediate speeds, like those allowed on the M2, M3 and M4, cannot be used on the M6 or M6 TTL! The shutter speed range, from 1s to 1/1000s and B, seems limited compared to reflex cameras, but does one really need 1/4000s, 1/8000s? Only if one is always using the highest-speed films in order to freeze the propeller blades of an aircraft on film for instance. But the highest-speed films are not universal films for all applications.

There is also the following argument for why the Leica's top shutter speed of 1/1000s is adequate even today. With the exception of the Tri-Elmar-M 28-35-50mm f/4 and the Apo-Telyt-M 135mm f/3.4, all Leica lenses have speeds between f/2.8 and f/1, f/2 being the standard. Leica's claim over the years has always been the ability to use fast lenses at their maximum aperture without loss of performance with slow or moderate films. One does not need extremely fast shutter speeds to remove an excess of light.

Beyond "1s" on the shutter speed dial is the option of "B" for exposure times of any desired length which are controlled using a cable release—the M6 still has a threaded socket for one—and a stopwatch. The Leica M6 TTL's shutter speed dial has an "OFF" setting by which the camera's electronics are shut off but the mechanically controlled shutter responds to the release as it does in the "B" setting. In the former Leica M6, the "B" setting of the shutter speed dial disconnected the electronics. In order to enable TTL control of fill-flash in long time exposures, the "B" setting had to be separated from the "OFF" switch. The mechanics under the shutter speed dial were redesigned at the same time to make the direction of rotation required to correct the exposure match the LED arrows.

The practicalities of a focal plane shutter mean that it is in motion for a longer time than the actual exposure time, and also longer than the time an electronic flash illuminates. The flash can only fully illuminate the film format if the gap between the two shutter blinds is wider than the 36mm length of the film format. That means the second shutter blind can only start travelling when the first blind has cleared the other side of the film gate. The Leica M6 TTL shutter achieves this condition starting at 1/50s, the speed marked with the flash symbol, and at any slower speed and "B". This relatively slow sync. speed is often listed as one of the Leica's disadvantages. But

Leica photographers seldom have problems with it. A characteristic of Leica photography is the ability to take unobtrusive and dynamic shots under low available light conditions, thanks to the combination of high speed films and the high maximum aperture of its fast M-lenses. Leica photographers only resort to the flattening effects of frontal flash illumination if there is no other choice. The fact that the Leica M6 TTL now offers TTL flash exposure control, as well as the Leica SF-20 flash unit, is a reaction to different photographic styles, requirements and everyday occurrences in photo-journalism.

Some photographers might consider the fact that the Leica M6 does not display the shutter speed in the viewfinder as a drawback. But guided by the concept of the Leica M6 TTL, everyone will soon find his or her own methodology whereby he or she will survive without needing a shutter speed display in the viewfinder, in contrast to aperture-priority mode on a reflex camera.

In cooperation with the aperture, the device controlling the amount of light striking the film is the Leica M6 TTL focal plane shutter. Its second task, also in conjunction with the aperture, is to ensure that exposure times are as short as possible in order to avoid camera shake and that fast-moving subjects are captured crisply on film. For the first requirement, the old rule of thumb still holds that the shutter speed in fractions of a second should be as short as the focal length of the lens is long in mm—i.e. 1/50s or 1/60s with 50mm lenses and at least 1/125s with a 135mm lens. The Leica M6 is practically tailored to your hand, its shutter release is on a hair-trigger, its extremely low-vibration shutter and its operation without a reflex mirror or spring aperture all combine to allow you to shoot at speeds slightly slower than those recommended. As long as the photographer's hands are reasonably steady, the chances are not bad. But this does not change the recommendation to keep the shutter speed as fast as possible given the lens and the dynamics of the subject. An excellent image spoiled by camera-shake is still only good enough for the waste basket.

The second requirement touches on the creative aspects of dealing with the M6 TTL shutter. Water droplets, or motorcross riders frozen in midair are an opportunity to show movement and speed in a picture. Blurred hair and costumes of dancers and athletes, bicycle races reduced to coloured streaks, cottony-soft foam on a fast-flowing stream always were and still are the other, extremely effective method of expressing movement, speed and temperament.

The question remains where to draw the line between still-sharp and not-really-that-sharp. Oskar Barnack answered that question in his "Small negative—large image" philosophy as follows: everything on a 35mm negative that is to be in focus when blown up to a size of

18x24cm can only exhibit circles of confusion with a diameter of 0.033mm or less on the negative. At an eight-times magnification to 18x24cm, they increase to 0.26mm and are therefore just under the resolving power of the eye at a viewing distance of 30cm.

The operational principle of the M6 TTL focal plane shutter is easy to understand. At 1/125s, the gap between the first and second blinds is twice as wide as at 1/250s, but only half as wide as at 1/60s. It therefore allows twice as much light to strike the film at 1/125s than at 1/250s, but only half as much as at 1/60s.

The Diaphragm in the Lens

The variable diaphragm in the lens, made of wafer-thin blades, is the other method of limiting the amount of light to strike the film. It also allows more light to pass through at a larger opening and less at a smaller one. Unlike the shutter speed, it does not have a time component but has the geometrically determined feature that its area increases or decreases in all directions when the diameter changes. As a result, the area of the circular opening doubles when the diameter is only increased by a factor of $\sqrt{2}$ (approx. 1.41) and thus allows twice as much light to strike the film. Conversely, the area of the opening and therefore the amount of light allowed to pass is halved if the diameter of the opening is reduced by a factor of 1.41. The light-control effect of the aperture is inseparable from its distance to the film. In order to be able to compare the optically effective diameter of the opening of lenses of varying focal lengths and to

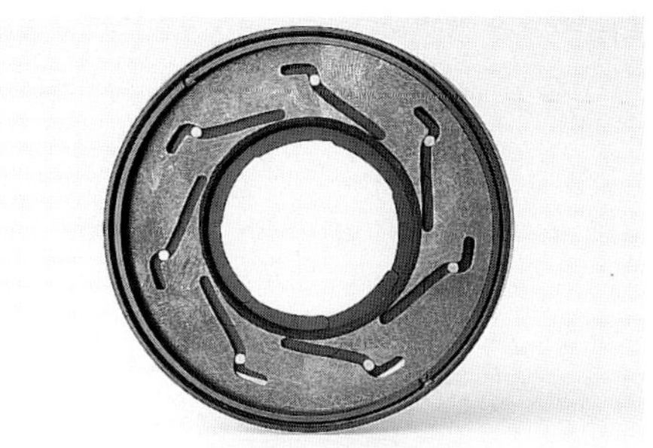

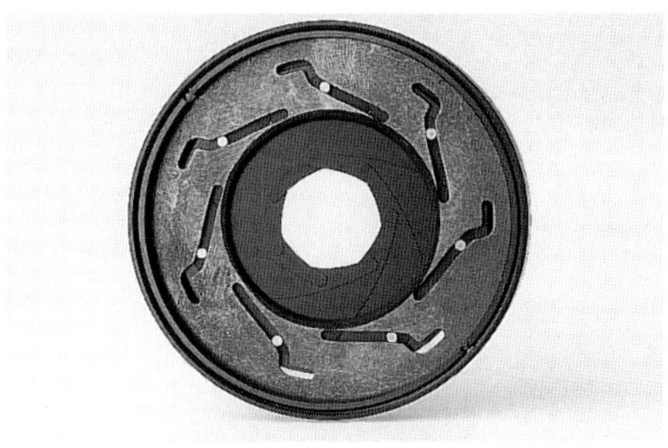

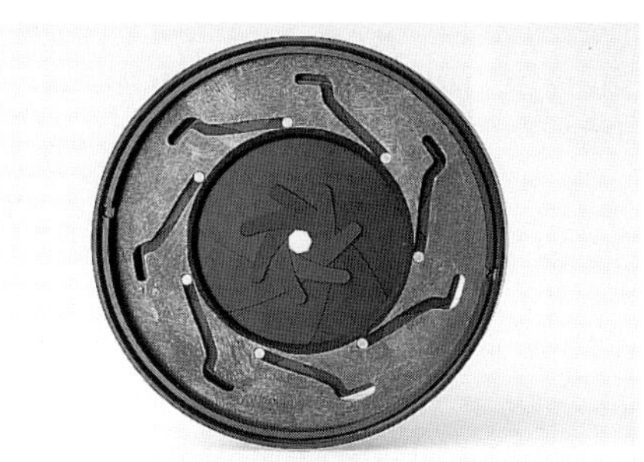

The diaphragm in the lens is the second element that one can use to control the amount of light so that the correct amount strikes the film for a perfect exposure. The smaller the aperture, the less the amount of light allowed to pass through and the larger the depth of field.
Leica R, Apo-Macro Elmarit-R 100mm f/2.8.

be able to use this number in exposure calculations, the size of a lens's aperture is not quoted in millimetres, but rather as a ratio of the opening to its focal length. Focal length divided by the diameter of the opening equals the aperture number. One can use this value directly in determining the division of the exposure value. An aperture of f/2.0 or f/5.6 or f/11 or f/32 means that in a lens of any focal length, the diameter of the opening, while of various physical sizes, is always contained in the focal length by a factor of 2.0, 5.6, 11 or 32 times. Now you know how the unusual series of numbers on a lens's aperture ring came into being.

Why these numbers are what they are you can forget. What you should not forget is that the smallest number corresponds to the largest opening and the largest to the smallest. And: if you turn the M-lens's aperture ring one stop to the right—when looking from the top—the aperture allows twice as much light to strike the film. Turn it one stop to the left, and the film only receives half as much light.

Leica M-lenses are consistent in this orientation: turned to the left you obtain a smaller aperture and less light, to the right a larger aperture and more light. The only exception is the old Summicron 90mm f/2—no "M" in its nomenclature at the time because "R" did not yet exist—whose aperture ring works in the opposite direction. I will not give up my wonderfully baroque, in no way outmoded 90mm f/2 simply because I have to turn the aperture ring in the opposite direction of the LED arrow in the viewfinder. Also I can unscrew its head from is helicoid and attach it directly, or via an adapter, to a bellows unit for close-up work on a Visoflex II or III.or a Leica reflex camera.

Leica M-lenses have the internationally standard aperture scale of 1—1.4—2—2.8—4—5.6—8—11—16—22—32. The aperture ring also clicks in at half-stop increments.

As an image composition tool, the aperture is a function of what it achieves: depth of field. If one shoots a subject with the smallest aperture, the subject will be captured in focus from front to back on the film. A completely different image results if one uses the largest aperture from the same spot and places the now very narrow plane of focus on a certain part of the subject. This part is a captivating item in the image and the other components of the image dissolve into greater degrees of blur, depending on how far away from the plane of focus they are

Cloudy sky, maximum aperture for a safe hand-held shutter speed and minimal depth of field were the "ingredients" of this picture. Summicron-M 90mm f/2.

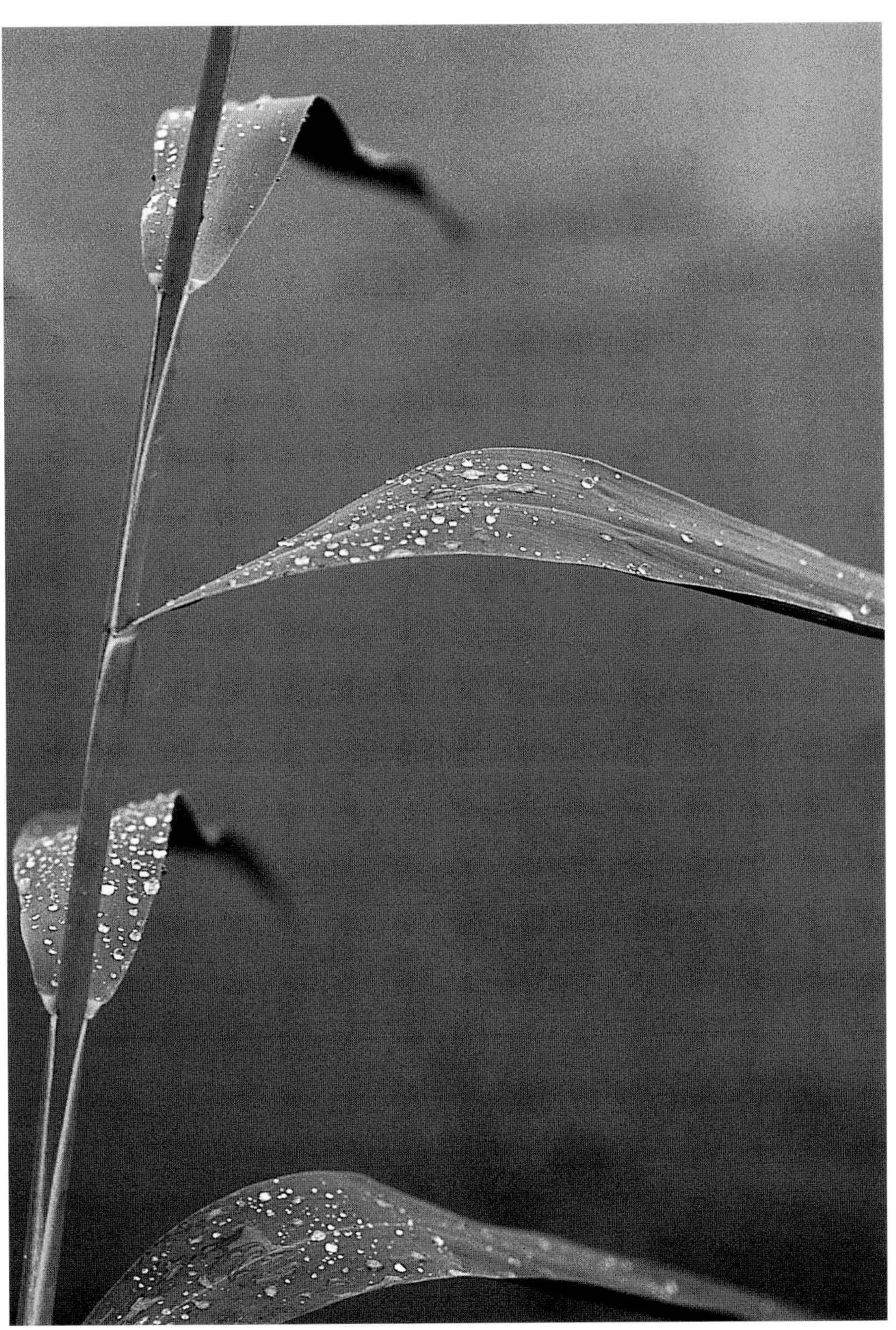

located. Control of depth of field is the tool of image composition.

Three Fingers for Total Control

All you need for your trip to a correctly exposed slide or negative with the Leica M6 TTL is the shutter speed dial and the aperture ring. In a reflex camera this is called "match metering." It is something like "back to basics" and gives the user the freedom of thought that comes with not worrying whether or not the correct program is functioning right now. This kind of freedom is the only thing one experiences with the Leica M6 TTL. Your brain behind the camera alone determines the positions of the rings and thus the photographic image. You alone are responsible for the creative, informative, documentary, storytelling qualities of the picture. If you are not happy with the picture when you see it, the blame rests wholly with you. This knowledge leads to asking the same question while contemplating any subject: is a carefully located plane of focus more important or is motion blur and camera shake to be avoided by using fast shutter speeds with their attendant apertures and the depths of field that result?

If the fast shutter speed takes precedence—and this is the case for a great many more subjects and scenes than one would think at first glance—set the M6 TTL shutter speed dial to the speed that your experience suggests is best, hold the camera to your eye, aim the centre of the metering field at the important part of the subject, and press the release lightly. The arrow that lights up in the viewfinder tells you in which direction you have to turn the aperture ring until the arrow disappears and the dot lights up. And that's it. You used three fingers on the aperture ring and shutter speed dial to do something that an automatic reflex camera would have done in slightly less time in shutter-priority mode.

If the LED's do not light up when you press the release, it could be for one of three reasons:

1 the M6 TTL's battery is flat or there is no battery fitted

2 the M6 is not cocked and the metering system is off

3 the shutter speed dial is in the "OFF" position and the metering system is disconnected from the battery.

If the left-arrow LED is flashing, the lens cap is still on the lens or the light striking the metering field is below the metering system's working range—perhaps because the aperture is too small.

Whether you need a very narrow or a broad depth of field for your subject, turn the aperture ring until your experience, or the depth of field scale on the M-lens, tells you that the desired setting is reached. But humans do not have an instinctive feel for what aperture f/5.6 or f/16 is, nor for the depth of field corresponding to each. Information and assistance for all Leica M and R lenses can be found in the Leica publication 920-003 Depth of Field Tables. Don't take too seriously the derision voiced by reflex camera owners "That's what you get for having a rangefinder camera where you can't see the depth of field in the viewfinder". An aperture closed to a moderate value will have already made the ground glass of a reflex camera so dark that it becomes difficult to determine precisely where the sharpness zone lies. This estimation also has to include the amount by which the negative or slide will be enlarged later. Practical experience shows that one should not overestimate the usefulness of the depth of field preview button on a reflex camera. Is this why some reflex cameras have lost that button in their evolution? Depth of field only became an important term for me when I surrendered to pressure and brought home a reflex camera in addition to my M3. The fact that it was a Leica R3 does not enter into the discussion. But it is an aperture-priority system and one has to select the aperture oneself. With the M3, I selected the desired shutter speed appropriate to the subject and let the aperture have whatever was left of the exposure value. I focused perfectly accurately with the rangefinder and never had any problems with the depth of field that chance allotted me.

Perhaps depth of field is held in too high a regard as a result of cameras with aperture-priority modes where one has to select an aperture in advance. The Leica M photographer should not allow him- or herself to be bound into thinking in terms of depth of field zones so that the M6 TTL can be used and enjoyed as it should be: as an unobtrusive and dynamic camera for photography in the thick of the action.

Select the aperture required for the desired depth of field, raise the M6 TTL to your eye, aim the centre of the metering area at the most important subject detail and touch the release. If you're in luck, the dot LED will light up and you can push the trigger down all the way immediately and take your shot. If an arrow-LED appears, turn the shutter speed dial in the direction indicated using the tip of your finger—the aperture ring has to stay where it is because of the desired depth of field—without lowering the camera. Since the knob must click into one of the stops, you have a choice between two settings that are a full stop apart if either one of the arrows lights up along with the dot. Moving the shutter speed knob in the direction indicated by the arrow will cause the other arrow to appear along with the dot. You now have to choose between one of the two speeds—normally the faster one to avoid camera shake—and eliminate the arrow by opening the aperture by half a stop. The resulting slight decrease in the depth of field will certainly not affect the image compo-

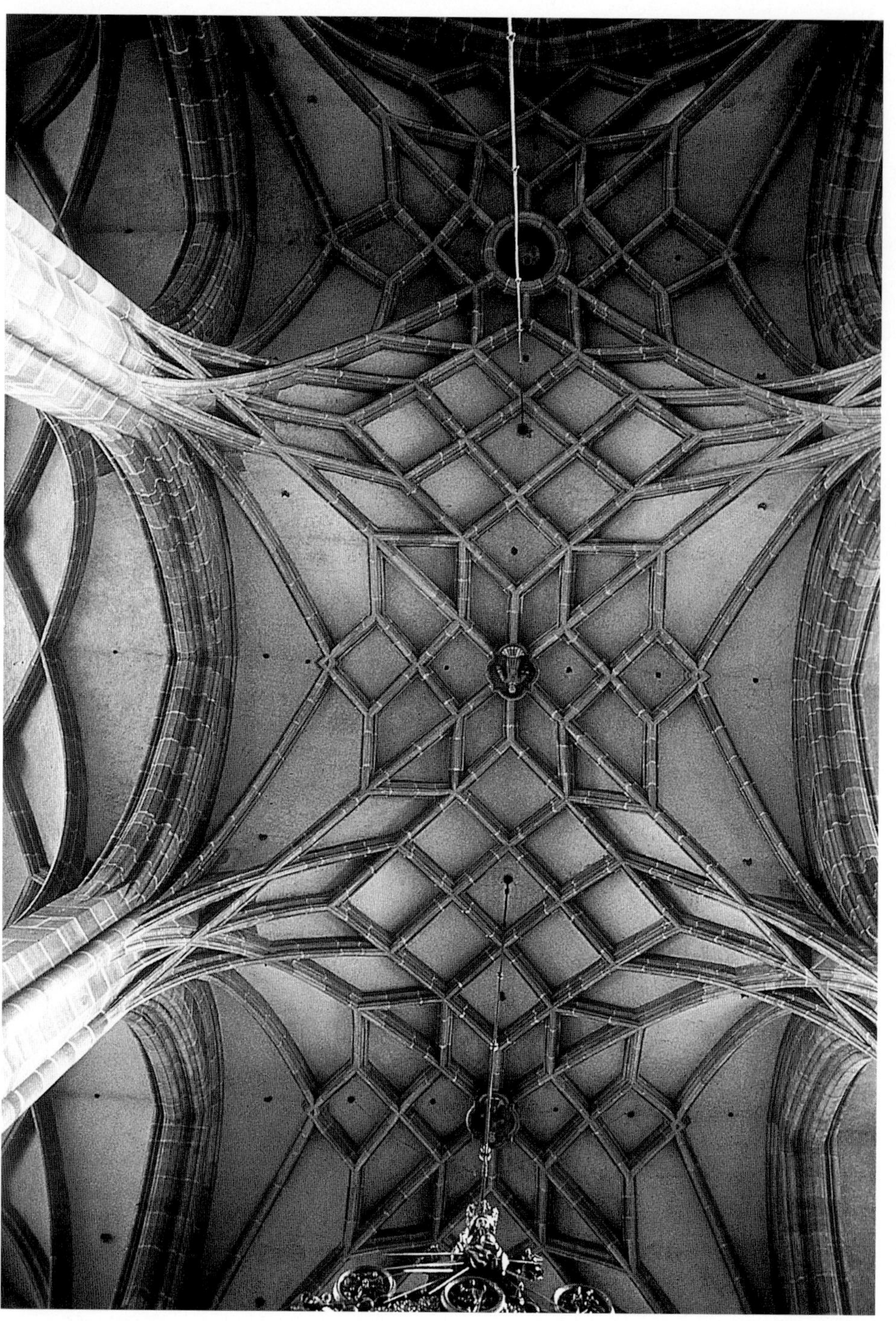

sition. The distance between the click-stops on the aperture ring of an M-lens is so great that one can practically adjust steplessly to any shutter speed.

One can also gain experience using the Leica M6 TTL's match-needle system: if black clouds are not chasing across the sky and creating sudden bright patches of sun, the subject illumination will remain constant for more than the next twenty seconds. You therefore do not have to turn the shutter speed and/or aperture dials to maintain a balance on the match metering system. Don't be worried if one arrow or the other lights under otherwise constant lighting conditions just because a slightly different area of the subject happens to be in the metering zone at the moment: the shutter speed/aperture pair selected a few moments ago for this shot will still be correct. If you react to change by adjusting the aperture slightly, the subject will appear a bit brighter or darker in the image.

I experienced a very personal kind of surprise when I went back to shooting with my M3 after many years of working with an autofocus reflex camera. The slides were exposed so consistently correctly that they could have been taken with an automatic camera boasting one of the best metering systems available. Another factor in this equation, no doubt, is the fact that I have used the same slide film for years and always have it developed in the same E-6 process. The result could have been a kind of seventh sense which lights a warning signal in my head if it thinks that the subject and viewfinder reports don't quite match.

For a shot into the high vaulting, I laid the M6 TTL on the floor. Elmarit-M 28mm f/2.8.

Anyone who is eagerly waiting for me to explain the Leica M6 TTL equivalent of the secret handshakes required to master the complexity of buttons on a reflex camera, I will have to disappoint. One does not need buttons on a camera for something that needs heart and brain, together with fantasy, knowledge and wit. But one cannot avoid the question any longer, that what is it exactly that makes the Leica M6 TTL so timelessly fascinating? How does it give the impression of being able to take better pictures? It only offers 14 lenses, one of which is the amazing Tri-Elmar 28-35-50mm f/4 with it variable focal lengths, but a true zoom it will never have—I have not missed one yet in my almost 40 years of Leica M photography.

The M6 does not have autofocus, no auto-exposure modes, no programs, no DX-code reader. The M6 TTL's only concession to modern camera technology is its TTL flash exposure control system, in conjunction with either the SL-20 flash

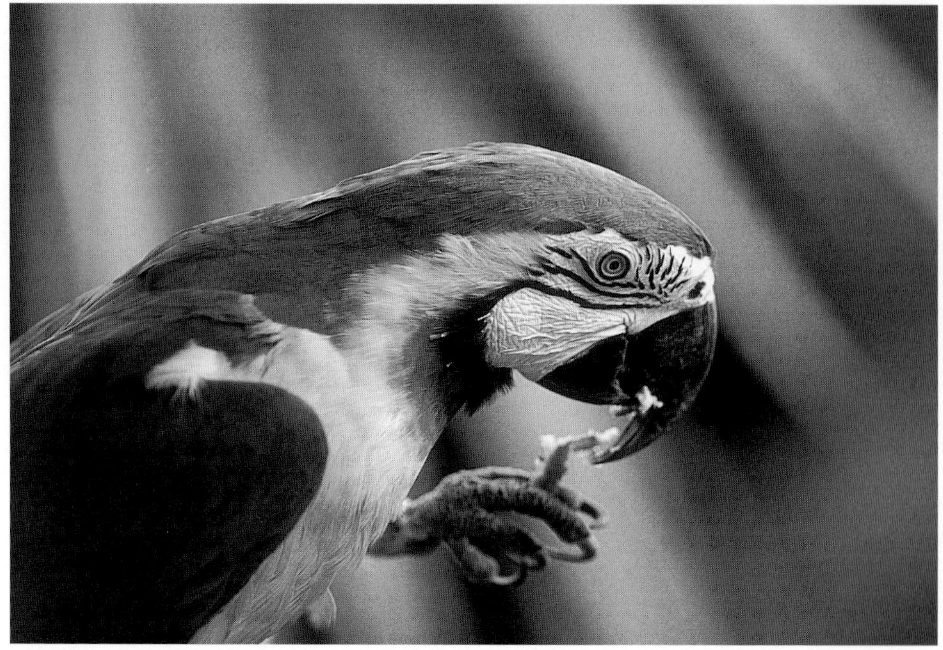

Only maximum aperture under the veranda led to a short enough exposure time for the parrot playing with his claws and beak. The roof removed the high contrasts from the subject. Elmarit-M 135mm f/2.8.

specifically designed for it, or flashes using the SCA 3000 system via the 3501/M1 adapter. Anyone who wants to use a lens longer than 135mm on the M6 needs a bit of patience to travel the distances required to reach the goal.

All this is offset by the hard-to-describe feeling of holding the ultimate in fine-mechanics and optics in your hand,.and the feeling of being able to rely completely on the M6 in the toughest circumstances. In its wonderfully simple concentration on the important and necessary and the ease with which one can learn how to use it, the M6 TTL confirms an old adage: only the image that one has had in one's head for minutes, hours, days even, or sometimes only seconds, that is the image created by one's imagination, should be captured on film. No computer can take that away from you.

Leica M6 TTL Technical Specifications

Type:

35mm rangefinder camera with mechanically controlled shutter, interchangeable lenses with focal lengths between 21mm and 135mm, through-the-lens spot metering and TTL flash control.

Camera Body:

Compact all-metal body, with hinged door in back, covered with easy-grip, textured PVC. 0.8mm zinc die-cast top-plate and 0.8mm brass base-plate. Die-cast shutter crate for maximum stability. Quick-mount M-bayonet for lens mount, mechanical connections for the Leica Winder M, Leica Winder M4-P, or Leica Winder M4-2 from serial number 10350.

Viewfinder and Rangefinder:

Bright, contrasty viewfinder image independent of focal length. Viewfinder magnification with the Leica M6 TTL/0.72 = 0.72x, with the Leica M6 TTL/0.85 = 0.85x with all lenses. Viewfinder calibrated for –0.5 dioptres, thread for correction lenses.

Format frame boundaries are indicated by projected frames which appear in pairs depending on the mounted lens: 50mm + 75mm, 35mm + 135mm, 28mm + 90mm. The Leica M6 TTL/0.85x does not have a 28mm frame. Frames can be projected at will using a selection lever without changing lenses.

Format frames enclose the angle of view as seen by the mounted lens; parallax correction is achieved by the rangefinder's control system. The interior edges of the format frame correspond to a 23x35mm film size (= the cutout in a slide frame) when the lens is at its close-focus point.

Large-base rangefinder using split-image and coincident-image methods. Bright measuring area in the centre of the viewfinder, mechanical measuring base 69.25mm, effective measuring base through viewfinder magnification 49.9mm, 135mm with the M6/0.85x.

Exposure Metering System:

Spot metering through-the-lens (TTL metering) at the working aperture, is activated for about 12 seconds by touching the release when the shutter is cocked. The system is turned off after the exposure and when the shutter speed dial is in the "OFF" position. A silicon photocell with a concentrating lens and filter to adjust to the sensitivity of the eye measures the light reflected off a metering spot, located on the first shutter blind, whose diameter is 12mm (about 13% of the film format), exposure matching with an LED system in the viewfinder after aperture and shutter speed between 1s and 1/1000s have been selected manually. The shutter speed dial must be set to one of the engraved settings, partial stop settings are not possible.

Careful matching of exposure to subject using shutter speed and aperture is achieved using LEDs: only a dot = correct exposure, left or right arrow + dot = about 1/2 a stop over or under exposure, only the left or right arrow = over or under exposure of at least one stop.

Metering range: from 0.063 to 125,000 cd/m2 at f/1. Left LED flashes when the lower boundary of the metering range has been passed.

Film speed: manual selection from ISO 6/9° to ISO 6400/39°.

Working range: at ISO 100/21°, exposure values from -1 to +20, that is 2s (shutter set to "B") and f/1 to 1/1000s and f/32.

Rangefinder / viewfinder image: the metering cell covers about 23% of the current format frame, its diameter is approximately 2/3 of the short side.

Power: two IEC SR 44 silver-oxide button cells or one 1/3N 3V lithium battery. Fresh batteries last for about 2900 meterings assuming 10 seconds activity per metering or about 80 36-exposure films. Automatic battery check: if the remaining battery power is lower than the required minimum, the right hand LED blinks.

Shutter:

Horizontal-travel, rubberised cloth focal plane shutter, extremely quiet and vibrationless, with speeds of 1—1/2—1/4—1/8—1/15—1/30—1/60—1/125—1/250—1/500—1/1000s and "B" for exposure times of any desired length. The shutter speed dial clicks into the engraved settings, half-stop settings are not possible.

Flash synchronisation: for electronic flash 1/50s, marked with a flash symbol, all longer exposure times and "B," for non-electronic flash from 1/30s to 1s and "B". Sync. socket for electronic and non-electronic flashes, X-contact in the hot shoe, both can be used simultaneously.

TTL Flash exposure control with centre-weighted average metering using SCA-3000 flash units and the adapter SCA 3501/M1. Flash exposure correction from -31/3 to +31/3 EV, set on the SCA 3501 adapter. Flash-ready display in the viewfinder via a flash symbol, it blinks for about 4s when the exposure is correct.

Shutter release: with a thread for cable release, depressing it about 0.25–0.45mm the exposure metering system and LEDs are activated, depressing to about 1.3–1.7mm the shutter fires.

Film Transport:

Rapid-advance lever with hinged thumb piece, can be swung out about 30° when in use. Rotation angle for advancing film and cocking shutter is 120°, can be done in one movement or in several partial ones.

Loading film: insert cartridge with about 11cm of film leader into the cartridge slot, insert leader into the slit in the take-up spool and mount bottom plate.

Frame counter: with magnifier, counts forward from -2 to 40, automatically resets when the bottom plate is removed.

Film transport control: rewind knob rotates when film transport is normal.

Rewinding film: using flip-up rewind crank after switching the R-knob on the front of the camera. Rear door and removable bottom plate for easy film loading.

Film window: 23.8 x 35.6mm, the image size changes slightly depending on the image angle/focal length of the lens.

Film transport motor: Leica Winder M, Leica Winder MP-4, Leica Winder M4-2 starting at serial number 10350 can be mounted onto the M6 TTL instead of the bottom plate, film transport and shutter cocking at a rate of up to 3 frames per second.

Size, Weight, Other Features:

All Leica M-lenses can be used on the Leica M6-TTL. The following lenses protrude too far into the camera body and the metering and TTL-exposure control systems are therefore not operational:

Hologon 15mm, f/8
Super-Angulon-M 21mm, f/4
Super-Angulon-M 21mm, f/3.4
Elmarit-M 28mm, f/2.8 below serial number 231.4921

Rings for a carrying strap
Tripod socket: A 1/4, DIN 4503 (1/4")

Dimensions:

Height:	27.8mm
Length:	138mm
Depth:	38mm
Flange-focal distance:	27.8mm
Weight:	560g.

All specifications without lens.

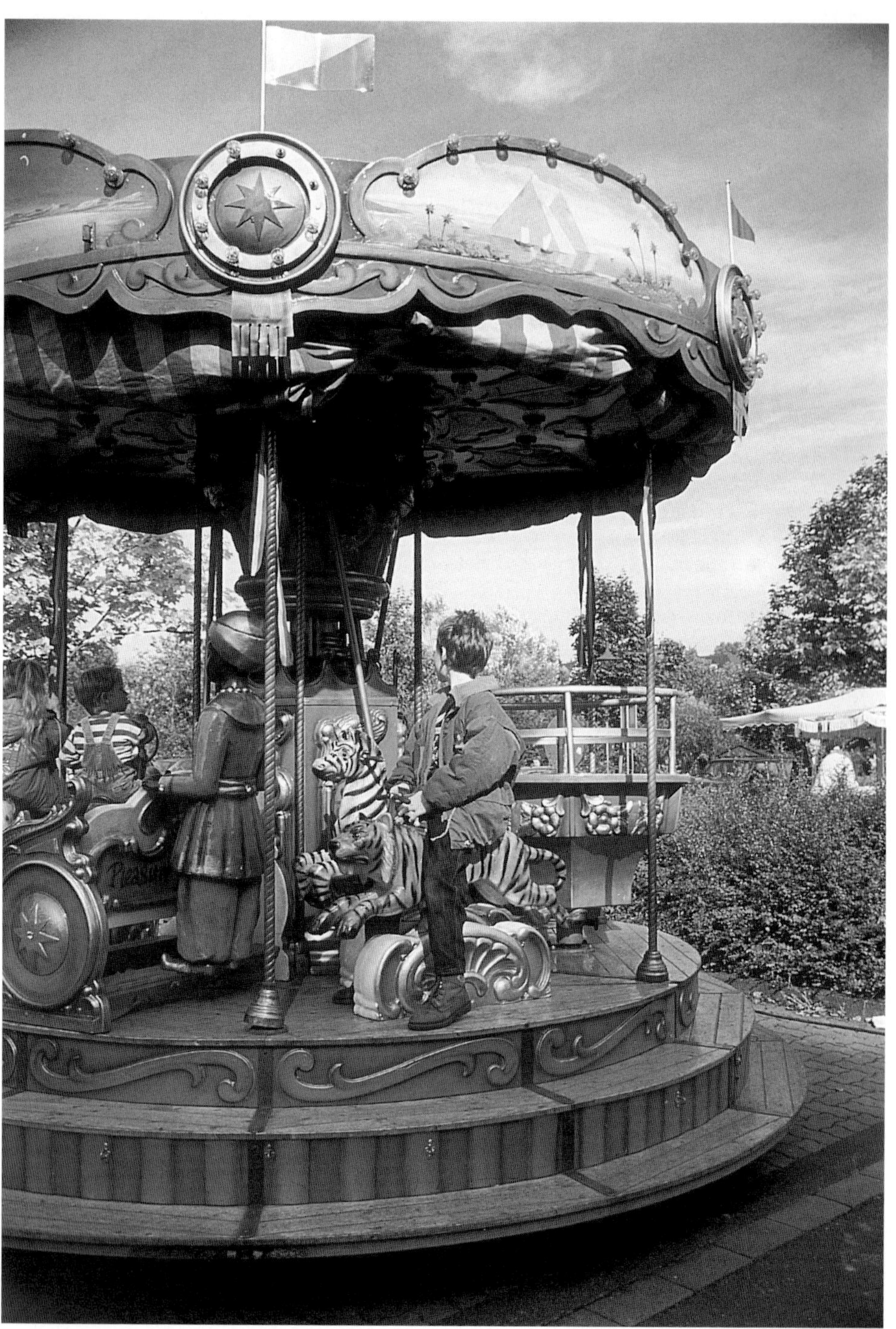

Chapter 3

The Motor for the Leica M6 TTL

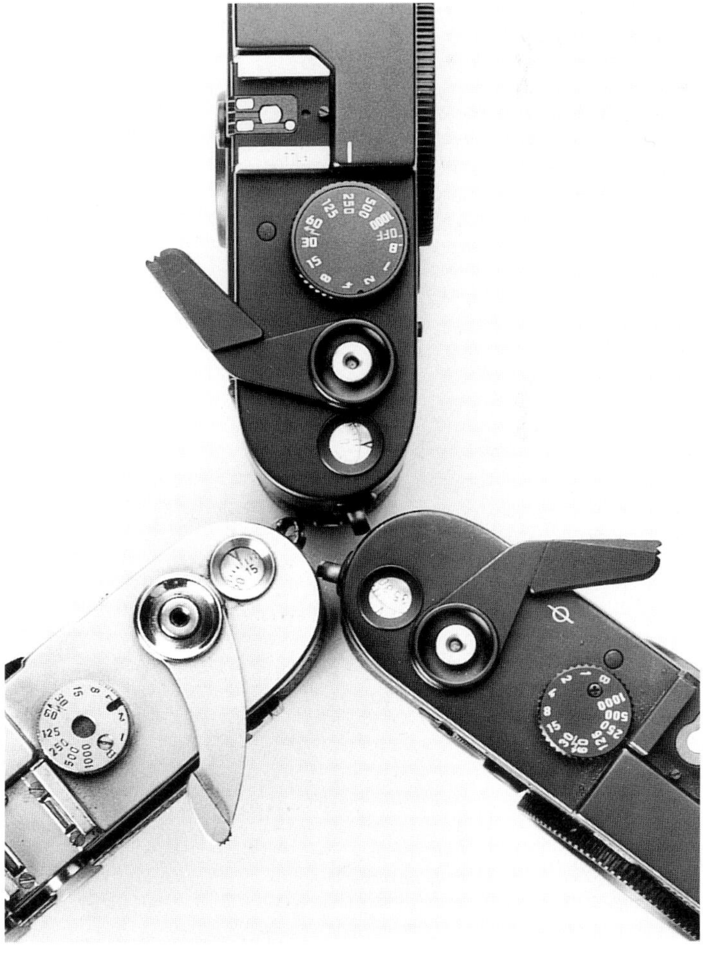

The silver Leica M3 and the black M6 (lower right) are 30 years apart and another 14 years passed before the M6 TTL mounted the photographic stage. The exterior differences are minimal: the curved rapid-advance lever had to cede to a cranked successor—I still prefer the M3. The M6's shutter speed dial and the M6 TTL's larger one are missing the slit for the Leicameter that was found on the M1, M2, M3, M4. The significant differences between the M3 through M6 and M6 TTL are under the top plate.

The soft fall sun emphasises the charm of the elaborate childrens' carousel. Summicron-M 35mm f/2.

Only three ways to advance to the next frame have been developed for the 35mm camera. Firstly, there was the knob on the right-hand side of the camera which became the hallmark of dynamic Leica photography. Made of solid brass, 18.5mm in diameter, 9.3mm high and with a handy rounding on the top edge, it was an unmistakable feature of screw-mount Leica cameras. After 39 years of service, it was retired with the Leica Ig. Reporters are said to have prided themselves, and set themselves apart from "mere photographers", in being able to fire off two shots in three seconds, thanks to a nimble trick with thumb and forefinger. I must say that I have never seen it done myself. And now listen to the noise a motorised 35mm reflex camera makes to manage two shots a second...

The Leica M3 of 1954, with its rapid advance lever, introduced a completely new Leica feel. It represented a large step in the development of Leica technology. Everything hidden inside it, refined over subsequent decades, is included in the Leica M6 TTL. The wonderful handling of the M rapid-advance lever can truly only be experienced: simply moving one's thumb along the edge of the camera body moves the lever out to its 30° ready position. The thumb automatically stays in this spot between the camera and the lever, giving the camera enough stability for firing if the left hand is indispensable elsewhere for some reason. Now one just has to slide one's thumb forward and around to the right for the 120° motion of the lever and the film and shutter are ready for the next shot. Small thumbs cannot quite manage the entire 120° swing. No matter, you can divide it into two, three, four small steps. Only those who have never had the chance to experience the advantages of a multi-step advance lever will consider this feature mere mechanical foolery. The sound of the M6 TTL shutter can hardly be heard over normal conversation and no-one will notice the tiny movements of your thumb.

Two shots in three seconds are not an impossibility with the Leica M6 TTL, given a coordinated thumb and index finger. Even one shot per second can be achieved—of course only with concessions in terms of image location and without adjust-ing focus.

The third transport method on 35mm cameras is motorised drive. One has limited freedom to choose between its two current versions: one can pick a camera onto which a motor drive can be mounted or one can select a camera with a built-in motor—and has to change one's entire system for the one or the other. Cameras with built-in motors are usually smaller and lighter but not necessarily quieter than a reflex camera with an external motor drive. The issue of sound is more than just noise. A photographer will find this out too late when he or she successfully smuggles a camera past the "No Photography Allowed" sign only to be quietly but firmly escorted from the building after the second shot because the camera gave him or her away. One cannot turn the motor off in the fully electronically-controlled camera in order to achieve a quieter mode of operation. A feature of high-tech cameras that the guards particularly enjoy is the treble peeping that the camera emits to advise of successful or unsuccessful metering and autofocus. This alerts the watchers to the misdeed before it has even taken place.

My preference therefore lies with a motorised transport that can be mounted onto the bottom of the camera. Whenever necessary, I can turn it off and work much more quietly by hand. But even so, the rattle of the reflex shutter, the automatic aperture and the high speed shutter blades still sound like a thunder clap in the stillness of the cathedral or the sparsely populated museum. These are the situations in which one desperately needs a whispering Leica M6 TTL!

The Leica Winder-M

It mounts on the bottom of the camera in place of the base-plate with the same fitting. Those who wish to use a Winder-M on two or more Leica M4s or M6s should keep this in mind: you cannot remove the base-plate from the M6 or M6 TTL in the middle of a film in order to attach or remove the winder! You first have to rewind the film then advance it again after the winder is attached. Should the, albeit minimal, noise of the winder be intrusive, the same lever that locks it onto the camera has an intermediate setting which keeps it on the camera but does not connect it to the power supply. The M6 or M6 TTL then works in conventional manual mode.

The Winder-M does not change anything in the standard operation of the camera—the only difference is that the right thumb can take a bit of a break. The first thing you will notice with glee: the motorised Leica M6 TTL is still orders of magnitude quieter than any non-motorised reflex camera and even quieter than most compact cameras. The Leica Winder-M is controlled mechanically via the M6 TTL shutter release. One should therefore cock the shutter with the manual advance lever before attaching the winder. If you do not do this, the control lever projecting into the camera performs this function before you have the chance to fully close the lock. While this does not have any adverse effects, the surprise of the moment can be avoided.

Switching from single-shot to series exposures on this winder is simply a function of sensitivity in your fingertip. The winder motor starts after the shutter has completed its task; it advances the film and sets the shutter for the next shot—and then pushes the release up again. If your finger follows this movement and lifts off the release, you will obtain only one shot. If, however, the fingertip maintains some back-pressure on the pulsating release, the M6 TTL and its winder immediately attack the next shot: hence fingertip-

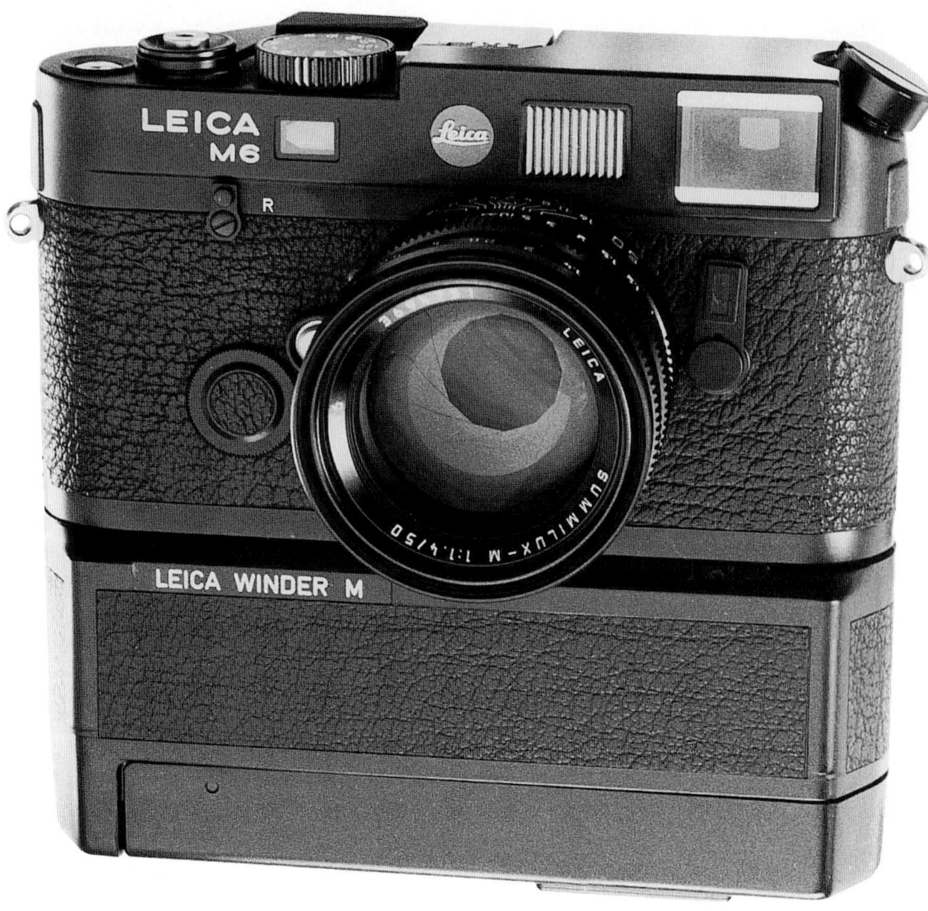

The Winder-M locks onto the bottom of the M6 TTL in place of the bottom plate and couples directly with the camera's control system. The M6 is handy and quiet even with the Winder! Constant pressure on the release makes the M6 take three shots per second.

controlled series shots. You can use all the shutter speeds the M6 offers for this function. The Winder-M manages up to three shots per second with a fresh set of batteries, provided the exposure time is at least as fast as 1/30s. If you hold the release down at its bottom point with stronger pressure, you will stop the Winder-M completely in its tracks until you release the pressure and let the release come up. At the end of the film, the Winder-M turns itself off automatically, regardless of the number of frames shot, as a security measure. It will even turn itself off if the winding process has not been completed. When this occurs, please use the intermediate setting of the lock lever to disconnect the winder from the battery to prevent unnecessary battery drain.

The Winder-M is powered by four AA 1.5V alkaline batteries. A fresh set will last for about 150 36-exposure films. Ni-Cad rechargeable batteries can also be used.

Should One Motorise the Leica M6 TTL?

While the Leica Winder-M fits in form and structure to the Leica M6 TTL, I find it does detract from the elegance of the system. Please feel free to disagree. For those who need a winder under the camera, appearances are secondary.

The Winder-M can manage a maximum of three shots per second. Will this shot frequency enable one to capture all the phases of a triple-flip off the 5-metre board? Three shots per second mean that the interval between shots is a bit less than a third of a second—and thus too long to capture a fast-moving event on film without interruptions. How much a subject changes within a quarter second is easy to determine. Mount your M6 on a tripod on a street corner and shoot afternoon traffic controlled by a light at a speed of 1/4s and an appropriate aperture. The varying lengths of motion blur accompanying passers-by and cars will immediately show you how much a subject changes, depending on the speed of motion. You will also see that increasing speeds make it less and less certain that you will capture the crucial point of the movement when shooting with a relatively low frequency. A dark phase of 1/4s, or 250 milliseconds, is always long enough to miss the important part. The rate of success is determined by the relationship between the pause between shots and the speed of the subject. Even with a motorised Leica, one must therefore adhere to the time-honoured professional maxim and use cool judgment and even cooler hands to evaluate the scene in front of the camera and use your sixth-sense to fire a brief spurt of three or four shots when the climax of the movement is almost upon you. A constant pressure on the trigger will chase a 36-exposure film through the camera in about 14 seconds—and the most amazing scenes will be taking place in front of the camera while you are reloading your film!

Wasting film is therefore not the primary task of the winder under the Leica M6 TTL. Its much more important task is to prepare the camera for the next shot immediately after the last one. The Winder-M can do this faster than even the most skilled Leica M photographer. When and how often you will need the assistance of the winder depends on your experience and the current situation. If you tend to shoot a large number of longer series, for comparisons, for example, the winder is a good aid. But please don't forget: at full tilt, it takes only 14 seconds to run a 36-exposure film through the M6 TTL!

The Leica Winder-M does not have a socket for a cable release. In order to fire the M6 from a distance, you have to use a mechanical, electromechanical or pneumatic release screwed into

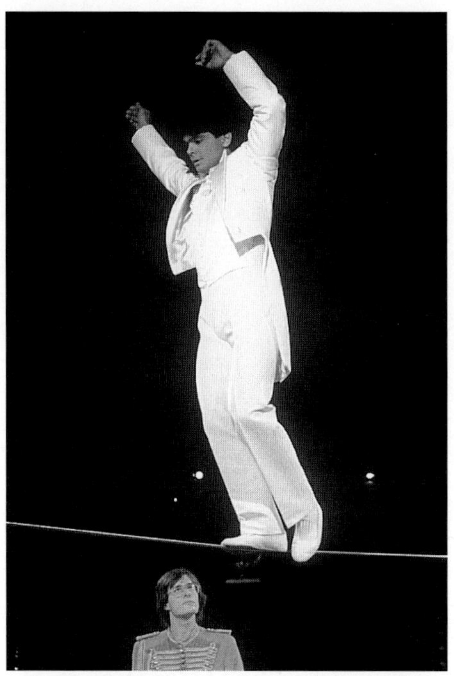

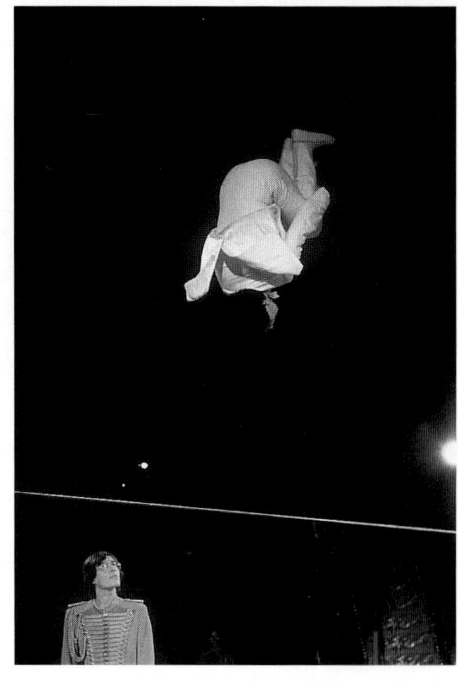

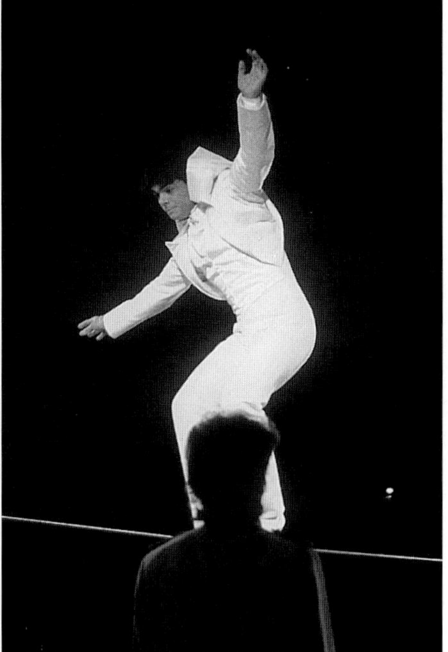

A flip in three phases on the tightrope in the Circus Roncalli, frozen with the Winder-M and the Noctilux 50mm f/1.

the M6 TTL release. But please take care that the plunger of the release is not overlong because it could damage the camera's mechanics. Also ensure that the plunger can follow the pulsation of the release! Before you risk damage to your camera with your own concoctions, contact Leica's Technical Service department.

The Winder M4-P and the Winder M4-2 from serial number 10350 are also compatible with the Leica M6 TTL. They are practically identical to the current Winder-M in terms of appearance and function.

Chapter 4

The Leica M Lenses

Limited but distinguished is the club of fourteen lenses for the Leica M6 TTL. The focal length range starts with the Elmarit-M 21mm, f/2.8 ASPH and ends with the Apo-Telyt-M 135mm, f/3.4. This collection of optical treasures does not include a fish-eye nor the beloved compact-zoom 28-105 whose appeal has lured many a photographer into accepting maximum apertures as slow as f/4 or worse. Fourteen lenses covering seven focal lengths—compared to the 35-lens palettes offered for most reflex cameras, this selection for the Leica M6 seems very limited. But an overwhelming selection of lenses and focal lengths does not determine a camera's power or usability, but rather a well-chosen array of focal lengths that correspond to the performance and application range of the camera.

The eight focal lengths from 21mm to 135mm do not leave room for needing a zoom—in my almost 40 years of shooting with the Leica M3 and M6, I have not missed one yet. A few steps towards a subject or away from it move it to an optimal position in the projection frame in the viewfinder. Furthermore, one generally benefits in terms of a more effective arrangement of foreground and background. A zoom increasingly encourages the photographer to forget these often crucial steps.

Driven by their designers to the ultimate of the achievable, the Leica M-lenses—and R-lenses—are truly the best. They are not terribly light or small. But what would you expect from lenses that are built to the toughest precision machining rules and made almost entirely without plastics?

The highlights of the Leica-M lens palette are evident at first glance. The Summicron-M 35mm, f/2 ASPH is still the smallest and lightest lens in its class, the Summilux-M 35mm, f/1.4 ASPH offers a fast maximum aperture together with incomparable imaging quality. The Noctilux-M 50mm, f/1 was for twenty years the fastest, mass-produced small-format lens. Only in the fall of 1989 did an autofocus small-format reflex camera step up to the podium with a 50mm f/1 AF lens. The Apo-Telyt-M

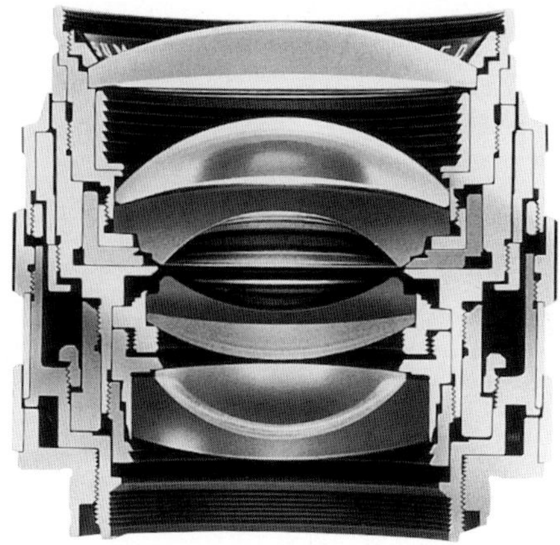

Leica M-lenses represent the highest standards of optical and mechanical precision and performance at the very edges of the physically/technically possible. Each lens is carefully adjusted after a long and rigorous testing program. Cross-section of the Summilux-M 50mm f/1.4.

135mm, f/3.4, although the slowest lens in the Leica M palette, is just slightly slower than the discontinued Elmarit-M 135mm, f/2.8. The Telyt-M's apochromatic correction, which is coupled with a lens system of slightly greater light transmission, more than makes up for the shortfall. In the classic focal length range between 35mm and 90mm, the standard aperture is f/2. Then why not a 135mm, f/2 for the M6? Building a 135mm, f/2 to the high standards required by Leica designers would not be a problem. But it would be a bit too large, a bit too heavy and somewhat cumbersome on the delicate (in the aesthetic sense!) Leica M6 TTL. It would also encroach too far into the viewfinder image.

The Common Features of all Leica-M Lenses

First is the mere 30° turn required to mount the lens and the 5.3mm long distance between the start of the bayonet flange and the inside of its grooves. It is responsible for the unique positive lock which does not loosen even after decades of use and holds M-lenses securely in all M-cameras. Despite its tight fit, the Leica-M bayonet turns as easily and smoothly as a spoon is liquid honey. And it will stay that way for the next thirty years.

The Leica M-bayonet does not have any protruding levers or posts that could be damaged in a rushed, somewhat-less-than-careful handling of the lens. Even the rangefinder's sensor mechanism operates inside the bayonet ring. One can and may therefore set any lens down on its bayonet ring! Many a reflex camera's lens would be ready for the repair shop after one such placement! Care is required only with the M wide-angle lenses whose rear elements protrude beyond the bayonet.

The focusing helicoids are made of brass and a brass alloy or brass and a special aluminium alloy. Exterior and interior helicoids are matched to one another with the tightest of tolerances. As a result, a wafer-thin layer of a special lubricant is enough to ensure smooth operation of the elements between temperatures of –25°C and +60°C for decades. M-Lenses can even survive brief exposure to even colder temperatures. Those who must subject their lenses to protracted periods below -25°C should have them adjusted at the Leica factory.

All Leica M lenses boast a focusing mechanism that offers decades of wobble-free and resistance-free movement, even with intensive use! The focusing system ensures that the optical system, including the front element, does not rotate during the focusing operation but travels in a straight line front to back. As a result, the lens hoods for the wide-angle lenses can be made rectangular and matched as tightly as possible to the angle of view. Guides ensure that the hood cannot be mounted incorrectly onto the lens. Focusing and aperture rings on all M-lenses turn in the same direction: the largest aperture is located at the leftmost end, the smallest on the right. The aperture ring is located in a very ergonomically appropriate location fairly close to the front of the lens. This is a feature that reflex cameras cannot boast, as the aperture ring is generally jammed between the focusing ring and the relatively bulky camera body.

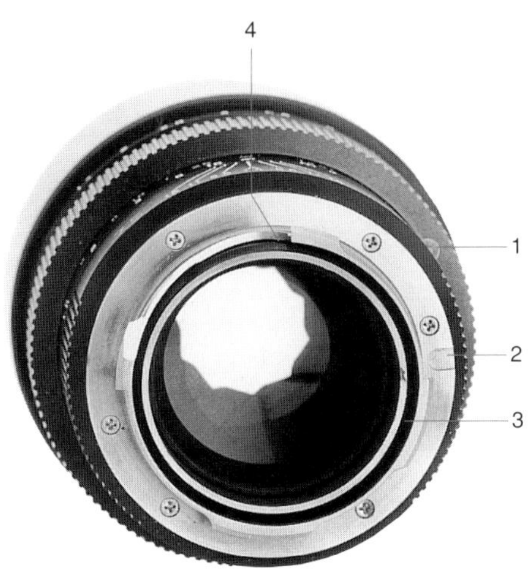

The lens part of the Leica M-bayonet: No levers or probes stick out the back of the bayonet and even the helicoid for the rangefinder always stays inside the protective ring. One can rest the lens on the bayonet without adverse consequences!

1—Index mark for lens mount
2—Detent for locking the lens
3—Individually, manually adjusted helicoid for the rangefinder's sensor
4—Cam for the rangefinder's sensor

Close examination will show traces of the matching of the focusing helicoid to the actual focal length of the lens—it corresponds to the unavoidable production deviation from the stated focal length, generally accurate to two decimal places—and the measuring optic in the Leica M6's rangefinder. You will notice that the lateral motion of this ring, or the lever corresponding to it, is not the same as the lateral motion of the optical system moved by the focusing ring. This has to be the case as the wide-angle movement of the rotating measuring optics, which is controlled by the sensor monitoring the lens's movement, is independent of the focal length of the lens. The measuring optic's movement from infinity to the close-focus setting is always the same. On the other hand, the movement of a lens from infinity to 1m varies greatly depending on focal length: about 0.5mm with a 21mm lens, about 3.1mm with a normal 50mm lens and 9.8mm for a 90mm lens. A 135mm lens travels about 15mm between its close-focus point and infinity. Matching these varying movements to the constant rotation angle of the measuring optic is accomplished by a double-threaded ring coupled to the helicoid. The Leica M-lenses are therefore not in any way less complicated, and in some details they are more custom-made than those of reflex cameras. A number engraved in small digits on the focusing ring indicates the correction required to correct the rangefinder to the actual focal length.

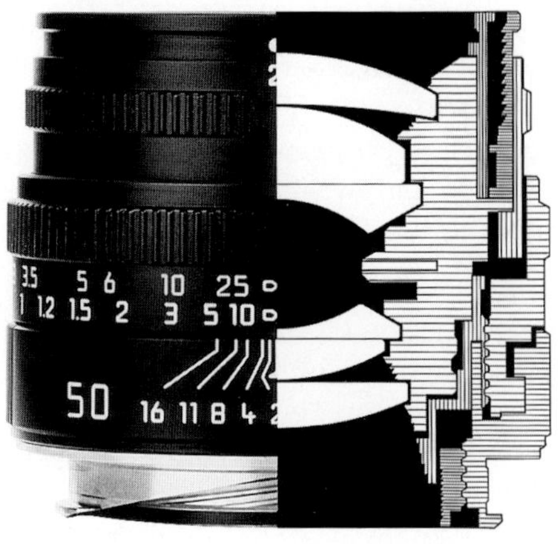

Summicron-M 50mm f/2: Standard lens for all Leica M-cameras with excellent imaging qualities. Still the best lens in its class in terms of highest performance and balanced imaging qualities of the highest level.

A typical Leica trait is the naming of the Leica lenses: "Elmar" is the name given to M-lenses with a speed of f/3.5 or less. Leica lenses with a speed of f/2.8 are called "Elmarit": one exception is the Elmar 50mm, f/2.8 a redesign of the legendary Elmar 50mm, f/3.5. A maximum aperture of f/2 is awarded the name "Summicron." while the super-fast lenses whose maximum aperture is f/1.4 are called "Summilux." The even faster 50mm, f/1 is called "Noctilux", with its suggestion of a lens for the night. Leica lenses boasting unique construction and of telephoto focal lengths are named "Telyt."

All Leica lenses show excellent imaging quality even at their maximum aperture. Maximum aperture is truly a usable aperture. The imaging quality of the fastest M-lenses for the M6 TTL increases even further if one closes them down by one or two stops. But this increase in quality is at such a high level and is so slight that the depth of field required by the photographer's imagination plays the controlling role. Leica lenses are absolutely top-class and are driven to the limits of optical and mechanical technology.

Single or multi-layer coating? Leica designers do not approach this question with the philosophy "the more, the better." The number and type of coatings placed on an element are, for them, important construction and correction tools. Combined with new optical glasses, one can achieve a high degree of UV-absorption. One can therefore do without a UV-filter on the front of a Leica lens, even at the sea or on the top of a mountain—or just use it to protect the front element.

The Standard Lenses

The Leica M-series lenses offer 50mm focal length as the midpoint between the wide-angles, whose generous angle of view captures a large amount of the scene, and the telephotos with their narrow angle of view. Today's entry-level lens into the Leica system is still a 50mm. The 50mm lenses are called "standard" lenses because their angle of view of 45° deviates only slightly from that of the human eye which nature decrees to be between 45° and 50°. Pictures taken with these lenses are therefore found to look "just what I saw." The standard lenses, whose focal length is about the same as the diagonal of the film format, capture subjects on film without any focal length or angle of view effects; they are exactly as one sees them. They do not over-emphasise the main subject in front of a not-small-enough or not-distant-enough background. This is probably why most people have their first photographic successes with a standard lens. But the standard lens is more than just a beginner's tool. Advanced users create captivating pictures using it. Not only Henri Cartier-Bresson, but countless other famous and not so famous Leica photographers have used the 50mm to take wonderful pictures and produce photo-journals that young photographers use as a guide.

Which of the four 50mm M-lenses is the "right" one is a subject that could monopolise an entire evening's discussion. Not to mention that the first M-lens offering variable focal length also embraces the 50mm focal length.

Since the inception of the Leica M-system, the SUMMICRON-M 50mm, f/2 has been the top-performer in terms of superb image quality and contrast all the way into the corners, even at maximum aperture. Its optical construction is a typical Gaussian 6-elements in four groups design. It has been, and still is the normal lens for the Leica M3 through to the M6 TTL. Stopping down to f/2.8 or f/4 produces only a slight increase in contrast. These wonderful imaging qualities change only slightly in the close-up range: the Summicron M 50mm f/2 shows a very even image field with top performance.

The SUMMILUX-M 50mm f/1.4 is, even in its new version, designed for photography at maximum aperture under low or poor lighting conditions: high contrast at maximum aperture, superb internal reflection control, no ghost images in extreme back-lit situations or with a strong light source in the image, high detail resolution. But even the best lens cannot do everything: in the close-up range, slight barrel distortion is evident with tricky subjects.

So which of the 50mm should you choose? The Summicron-M 50mm

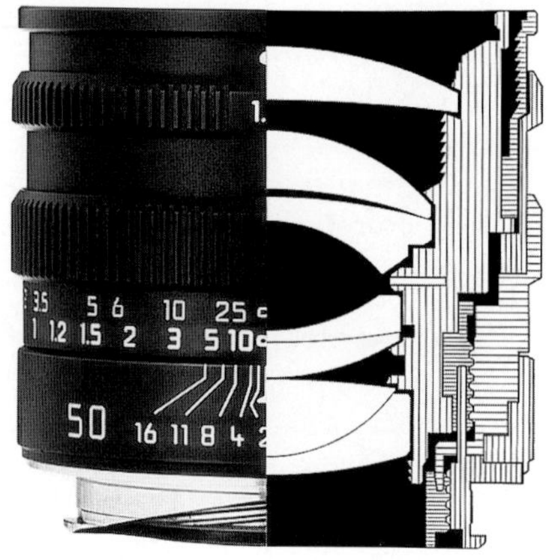

Summilux-M 50mm f/1.4
Very fast standard lens for all Leica M-cameras with very high imaging qualities in sharpness, contrast and resolution, even at maximum aperture under poor lighting conditions.

f/2 is a fast normal lens with overall high performance, even at maximum aperture, thanks to its excellent overall design: its length is normal, its two main planes are symmetrical with the aperture and it is almost 50mm, i.e. the focal length, removed from the film plane. This is why photographers using the older version of the Summicron 50mm f/2 happily attach the lens head to a bellows unit for perfect macro shots.

Summicron-M 50mm f/2 or Summilux-M 50mm f/1.4—the choice is really not easy and depends on the answer to this question: how often do you need an aperture of f/1.4 for photography under poor light, and are you willing to pay almost twice as much as for the Summicron-M 50mm f/2 for those few shots per year? Maybe this will make your decision easier: I never felt unprepared in terms of speed with my Summicron-M 50mm f/2 in my entire Leica career.

The elite NOCTILUX 50mm f/1 is the lens for nighthawks; circus fans; lovers of subjects in the quarter-hour before and after sunset when the already-set sunlight reflects off the clouds and blends with the street lights, shop-window lights and illuminated signs to create an overwhelming mixture of colour; for the romantic hour in candlelight in a restaurant; or in the home. Those who stop the Noctilux-M 50mm f/1 down to f/4 or f/5.6 in these situations, and only use f/1 once or twice a year, have aimed too high with this costly piece of glass. For the same money one would be four fifths of the way to being able to purchase the classic Leica focal length pair Summicron-M 35mm f/2 ASPH and Apo-Summicron-M 90mm f/2 ASPH. But the desire for high-carat jewels like the Noctilux-M 50mm f/1 cannot be measured in dollars and cents!

The freedom afforded by the f/1 aperture on the Noctilux-M 50mm f/1 is impressive: even with a mere ISO 400/27° film, one can manage exposure times of 1/60s or 1/125s in dimly lit streets, living rooms or pubs! Depth of field at f/1 in the close-up range is practically zero and grows to a few centimetres at moderate distances. Only over a distance of 10 metres does it grow to cover about 2 metres. Simply

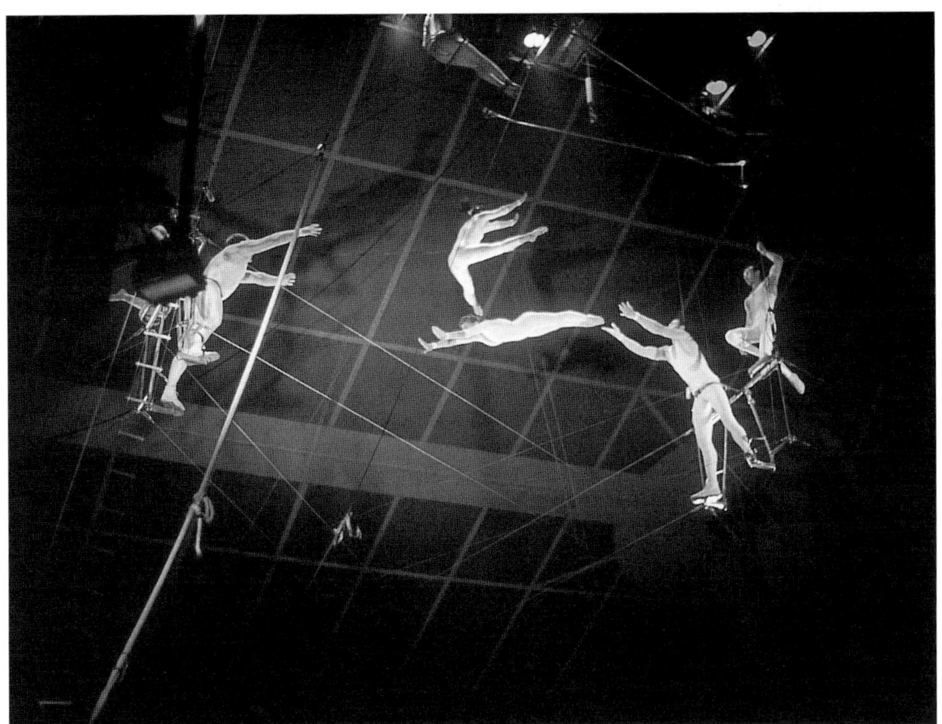

The dark roof of the circus tent could force the M6 TTL exposure meter to select an incorrect, excessive exposure. The solution is to read the information off a subject whose illumination is similar to that of the artists. In the interests of a sufficiently fast shutter speed, open the aperture as wide as it will go. Summicron-M 90mm f/2.

accepting this type of image with a narrow depth of field is not sufficient—one must feed it as one feeds one's best obsessions. The aperture f/1 in the Noctilux-M ensures that one concentrates on the most important aspect of the subject, to accent it with the few centimetres of depth of field and to separate it from the less important aspects of the scene. The necessary focusing accuracy is no problem with the Leica M6 TTL's rangefinder—the version with the 0.85x viewfinder magnification now shows a slight advantage over its sister with the 0.75x magnification. Stopping the Noctilux-M down to f/2.8 or f/5.6 creates the same depth of field as any other 50m lens.

The Noctilux-M, designed for photography at maximum aperture under low light conditions, shows surprisingly little vignetting, despite its exceptionally large maximum aperture, and that disappears completely at f/4. It shows slight barrel distortion in the close-up range. One should therefore not use the Noctilux-M 50mm f/1 for copying small or flat originals.

This high imaging quality, even at maximum aperture, combined with excellent suppression of internal reflections, even with bright light sources in the subject, was achieved by the Leica designers with what appears at first glance to be minimal effort: seven elements in six groups. This is normal for 50mm f/1.7 and 50mm f/1.4 reflex camera lenses. Its weight of 630g provides good dampening for slight movements during longer exposure times. The expensive secret hidden in these elements is invisible. They are ground from glass developed in the former Leitz glass research laboratories. This glass has a very high refractive index of n = 1.9005, combined with anomalous and relatively low dispersion. Only these expensive glasses enabled the Leica designers to come up with such a stunning lens made of only seven elements, with no aspherics, which captures subtle colour differentiation and the smallest subject details, even in low light.

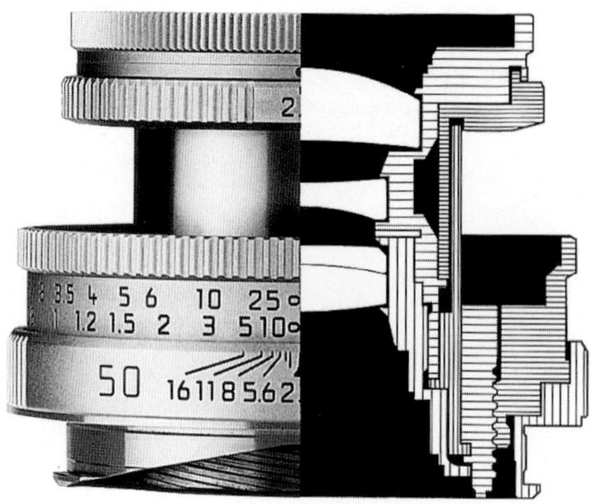

Elmar-M 50mm f/2.8
If compact size and light weight are more important than speed, then this lens, designed using the most modern techniques and highly refractive elements, is the right choice. Its excellent performance allows it to stand on the same level as the other Leica M 50mm lenses.

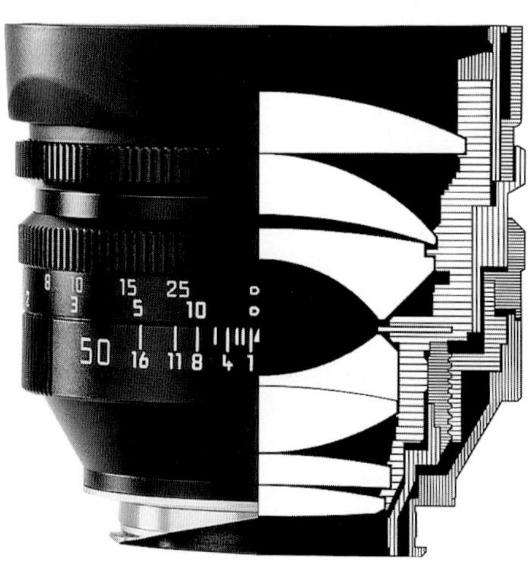

Noctilux-M 50mm f/1
An extremely fast lens for all Leica M-cameras. It offers outstanding performance in sharpness, detail resolution and contrast for scenes in the poorest light—an optical crown jewel!

The Noctilux-M 50mm f/1 had sole, undisputed possession of the distinction "fastest mass-produced small-format lens" for thirteen years. Since the end of 1989, it has had to share this title with an AF 50mm f/1 for an autofocus reflex camera. Because of the nature of the AF-reflex camera, the complexity of this lens is astounding: eleven elements, two of them aspheric, bring in a weight of 985g, 82mm of length and a 92mm diameter. The price is about 10% higher than that of the Noctilux. The Noctilux-M may have to share the "fastest mass-produced small-format lens" title, but it is still in sole possession of the smallest, lightest and most affordable 50mm f/1 lens award.

The fourth 50mm lens for the Leica M6 is the ELMAR-M 50mm f/2.8. According to the Leica naming convention, it should have been called "Elmarit" because of its maximum aperture of f/2.8. But the tradition and fame of this lens, which is closely related to Leica's ascension to world-class status, were stronger. Designed almost 80 years ago, it appeared on the photographic stage along with the first Leica with a speed of f/3.5. It was constantly improved until its aperture reached f/2.8 in the mid-fifties. About twenty years later, it disappeared from the M-program. It returned in 1995. In shape and handling, it is unmistakably the classic Elmar 50mm f/2.8, but redesigned for highly refractive new glasses with low dispersion and with new mechanics. The classic four-element lens thus rose to be on an even playing field with the other high-class M-lenses. Its unique characteristic—like that of its legendary predecessor—is its barrel that collapses into the camera. The result is that the Leica is slimmed down by 16mm and fits into a jacket pocket.

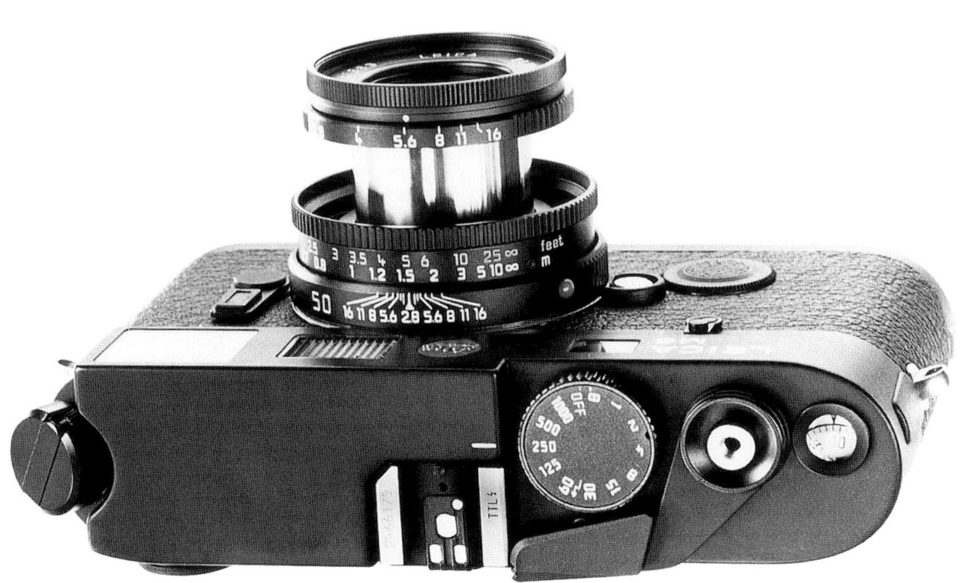

Elmar-M 50mm f/2.8
Extended to its working length, the Elmar-M 50mm f/2.8 is barely 38mm long and is therefore the smallest of the 50mm lenses available for Leica M-cameras.

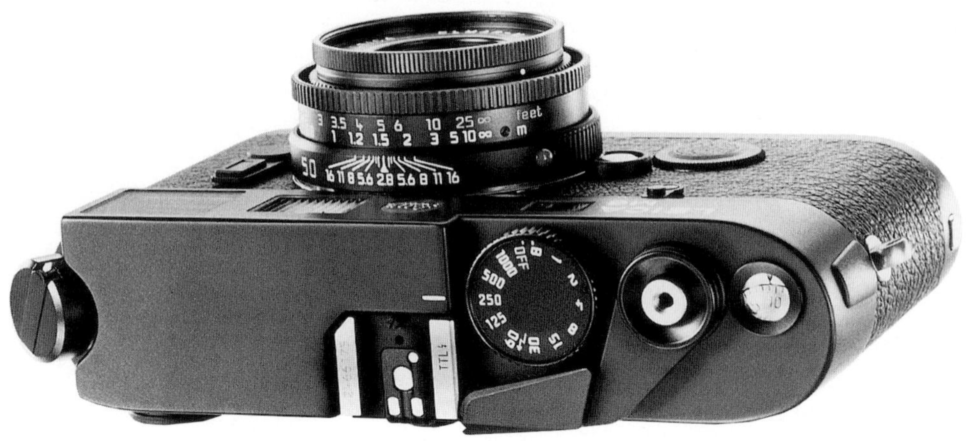

A short rotation to the right, and it allows itself to be collapsed into the camera body by 16mm. The Elmar-M 50mm f/2.8 now only sticks out 22mm from the camera body—perfect for shirt-pocket transportation.

Pulling the barrel out and locking it into place again takes only a second. The image quality of the Elmar-M 50mm f/2.8, even at maximum aperture, is outstanding—and how could it be otherwise. If light weight and compactness are more important than speed, the Elmar-M 50mm f/2.8 is the first choice.

Wide-angle—the Panoramic View of the World

But not only that, the wide-angle can magically create a different perspective between foreground and background that the eye can never see. Whether you mount the Elmarit-M 21mm f/2.8 ASPH or the Elmarit-M 28mm f/2.8 onto your Leica M6 TTL, the rules of the game for using a wide-angle are the same. Here is the first: if you think that you are close enough to the main subject with the 21mm or the 28mm, go a few steps closer. The golden rule of 35mm photography is particularly applicable to wide-angle lenses: fill the frame right up to the edges of the 24x36mm format! This does not mean, though, that the subject should be jammed into the entire area. Give its surroundings some room. Those shooting on negative film could reduce the amount of unwanted background by cropping in the darkroom. This also works when purchasing prints from an economical full-format printer: order a larger print than you actually want and simply trim off the unwanted area.

The photographer producing slides does not have this option. He can only remove the unwanted bits by covering the excess on the slide, thereby recklessly wasting image area, or by commissioning a professional duplicate that maintains the quality of the original but eliminates the unwanted area. Shooting a subject from close-up and allowing the background to become vanishingly small is the stuff dramatic images with altered perspective area are made of. The illusion of distance created by a disproportionately large fin of the classic car, for example, requires depth of field that encompasses the entire image. So turn the aperture ring on the Elmarit-M 21mm f/2.8 ASPH or the Elmarit-M 24mm f/2.8 ASPH to f/5.6 or f/8 and read the expected depth of field off the scale on the focus ring. If you cannot make the "OK" dot appear in the M6 TTL's viewfinder using the full-stop shutter speed dial, you will have to use the aperture ring to fine-tune the exposure. You will end up deviating a maximum of half a stop from the desired aperture. Whether up or down depends on how much latitude the exposure time still has before camera shake becomes an issue. A half-stop larger aperture reduces depth of field negligibly and is not even apparent with a large enlargement. The Elmarit-M 21mm ASPH at an aperture of f/4 and a focus point at 5m already offers a depth of field from 2m to infinity. The Elmarit-M 24mm at the same settings offers focus from 2.5m to infinity.

The Super-wide-angles

If one still considers the Elmarit-M 28mm f/2.8 a super-wide-angle today is a matter of opinion. In the days of the classic Leica I to IIIg, the 28mm lens was the widest available and was therefore considered a super-wide-angle. Let us leave it at that.

The Elmarit-M 21mm f/2.8 ASPH

Its 92° angle of view is larger than the subject displayed in the viewfinder of the Leica M6 TTL/0.72x and larger still than the image in that of the M6 TTL/0.85x. If time does not allow the mounting of the 21mm bright-line finder into the accessory shoe, one could use a bit of imagination and a bit of doubt to guess the area that the Elmarit-M 21mm f/2.8 ASPH would capture on film with nothing more than the M6 TTL/0.72x's viewfinder. [page 113] But the uncontrolled edges of the frame are downright large. With the Leica M6 TTL/0.85x, subject control is truly doubtful. The 21mm bright-line finder always produces better results! Exposure and focus control are performed as always using the M6 TTL rangefinder. If you never, or rarely use the accessory shoe for the Leica SF 20 flash unit, you can leave the 21mm finder permanently attached. This is also true for the bright-line finders for the 24mm and 28mm lenses.

Nine elements, one of which is aspheric, in seven groups are not excessive when one considers the 92°

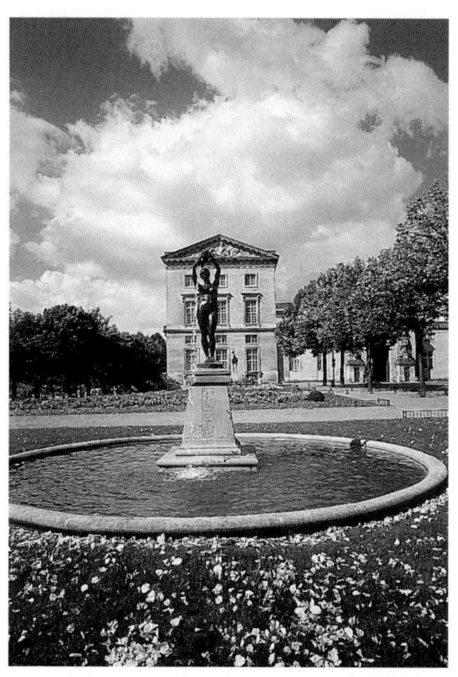

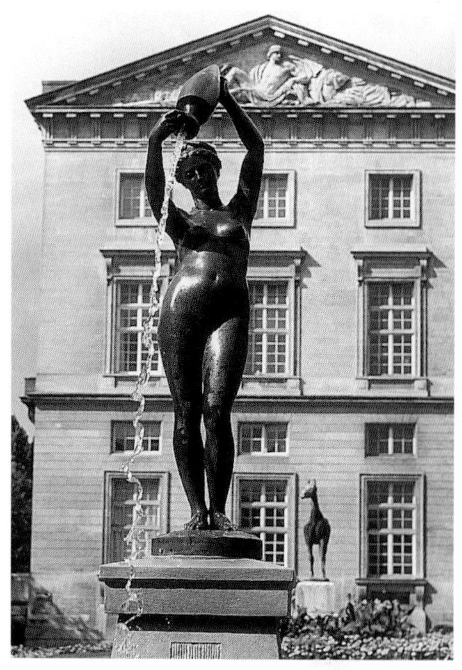

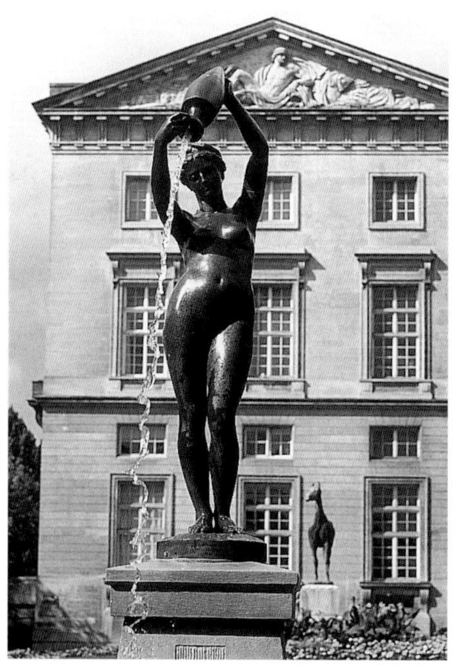

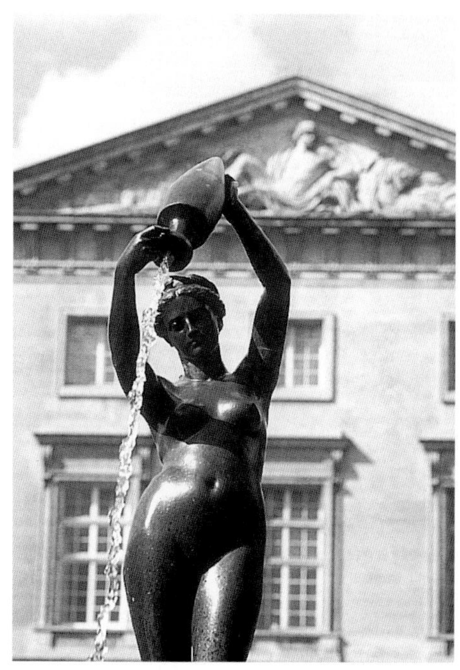

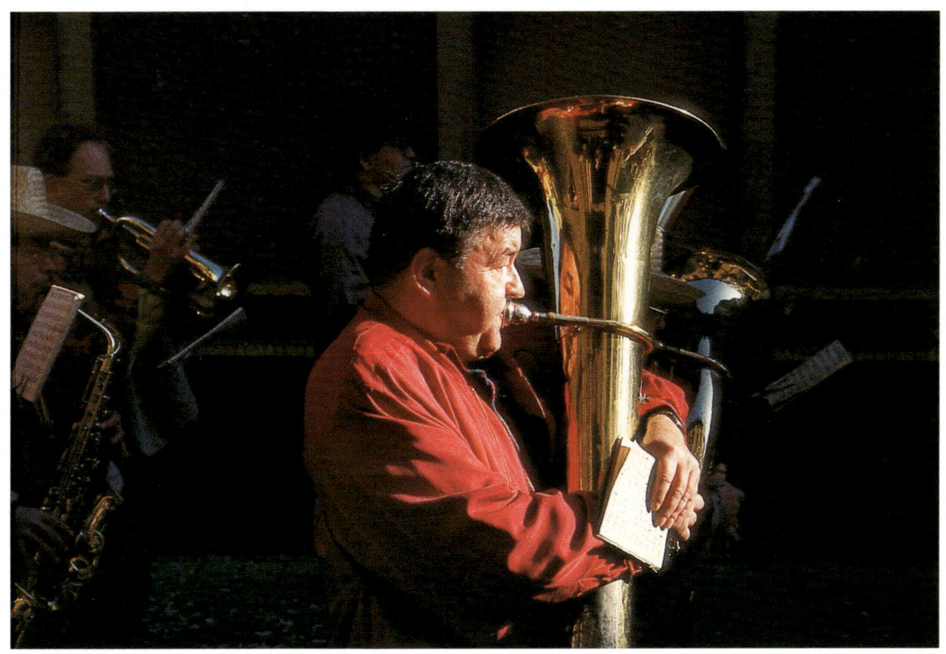

Only if one prepares exposure data and distance in advance does one have a chance of capturing the musician in the sun against the dark background. Summicron-M 90mm f/2.

Changing the focal length from 21mm through 50mm and 90mm to 135mm allows one to "wander" optically into the subject space. Ever smaller segments of the scene are captured. If one does not change one's position relative to the subject, then the relative sizes and perspective remain constant. Leica M6 TTL, Elmarit-M 21mm f/2.8 ASPH, Summicron-M 50mm f/2, Summicron-M 90mm f/2, Apo-Telyt-M 135mm f/3.4.

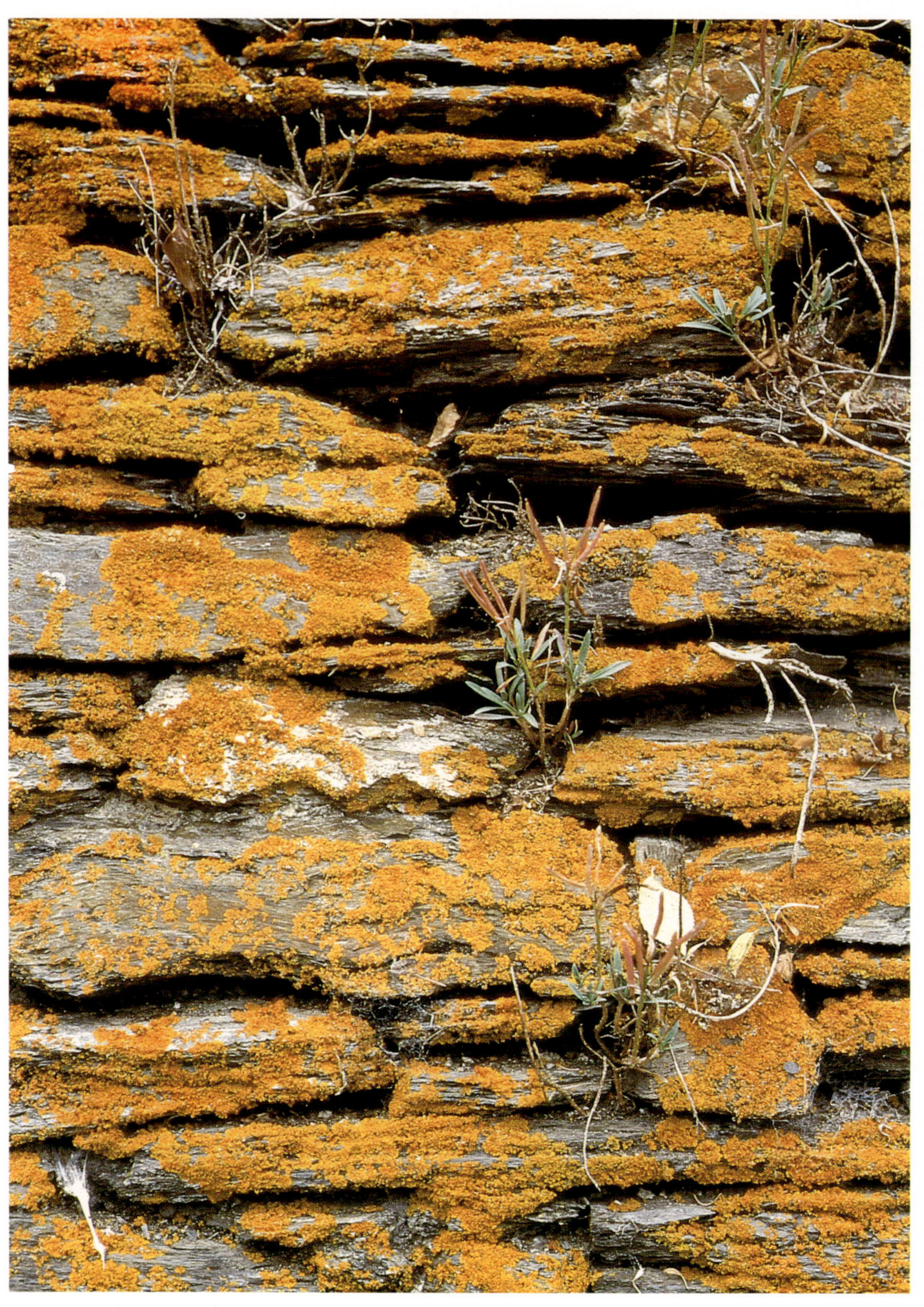

Nature's reclamation of a stone wall. A lightly clouded sky provided a very even illumination that still permitted 1/125s. Elmarit-M 135mm f/2.8.

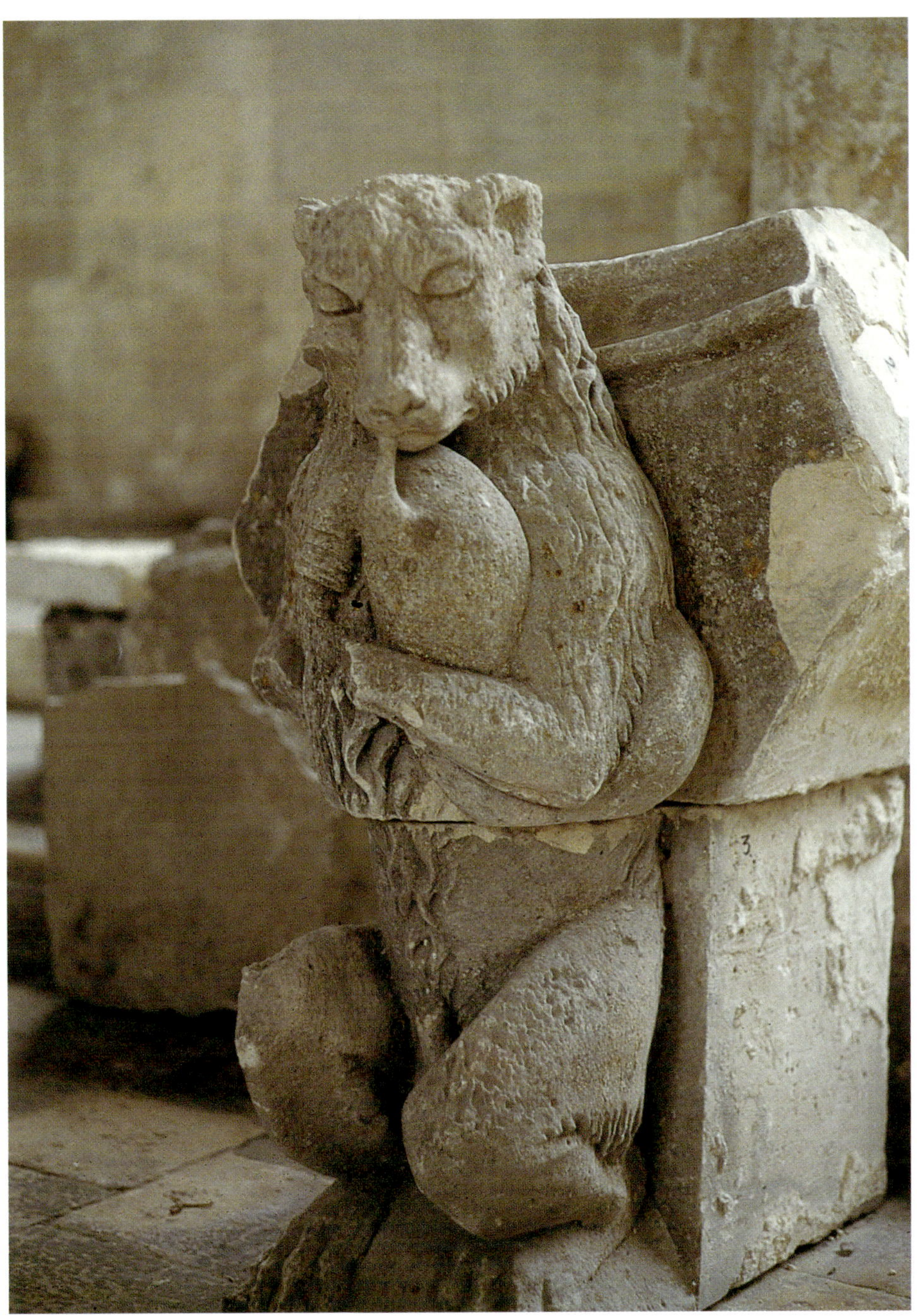

Collections of damaged pieces of medieval architecture usually contain some interesting subjects, and they tend to be located in pleasant, even illumination. Summicron-M 90mm f/2.

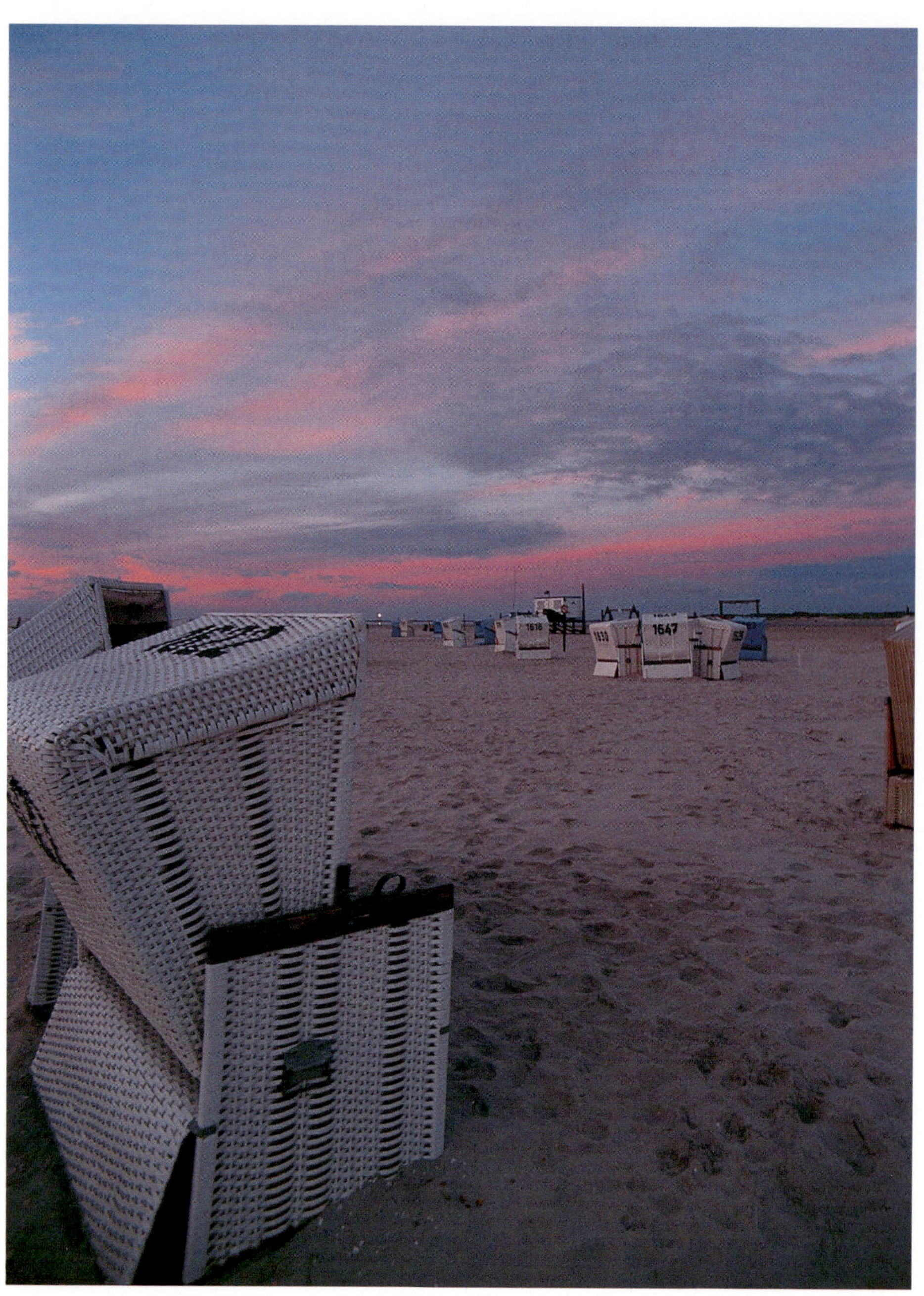

Ten minutes after sunset there is beautiful lighting on the beach—even though it is only enough for 1/30s at f/4. But that's still enough for depth of field almost all the way to the horizon. Super-Angulon-M 21mm f/3.4.

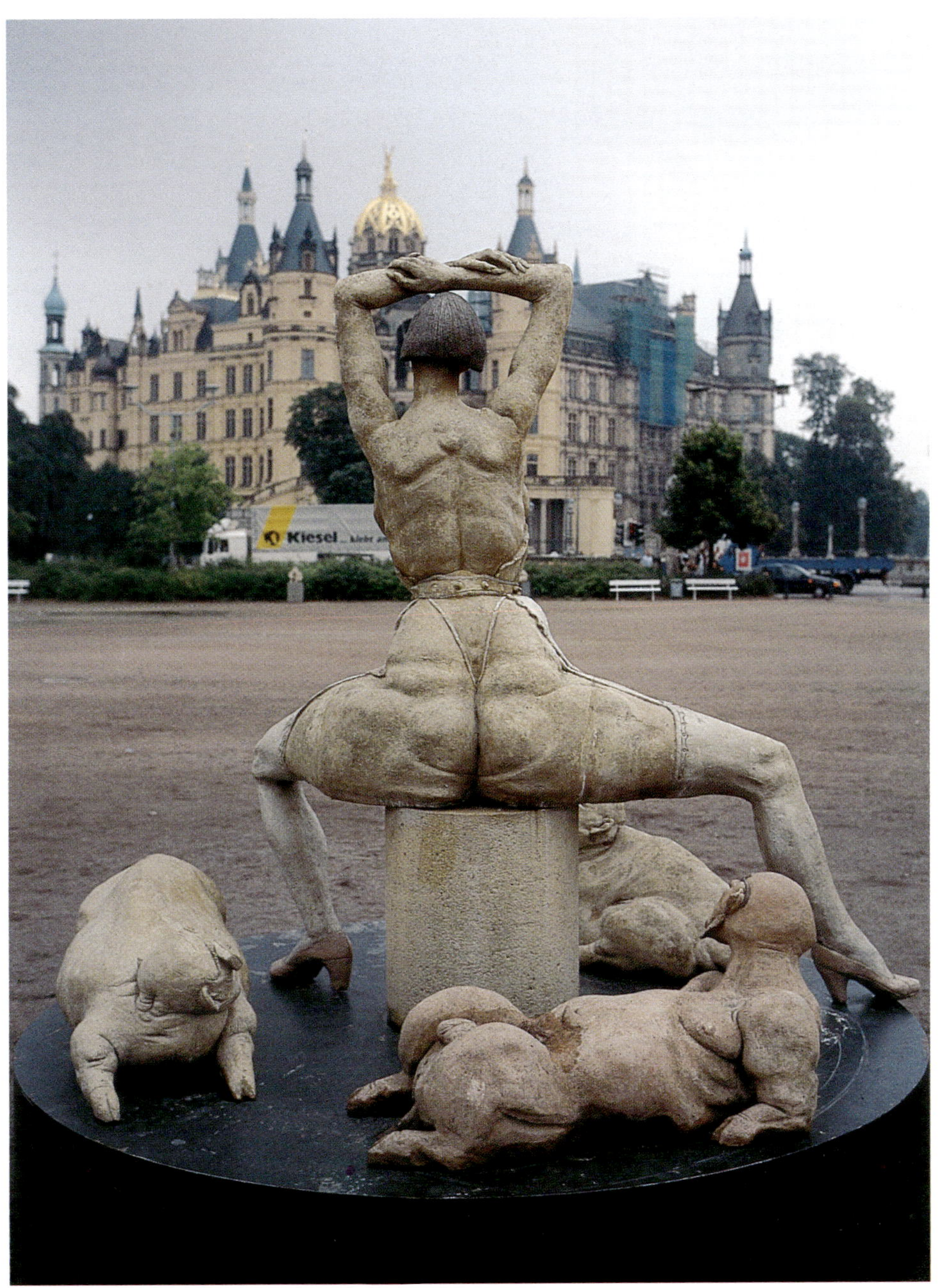

Open-air exhibition in Schwerin: shot with a short focal length at close range, the work of art appears large in front of the castle in the background. (Photo: Peter Lenk)
Elmarit-M 2.8/28mm.

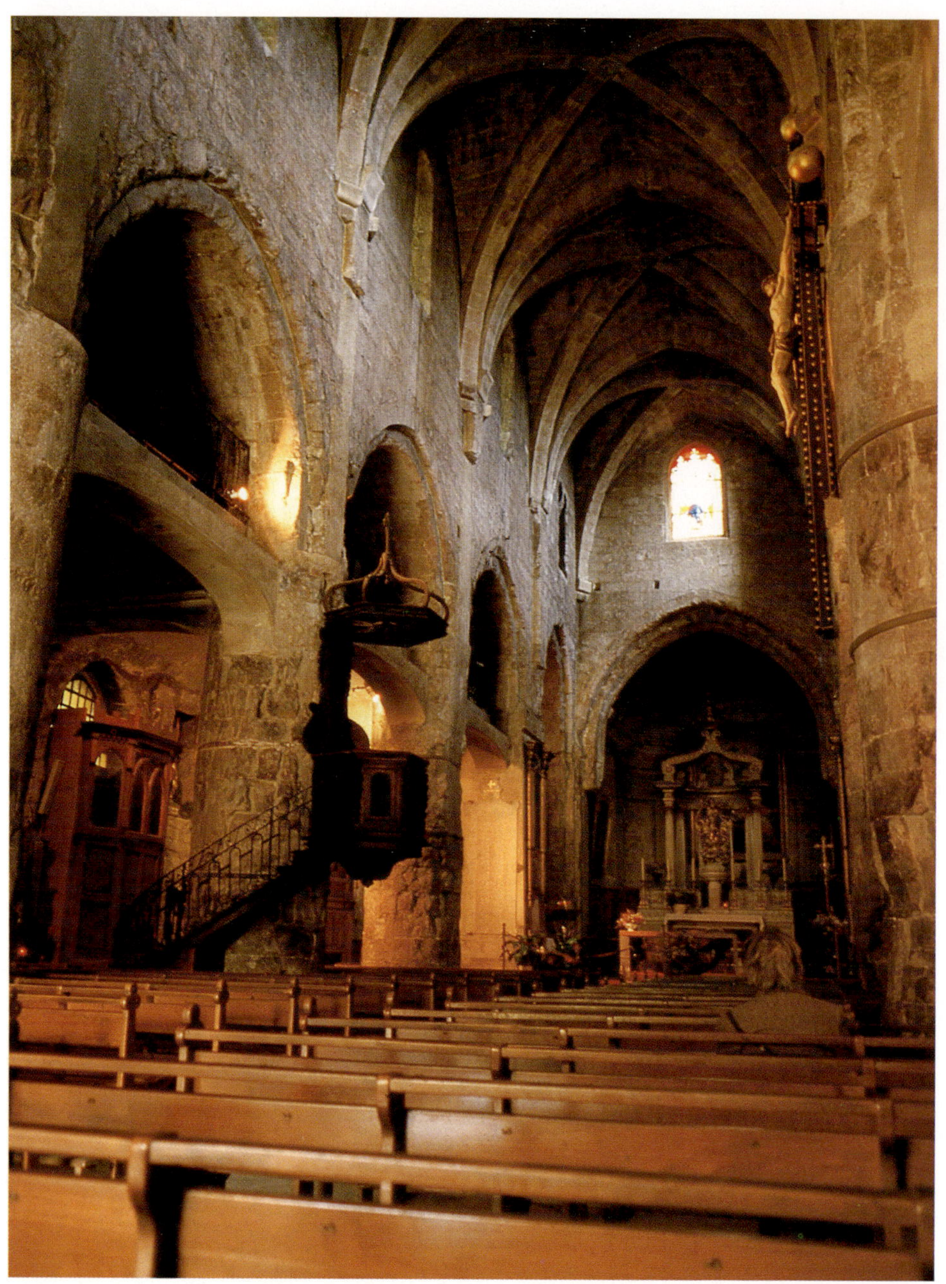

Despite bright sunshine, the interiors of romanesque churches are usually dimly lit. One should do without the flash. A wide-open aperture and an M6 supported against a pillar to enable exposure times that are not safe to hand-hold is how one captures atmosphere in a picture.
Elmarit-M 24mm f/2.8 ASPH.

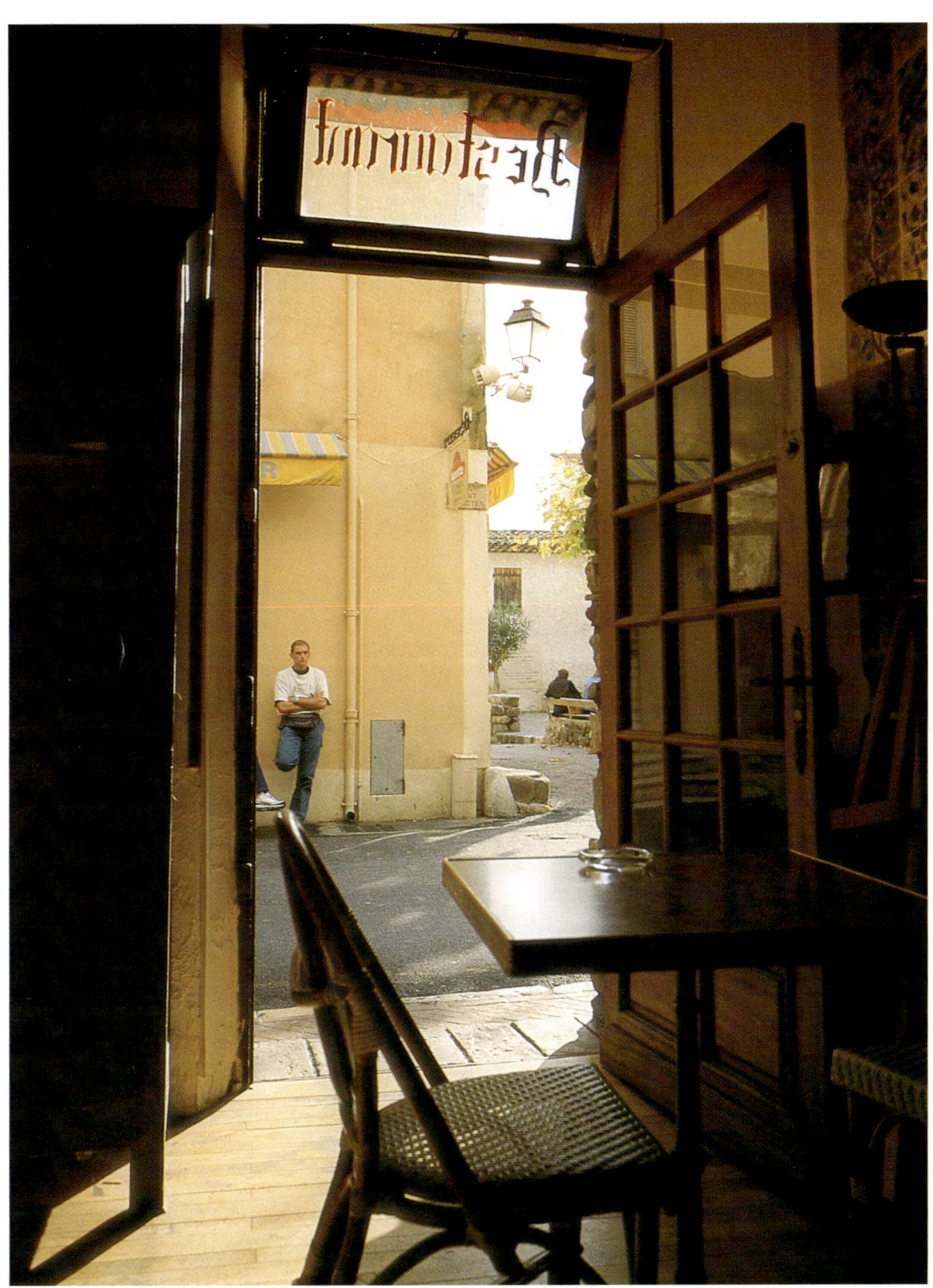

The view from the Bistro in Biot.
Elmarit-M 28mm f/2.8.

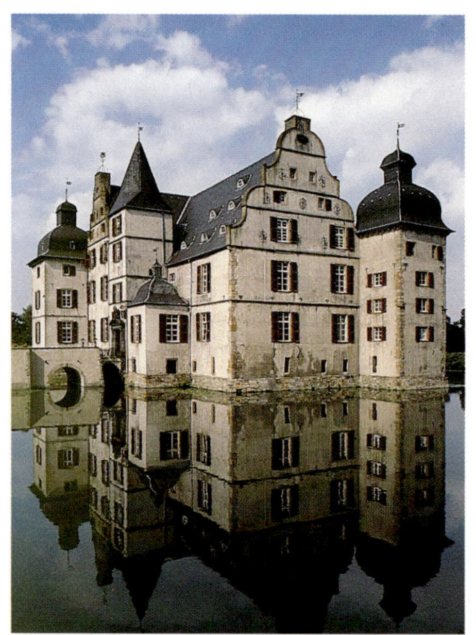

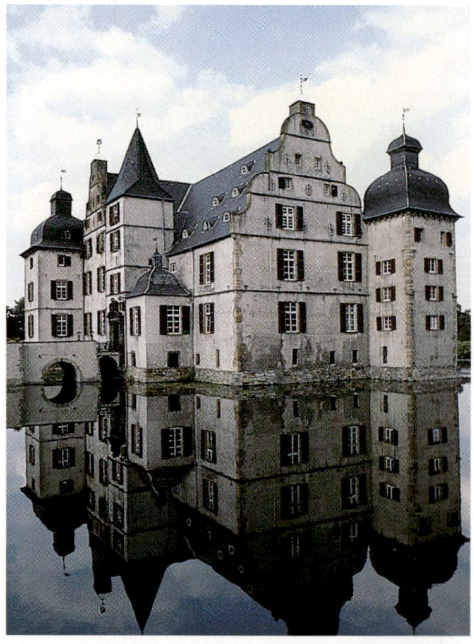

Only a tiny cloud in front of the sun—but it not only reduces the illumination, but also changes the colour temperature from "warm" (left) to "cool" (right). Summicron-M 35mm f/2.

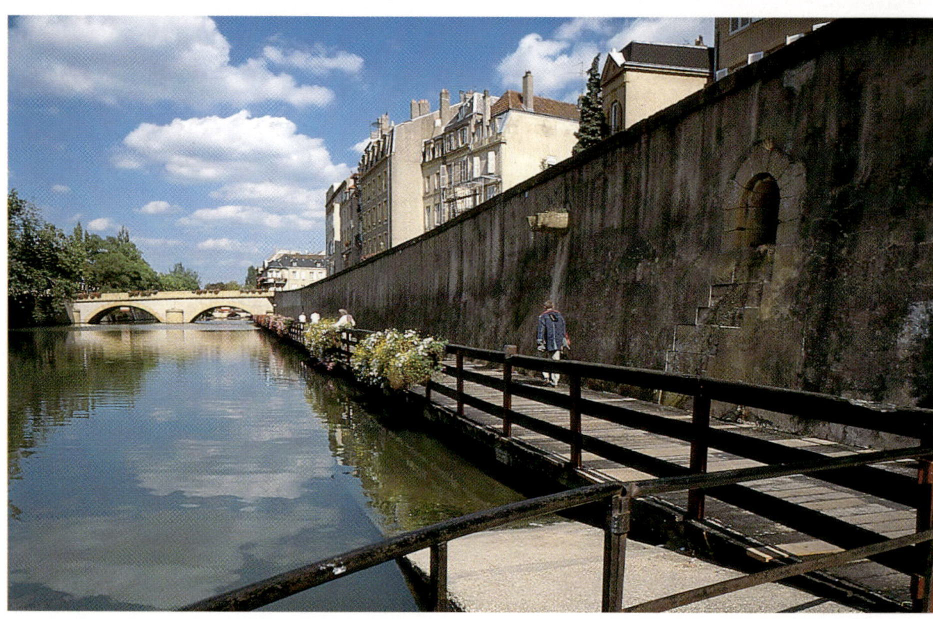

One can only tame this subject with a super-wide-angle lens, but one has to ensure that the exposure is balanced between the bright sky and the dark stonework. Elmarit-M 21mm f/2.8 ASPH.

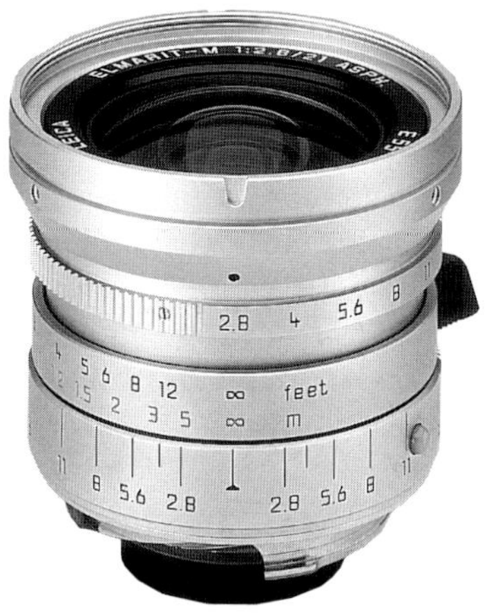

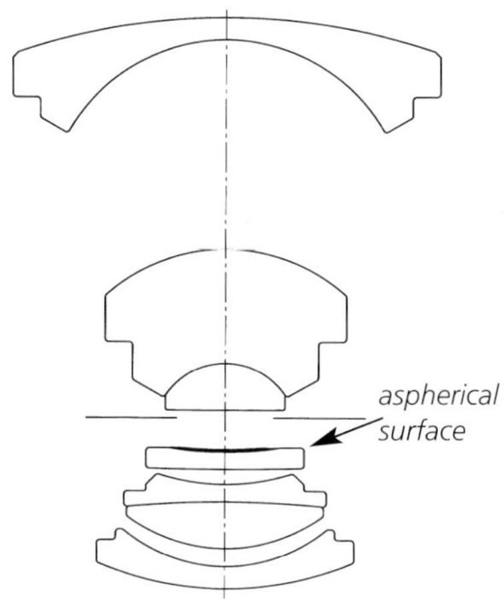

Elmarit-M 21mm f/2.8 ASPH
Highly refractive glasses, glass with anomalous partial dispersion and one element with an aspheric surface afford this super-wide-angle lens excellent optical quality. Photo-journalism, landscape and architectural photography, in small rooms or for large vistas from close up are the best applications for this lens. One definitely needs the 21mm bright-line viewfinder for this widest of lenses available for the M-cameras—the M6 TTL viewfinder is not capable of showing a 92° angle of view.

angle of view. The Elmarit-M 21mm f/2.8 ASPH is also not a retro-focus design as most 21mm's for reflex cameras are. The Elmarit-M 21mm f/2.8 ASPH can be focused down to 70cm or a magnification ratio of about 1:29 with an object area of about 69 x 104 cm. This is by no means close-up photography in the conventional sense, but the lens was not designed for that purpose anyway. This lens really comes into its own with a large-scale architectural model or a model railway. The lens is only slightly larger than the Summilux-M 50mm f/1.4.

The Elmarit-M 21mm f/2.8 ASPH is fully compatible with the Leica M6 TTL exposure meter. The 12mm metering disc on the first shutter blind corresponds to about 13% of the image area with this lens as well. But in relation to the subject area visible in the viewfinder, the metering cell covers an area about the size of the 50mm projection frame. In a 92° angle of view, this still counts as spot metering—but a whole lot of sky can force its way into the metering when shooting a high building. The result is an underexposed image of a bizarre silhouette of the building. As with any captivating effect, one should not overuse it. Tilt the M6 TTL with the Elmarit-M 21mm f/2.8 ASPH—and with other wide-angle lenses too—so that only the building appears in the metering cell and then adjust shutter speed and aperture. But do not be satisfied with only one shot. Two to four additional shots in which the aperture varies by a half-stop should capture the building correctly. Experience dictates that one will only get it right if one brackets the exposure. You have to ignore the LED-readouts in the viewfinder as the bright sky will cause the exposure meter to give erroneous readings.

The ELMARIT-M 24mm f/2.8 ASPH

We Leica M-photographers had to wait a long time for this lens—and the wait was worth it: the Elmarit-M 24mm f/2.8 ASPH produces images, even at maximum aperture, that one can only regard in awed silence! This 290g light lens is made of the very best optical components: one element with an aspheric surface, one lens with anomalous partial dispersion, two elements made of glass with very high refractive indices. Images taken with the 24mm f/2.8 ASPH are an art form of a high order.

The M6 TTL with a viewfinder magnification of 0.72x shows slightly more image than the Elmarit-M 24mm f/2.8 ASPH brings onto the film. With a bit of practice and imagination, one could do without the 24mm bright-line viewfinder on am M6/0.72x—results are naturally more exact and assured with it. Distance and exposure are, as always, controlled in the M6's rangefinder.

Regardless of whether you use your imagination to compose the image in the viewfinder or rely on the bright-line finder, you have to keep one thing in mind: keep the M6 with a super-wide-angle lens, 21mm or 24mm, horizontal. The slightest tilt in the camera will cause markedly converging lines in your subject. Converging lines are a photographic faux-pas if they look unpleasant in the image. Used carefully and intentionally as a compositional tool, they can lend a breathtaking appeal or even a surreal or humorous attitude to architecture shots.

If you want to or must shoot diagonally upwards, adhere to the following rule: as little as possible. Moderately tilted shots of buildings cause the architectural lines to appear as unattractive structures in the image. So go right up to the building and shoot almost straight up with a super-wide-angle. The post-modern facade rises steeply and dynamically into the infinity of the sky. And if the clouds are chasing

While in Leutershausen, I shot this memorial statue to Gustav Weisskopf, the designer of the first motorised plane capable of flight, with the Elmarit-M 28mm f/2.8 so that it would reach up into the sky and dominate in front of a small background.

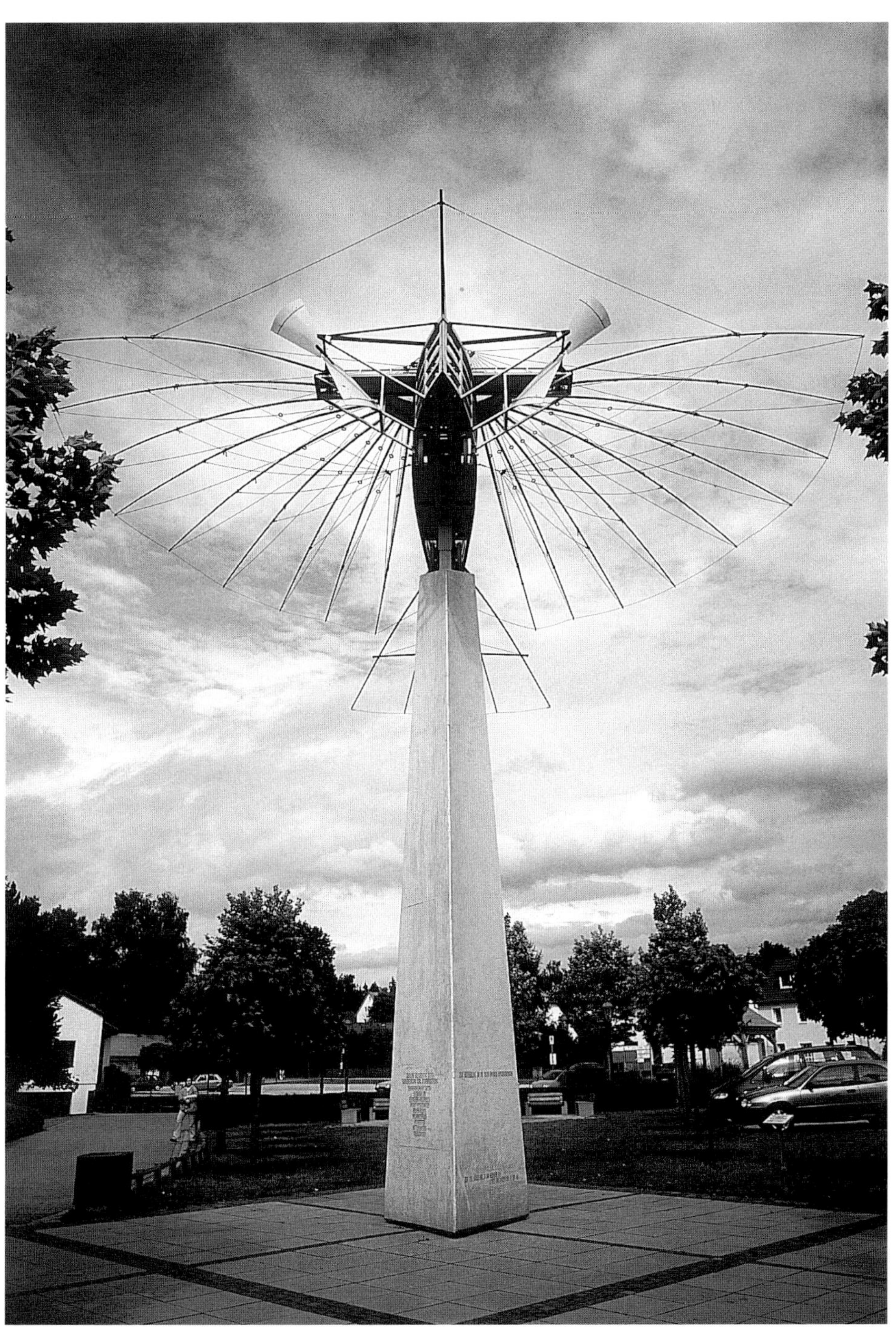

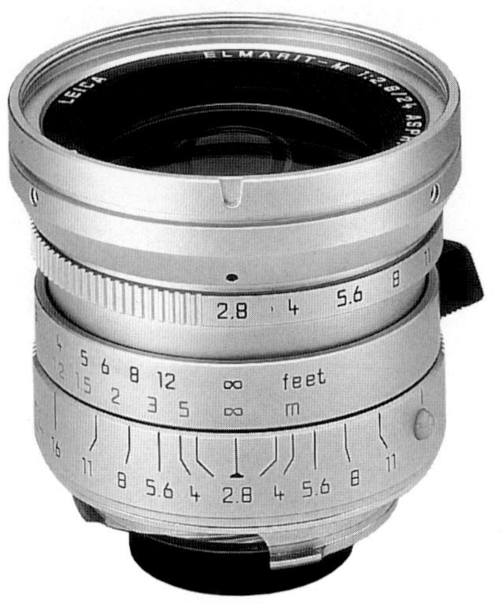

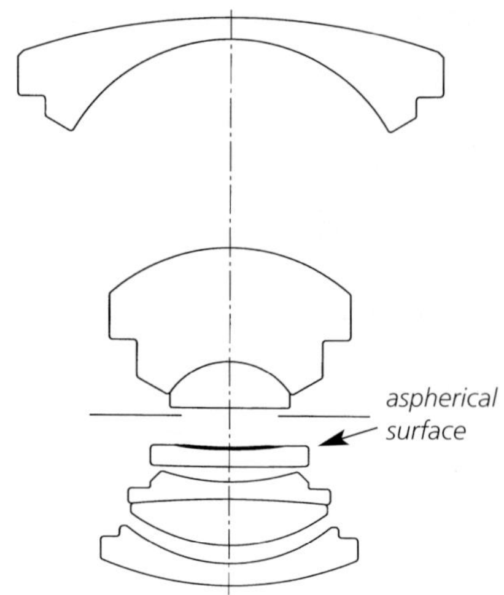

Elmarit-M 24mm f/2.8 ASPH
Super-wide-angle lens for all Leica M-cameras with excellent imaging qualities, even at maximum aperture! Here also the Leica specialities: aspheric elements, glass with anomalous partial dispersion and glass with high refraction indices. One needs a 24mm bright-line viewfinder with the Leica M6 TTL/0.72x and M6 TTL/0.85x.

across the sky and being reflected off the huge glass panels in the building to create confusion, no-one will accuse you of creating unpleasant converging lines when admiring your image.

The Elmarit-M 21mm f/2.8 ASPH and Elmarit-M 24mm f/2.8 ASPH both capture the desired image in tight spaces with their angles of view of 92° and 84°. But pay attention to the foreground: the six metres of asphalt in front of you are hardly apparent in the viewfinder, but on a 160cm projected slide, or a print enlarged to 60x40cm, it can stretch on forever. So fill this space, be it with a repositioned flower pot or the reflection of a fire hydrant in a puddle included in the image by taking a step to the side—save the day by filling the foreground!

ELMARIT-M 28MM F/2.8 ASPH

Since you are usually in the thick of the action with the Leica M6 TTL in order to shoot action and scenes up close and personal, many photographers consider the 35mm as the normal lens and the Elmarit-M 28mm f/2.8 ASPH as the "normal" wide-angle. It is further removed from the 50mm than the 35mm and, together with the 50mm and the 90mm, is part of the trio with which photo-journalists successfully travel the far reaches of the globe. The Elmarit-M 28mm f/2.8 ASPH does not offer such extreme perspectives

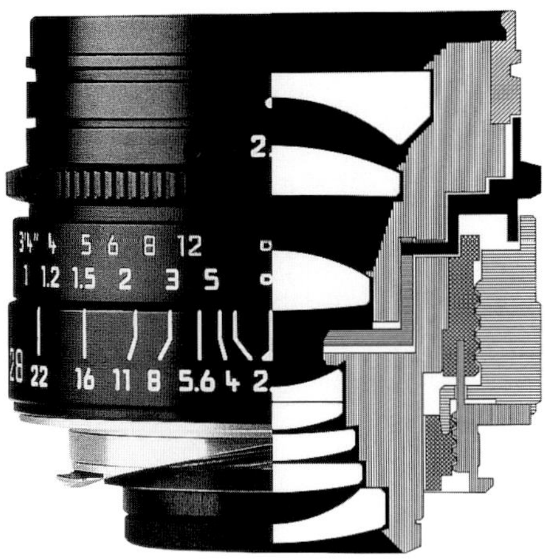

Elmarit-M 28mm f/2.8
The Elmarit-M 28mm f/2.8, together with the 50mm and 90mm, is part of the trio with which one is well equipped, even for longer trips.

as the Elmarit-M 21mm f/2.8 ASPH or the 24mm f/2.8 ASPH. A portrait taken of a person at the close-focus point of the 28mm f/2.8 is unlikely to foster the relationship between the person in front of the camera and the person behind it. But that is only a function of the relationship between focal length, angle of view and subject distance. The 28mm focal length is still short enough to produce unattractive lines when shooting architecture if the Leica is held at an angle.

Even at maximum aperture, the Elmarit-M 28mm f/2.8 shows excellent imaging quality—and that with only eight elements. Thanks to its optical design, it only projects a short distance into the M6 TTL and therefore does not interfere with the silicon photocell's metering angle for the exposure metering system and TTL flash exposure control. The earlier production version of the Elmarit-M 28mm f/2.8 with serial numbers below 2,314,921 project further into the M6 TTL and interfere with the metering angle of the silicon photocell and can therefore not be used in conjunction with exposure metering!

You do not need the 28mm bright-line finder for the M6 TTL/0.72x. The projected frame that appears for the Elmarit-M 28mm f/2.8 is slightly smaller than the entire viewfinder image on the M6 TTL/0.72x. This extra space is large enough for you to identify a passer-by in time. For the M6 TTL/0.85x viewfinder, which is designed to be slightly larger than the image area of the 35mm lens, the projected frame for the 90mm focal length will appear when the Elmarit-M 28mm f/2.8 is mounted. The frame for the 28mm is missing as the image projected by the 28mm lens onto the film is slightly larger than the entire viewfinder image on the M6 TTL/0.85x. With a bit of practice and careful examination of the viewfinder image right up to the edge, one can guess the subject area without too much difficulty—and not only when time does not allow for mounting the 28mm bright-line finder. I hardly ever shoot with the Elmarit-M 28mm f/2.8 on the M6/0.85x without using the bright-line finder and have yet to make an unforgivable error or an unusable image. So if you want to be absolutely sure you should mount the 28mm finder into the accessory shoe on the M6/0.85x.

Retro-focus—What Is It?

In an optically ideal system, the aperture is exactly one focal length distant from the film at the infinity setting. With fast lenses composed of many elements, the distance from the rear element to the film—the focal distance—is generally significantly shorter than the distance from the bayonet to the film—the flange focal distance. The flange focal distance is determined by factors other than the focal distance.

Even if the focal distance of a given M-lens was significantly shorter than the flange focal distance, the differential was unimportant in the Leica M-camera up until now: the only things between the bayonet and the film were air and the shutter blinds. That is why my Super-Angulon 21mm f/3.4, made in 1976, can protrude 20mm into the M3. The rear element is only 8mm from the film. It blocks the silicon photocell's view of the metering dot on the shutter blind and prevents it from seeing the light reflected off the film for TTL flash control in the Leica M6 and M6 TTL! As a result, the Leica designers had to select a different construction for the new versions of the 21, 24 and 28mm lenses whereby the rear element stays out of the way of the silicon photocell: retro-focus construction. Its main feature is a one or more element front group with dispersing qualities in front of a lens system with a shorter focal length. In order to ensure that this front element with a negative refractive index delivers a coherent bundle of light to the following wide-angle base lens, it has to be a great deal larger than the front element of a symmetrically-designed wide-angle lens of the same focal length and speed.

My old, non-retro-focus Super-Angulon 21mm f/3.4 has a filter thread of E 48. The old Elmarit-M 21mm f/2.8 needs E 60 filters. The new Elmarit-M 28mm f/2.8 ASPH, thanks to its aspheric element, high refraction glass and glass with low anomalous partial dispersion, needs E 55mm filters. The half-stop larger maximum aperture of the Elmarit-M 28mm f/2.8 ASPH naturally also affects the filter size. The optical magic of retro-focus has its price: compared to a normally designed symmetrical lens, the retro-focus design is often larger and heavier and the excellent imaging qualities over long and moderate distances are not achieved in the close-focus range. This can be equalised by stopping down to slightly smaller apertures. Or basically by using unique optical devices such as aspherical elements and extreme glasses. One does not need much imagination to figure out how many "optical gyrations" designers have to go through to design a 21mm super-wide-angle lens with excellent optical quality for a reflex camera where the flange focal distance and the focal distance are almost twice the focal length of the lens.

35mm and 64°— The Normal Wide-angle

That is the diagonal value of the 35mm wide-angle lens, whose angle of view is narrower than a "super" and wider than "normal" and which many photographers are now using as their "standard" lens. If the pressure of the moment causes you to hold the M6 TTL slightly at an angle, the world does not appear to come crashing in. Photographing a pretty girl up-close magically places a rather original nose into the attractive face. Both 35mm lenses for the Leica M6 TTL are absolutely top-class, the choice just as easy as the one between the Summicron-M 50mm f/2 and the Summilux-M 50mm f/1.4.

The black anodised SUMMICRON-M 35mm f/2 ASPH—you can also obtain it in the classic silver-chrome version—is still one of the smallest and lightest lenses for the Leica M6. Even though it is eight millimetres longer than the "old" 35mm Summicron-M, the M6 TTL fitted with the Summicron-M 35mm f/2 ASPH still fits in a jacket pocket—but without the clip-on lens hood that you should never be without! The only thing the design of the 35mm f/2 ASPH has in common with its predecessor is the number of elements—seven. The element with the aspheric surface and the unusual shapes of the front and rear elements indicate that the Leica designers have turned a new page in the construction of wide-angle lenses with excellent imaging qualities. The imaging power of the Summicron-M 35mm f/2 ASPH is so excellent that there is absolutely nothing to complain about. Together with the Summicron-M 50mm f/2 and the Apo-Summicron-M 90mm f/2 ASPH, it forms the classic, high speed Leica lens trio with which you are very well equipped for a trip across Europe, even in today's age of super-zooms.

The early Summicron 35mm f/2—at the time there was no "M"–with the optics to fit in front of the viewfinder and rangefinder windows, type 11,108 and 11,104, fits onto the Leica M6 TTL. These optics for the viewfinder and rangefinder windows were there to enlarge the Leica M3's viewfinder image with its magnification ratio of 0.7x designed for a 50m lens, to the image angle of a 35mm lens. Used with the Leica M6 TTL 0.72x, this produces an overall viewfinder magnification of 0.5x and reduces the viewfinder factor to 0.6x with the M6/0.85x. This reduction of the viewfinder magnification only has a negligible effect on subject control and range finding. The projection frame for the 50mm focal length appears with the "magnifier" 35mm.

The 35mm lenses also divide their efforts: if the Summicron-M 35mm f/2 ASPH is the all-round fast wide-

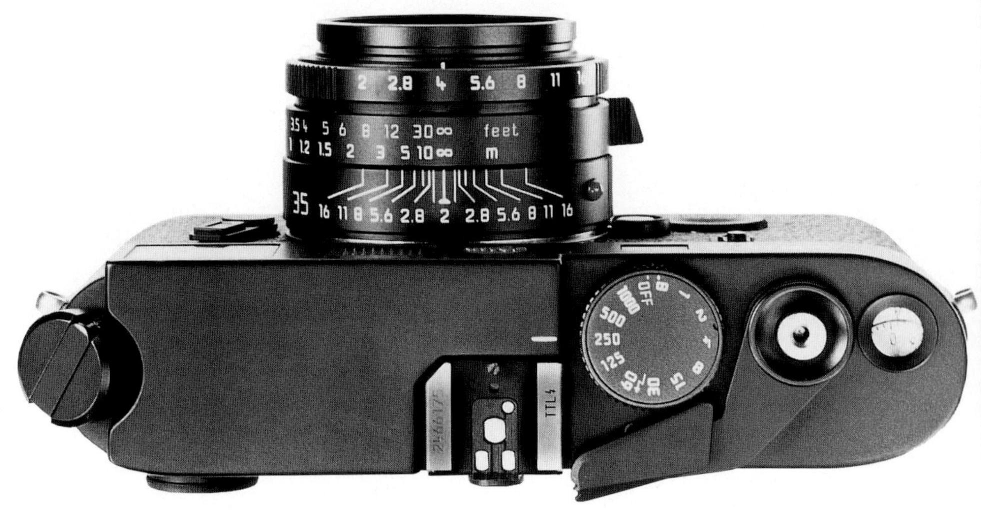

The Summicron-M 35mm f/2 ASPH and the M6 TTL are ideal for close-in and personal photography in the centre of the action. Since the 35mm f/2 ASPH is barely 35mm long, this combination still fits in a coat pocket.

angle, the SUMMILUX-M 35mm f/1.4 ASPH is for shooting at maximum aperture under low to poor light. Its imaging qualities are outstanding in any situation. Even light falling directly into the lens produces reflection or double-images only in the most extreme situations. With its concave surfaces on the front and rear elements and the aspheric element behind the aperture, its design is similar to that of the Summicron-M 35mm f/2 ASPH. Composed of nine elements in five groups, it is about 12mm longer and, in the black anodised finish, it is 5 grams lighter than the 35mm f/2 ASPH. Aspherics and glass with extreme characteristics drive the imaging qualities of the Summicron-M 35mm f/2 ASPH and the Summilux 35mm f/1.4 ASPH well beyond anything attained by other fast 35mm lenses. Even wide open they show outstanding qualities: high contrast, excellent overall detail resolution, good flatness of field, practically no coma. Closing down two stops only improves these qualities slightly. The system-defined vignetting is very slight at f/1.4 and disappears at f/4. The Summilux-M 35mm f/1.4 ASPH maintains these outstanding qualities right to its close-focus distance of 70cm. It is a "bad-weather" lens but still a universally usable wide-angle lens. But its price of two-thirds more than the Summicron-M 35mm f/2 ASPH makes the photographer ask: how often and when do I need an aperture of f/1.4?

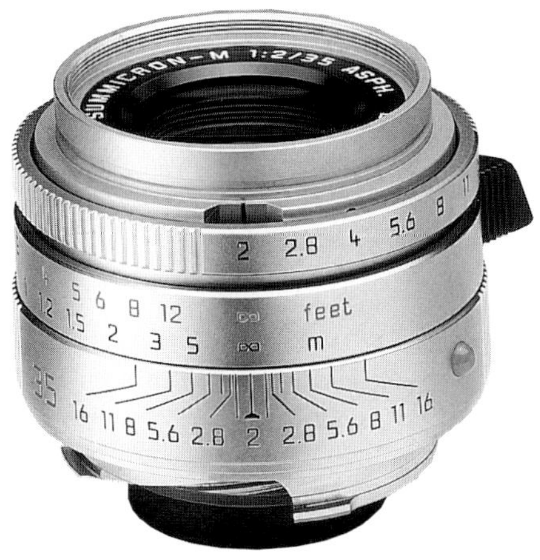

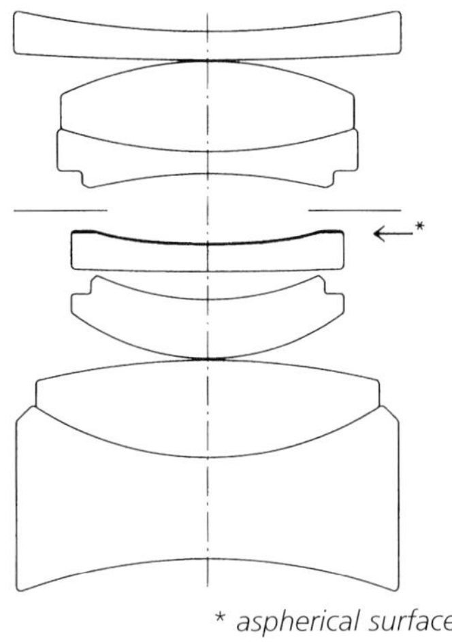

A noticeable characteristic of this Summicron-M 35mm f/2 ASPH is the concave nature of its front and rear elements. This unusual design, together with an aspheric element and glass with high optical qualities, produces exceptional imaging performance.

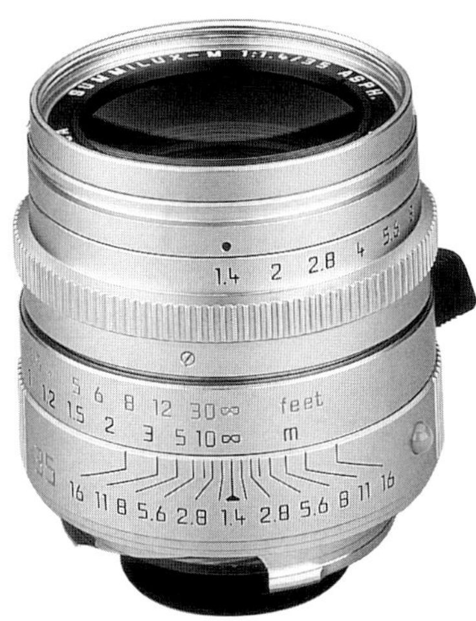

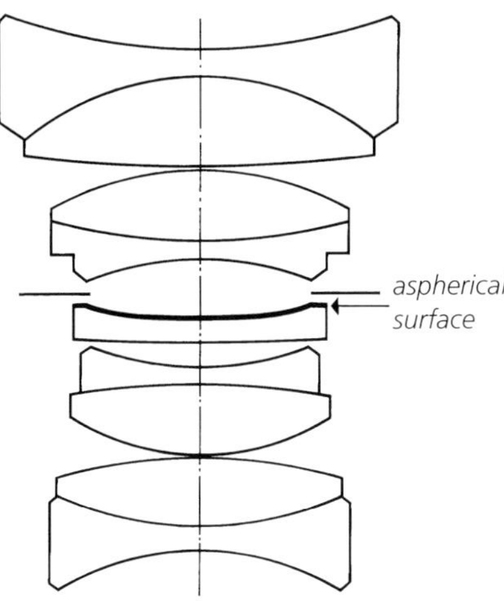

Summilux-M 35mm f/1.4 ASPH
The wide-angle lens with outstanding, incomparable imaging qualities, even at maximum aperture, composed of these ingredients: concave front and rear elements, glass with extreme properties, an aspheric element and an ingenious method of dealing with the inevitable tolerances in the lens mount system.

The early Summilux 35mm f/1.4 was available with a viewfinder attachment for the Leica M3. It fits perfectly onto the Leica M6 with the magnification ratios given for the Summicron 35mm f/2.

A 35mm's angle of view of 64° is wide enough to include enough sky in an architectural shot on the metering cell to bring the Leica M6 TTL metering system to report a subject-incorrect exposure. When faced with such a critical subject, project the 90mm format frame into the viewfinder in order to approximate the circle of the metering dot. If the contrasts are too high or the metered area is too bright or too dark, select a different spot for the exposure metering, but still bracket the exposure.

Not for Searching the Distance: telephoto Lenses

"Telephoto" actually stands for a specific design of long focal length lens. In a normal lens designed without a telephoto element, its nodal point, generally the location of the aperture, is a focal length from the film. Examples are the Hektor 135mm f/4.5 and the Elmar 135mm f/4. Focused down to 150cm, the lens hoods of these approximately 135mm-long lenses protrude into the lower right corner of the

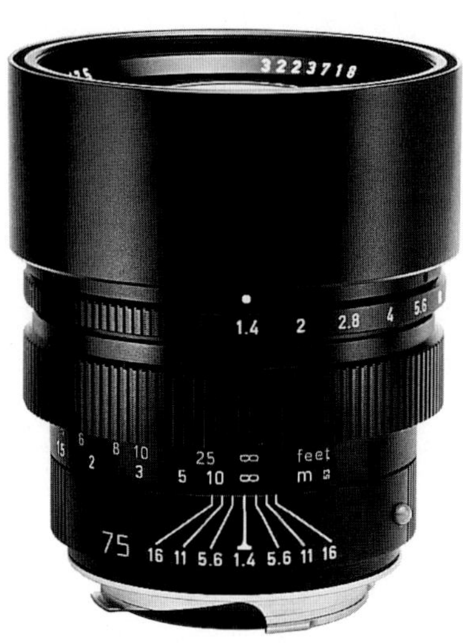

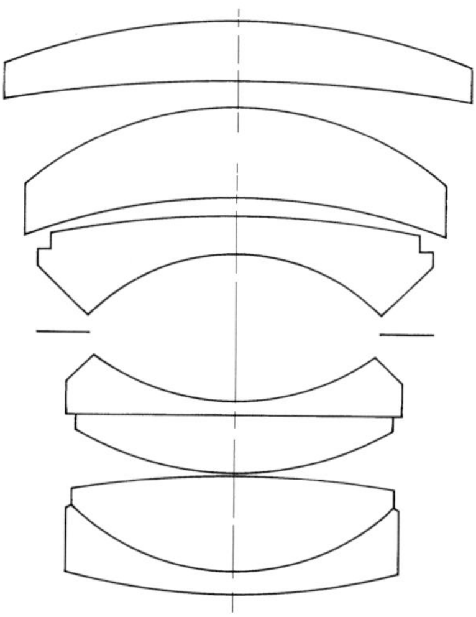

Summilux-M 75mm f/1.4
A very fast lens with a slightly narrower angle of view than the 50mm lens and with true all-round characteristics. Together with the 35mm f/1.4 and the Apo-Telyt 135mm f/3.4, it becomes a high speed focal length companion with the highest of imaging qualities.

M3 and M6 TTL 135mm format frame. The area of the subject covered by it can be guessed fairly accurately, however. There is no reason why one should not use these lenses on the M6 TTL. A normally designed 135mm f/2.8 and even more so a 135mm f/2 would, because of their design-constrained diameter, protrude too far into the viewfinder image. The only option for fast M-lenses with a long focal length is therefore an optical design that shortens the mechanical length of the lens, the telephoto principle. One places an element with a negative refractive index behind an element group with a long focal length. One can shorten the physical length of the lens in proportion to the amount that the element with the negative refractive index magnifies the image produced by the front group. If one desires optimal imaging characteristics from infinity into the close-up range, one has to add more elements.

The optical and mechanical limitations of the Leica M2 to M6 rangefinders mean that the longest focal length of lens that can still be focused reliably is 135mm. "Not much", will be the response of the reflex camera aficionados whose standard-tele-zoom lens has 200mm or 240mm as its top end. The rangefinder Leica was never intended for use with very long focal lengths, but rather for fast, unobtrusive shooting as close as possible to the event.

The Pleasing Little Ones

"Portrait lens" used to be a name given to a lens with a focal length about twice the diagonal of the film format. For the 35mm camera, diagonal 43.5mm, these are lenses between 80 and 100mm. These short telephotos force the superfluous out of the image, they emphasise the important while not removing it completely from the reference of its surroundings, they are simply ideal for the portrait, for the landscape shot where the eye does not get lost, for architecture and product shots, and one can shoot with them as easily as with a 50mm, hence the 90mm has become the usual "standard" lens for many photographers. This is true for the following lenses.

SUMMILUX-M 75mm f/1.4. The only longer Leica-M lens that is not a telephoto type but rather a modified Gauss-type with seven elements. Even at maximum aperture, contrast, resolution, detail sharpness, lack of distortion and internal reflection are outstanding. It is the telephoto for low-light conditions. 75mm is the perfect compromise between 50mm and 90mm and, together with the Elmarit-M 28mm f/2.8, forms the perfect lens pair for a stroll through town.

The 90mm focal length has a long-standing tradition in Leica photography. It and the 135mm lens helped 35mm photography, at the time limited to rangefinder cameras, make inroads against the larger film

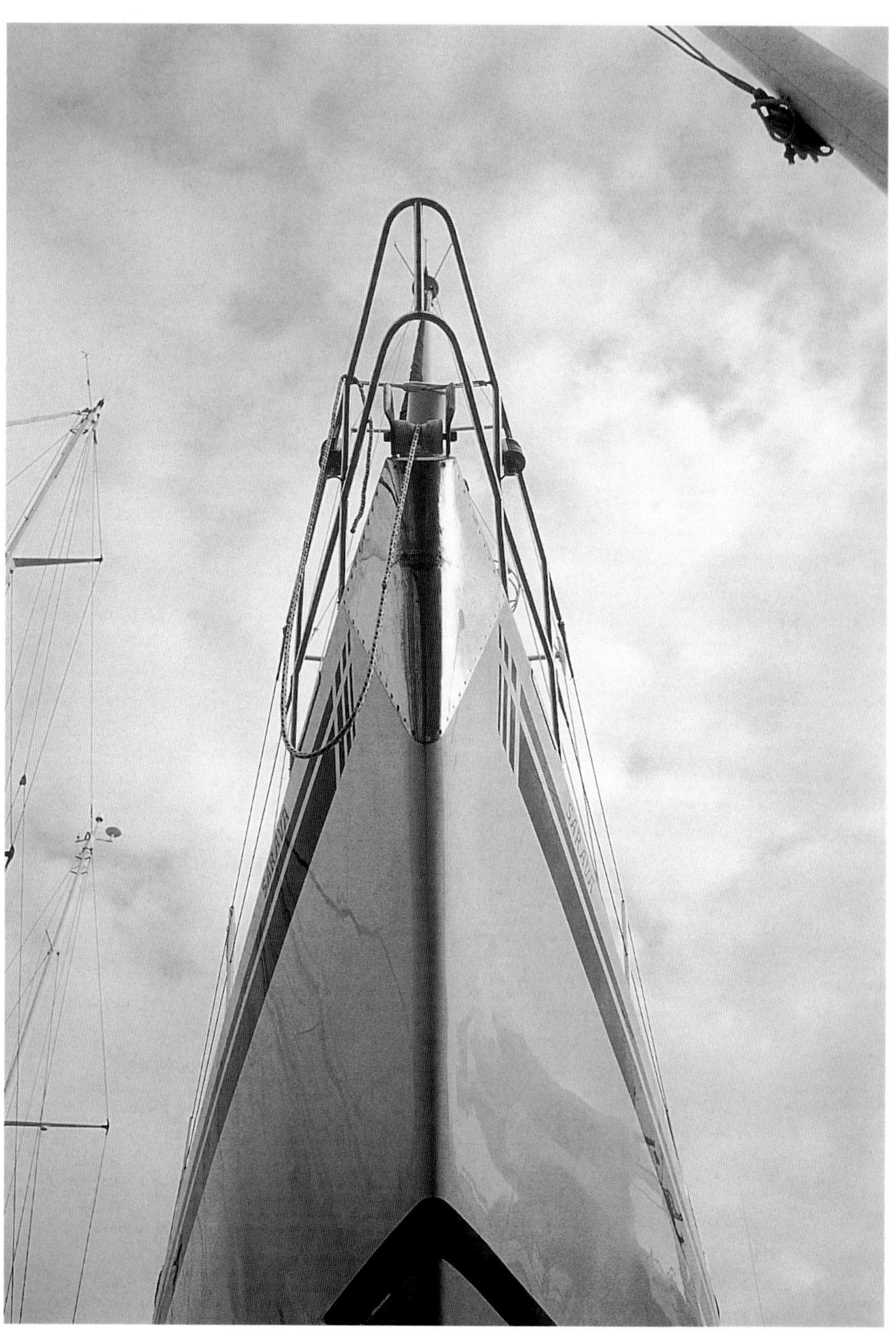
SARAVA

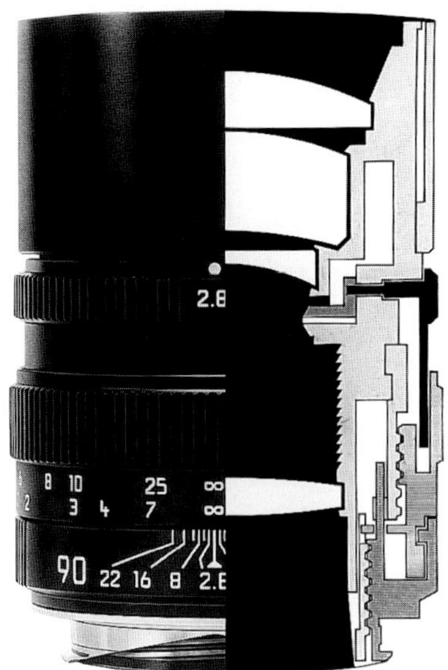

Elmarit-M 90mm f/2.8
The small telephoto with excellent imaging performance, a universal lens of unique character, the ideal partner for a short photographic stroll in combination with a 35mm wide-angle.

formats. Only these successes drove the development of the small format camera ahead. You can choose between the Elmarit-M 90mm f/2.8 and the Apo-Summicron-M 90mm f/2 ASPH.

The ELMARIT-M 90mm f/2.8 is somewhat smaller and, in the black anodised version, somewhat lighter than the Apo-Summicron-M 90mm f/2 ASPH. One can still tuck it into a jacket pocket if one wishes to stroll around with it and the Summicron-M 35mm f/2 ASPH. Even at maximum aperture, it shows excellent imaging characteristics thanks to its four elements made of high-grade glass. Stopping down by two or three stops increases performance further. For top-quality work in the close-up range, stop down to f/5.6—even high-performance lenses have their limits. An aperture of f/2.8 is not too small for available-light photography.

The APO-SUMMICRON-M 90mm f/2 ASPH replaces the treasured Summicron-M 90mm f/2 — and supersedes it significantly in all respects. Its five elements are the first to combine two of Leica's special technologies: apochromatic correction and one aspheric element. Two elements are made of highly-refractive glass with anomalous partial dispersion. The result is excellent contrast, extraordinary sharpness, detail resolution and brilliance. Colour dispersion that is a characteristic of fast, long focal length lenses is suppressed so well that

Only a super-wide-angle lens could make the bow of this sailboat reach up to the sky. The bright sky can confuse even the Leica M6 TTL's exposure meter and produce underexposures! An aperture one stop larger than the metered one will produce the best results.
Elmarit-M 24mm f/2.8 ASPH.

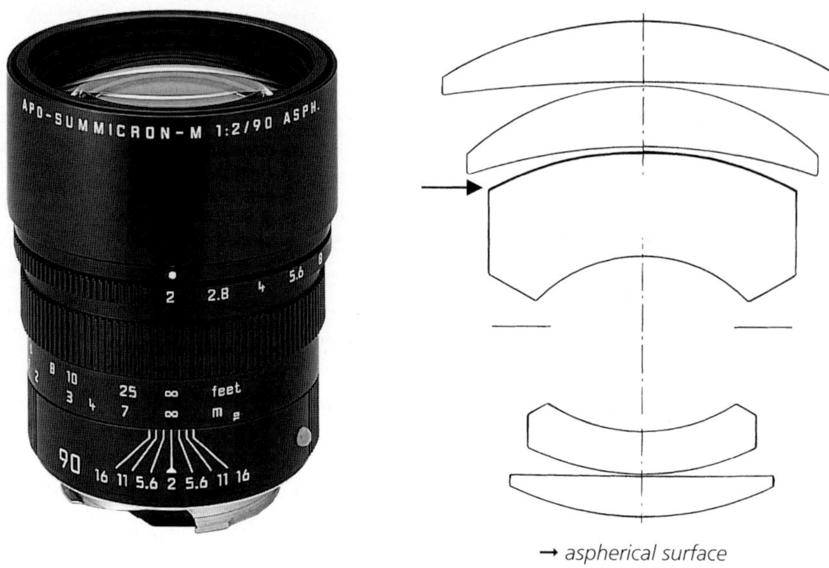

Apo-Summicron-M 90mm f/2 ASPH
The new quality and performance standard of the 90mm class: apochromatic correction, an element with an aspheric surface, highly-refractive glasses and glasses with anomalous partial dispersion guarantee superb imaging qualities in this photo-journalism and portraiture lens, even at maximum aperture.

even the finest details of a subject do not show evidence of colour-fringes. These outstanding optical qualities are evident at this high level throughout the entire image area at maximum aperture. Stopping down makes such slight improvements that the only reason to close the aperture is to increase depth of field. The Apo-Summicron-M 90mm f/2 ASPH is the absolute tops and the standard against which all fast telephoto lenses should be compared.

APO = Apochromatic Correction —What Is It?

Normal optical glasses refract or bend the various colour components of daylight by different amounts. Using a combination of elements made of different kinds of glass with different refractive indices, optical designers can only bring two colours to the same focal point; current choices are light-red, wavelength 656 nanometres, and blue-green, wavelength 486 nanometres. All other colours have their focal points slightly in front of or behind this focal point. Designers use apochromatic correction to bring a third colour to this focal point. The remaining partial spectra are now practically outside the visible spectrum. The level of difficulty is high if this correction is to hold not only for those details close to the optical axis, but be equally accurate for anything in the 864 square-millimetres of the small format image, as is the case with all Leica lenses. Aspheric elements, glass with high refractive indices and low overall dispersion, glass with anomalous partial dispersion, combined with a very stable and accurate mechanical lens construction to ensure that the precise mounting and alignment of the elements is maintained permanently even under rigorous use are required.

And What Does Anomalous Partial Dispersion Mean?

Glass with anomalous partial dispersion is used in high-performance lenses, particularly fast lenses with longer focal lengths, in order to reduce secondary chromatic aberration, also called the secondary spectrum, to zero or as close to zero as possible. The cause of the secondary spectrum is as follows.

White daylight is a natural mixture of seven shades of violet, blue, blue-green, green, orange and red, in other words wavelengths of light between about 380 and 780 nanometres. Glass has a different refractive index for each of these wavelengths. This is why an element or a prism bends or refracts each colour component of daylight differently: blue beams are always refracted more than red. A coherent beam of light projected into a prism will come out the other side split up into the colours of the rainbow—a visible "progression" of the glass's increasing refractive indices of red to blue, its dispersion curve. Even with today's best optical glasses, whose dispersion is practically identical and therefore considered "normal," designers cannot fully remove secondary spectra. In fact, even when using a combination of elements made of different "normal" glasses, they can only bring two colours to the same focal point. They already have trouble with the third colour, particularly if they want to achieve this concurrence not only with points at or near the optical axis but with those all over the entire small format frame. A generally adopted compromise is to bring the 656 nanometre wavelength for light red and the 486 nanometre wavelength for blue-green to one focal point. All other colours have their focal points slightly ahead of or behind it—and therefore make sharp contours unsharp, create small colour fringes around details of another colour. The focus differential is about 1/1000 of the focal length, meaning that it is more evident with longer focal lengths than with short ones.

The specialists at the then-Leitz glass research laboratories succeeded at what was considered impossible—they melted the very first glass with properties that diverged markedly from normal, with high refractive index, but low overall dispersion—and a drastically different dispersion in a specific spectral region, anomalous partial dispersion. This glass was the basis for subsequent glasses with anomalous partial dispersion transposed to other spectral areas. Optical designers always need paired or partnered elements with slightly different or even opposite partial dispersion characteristics in order to keep the secondary spectrum below a quarter of the hitherto normal size or, ideally, to reduce it to zero. A useful side-effect of these glasses, that cost DM1000 or more per kilo is that elements made from them can be ground flatter and therefore thinner and lighter. This in turn means that the lenses will be smaller and lighter.

135mm—The Longest M-focal Length

Photokina 1998 marked this expected change: the APO-TELYT-M 135mm f/3.4 replaced the Tele-Elmar-M 135mm f/4 and the Elmarit-M 135mm f/2.8. With its viewfinder magnifier, which enlarged the viewfinder and rangefinder images by a factor of 1.5x to ensure a very precise distance measuring, the Elmarit-M 135mm, f/2.8 was either loved or hated. I have never minded the viewfinder attachment. The increased focusing accuracy it afforded for the 135mm focal length was worth its size and weight for me. However, unchanged for over 30 years, the time of the Elmarit-M 135mm f/2.8 was over.

The Apo-Telyt-M 135mm f/3.4, coincidentally also consisting of five elements, some of which have anomalous partial dispersion, exceeds its predecessor in performance, with outstanding contrast, extraordinary sharpness, detail resolution and brilliance, thanks to its apochromatic correction. The chromatic aberrations evident in fast, long lenses are so well suppressed that the Apo-Telyt-M 135mm f/3.4 captures even the finest structures without any colour fringing. Even at maximum aperture, its amazing optical qualities are even over the entire image area. One cannot improve them by stopping down and they are just about maintained all the way into the close-focus range. Only around the 150cm mark does stopping down one or two stops bring an improvement in quality.

The 135mm focal length lenses have their own, distinctive characteristic image style in Leica photography. They compel the eye to see the scene or detail taken out of the subject area, seem to move the background close to the subject, compromise the appearance of distance and bridge larger gaps to the subject. Depth of field, as we know from 50mm lenses, is not evident for even moderate focal lengths and apertures. The 135mm lens, whether it be the Apo-Telyt-M 135mm f/3.4 or the legendary Elmarit-M 135mm f/2.8, is the lens for the portrait taken over an non-intrusive distance, for the architectural shot or landscape scene which typifies the whole, or for product shots.

Despite the excellent handling of the Leica-M 135mm lenses, one

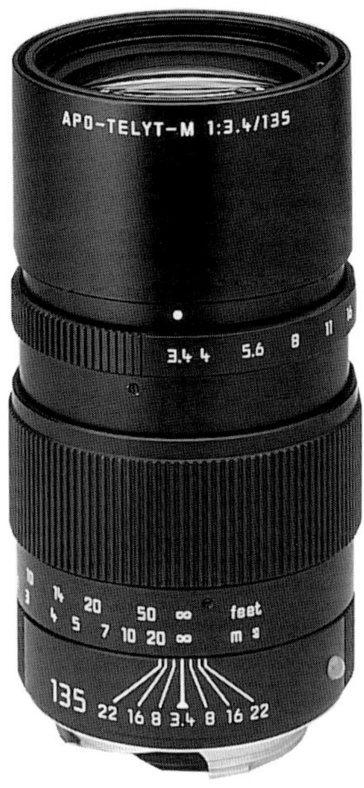

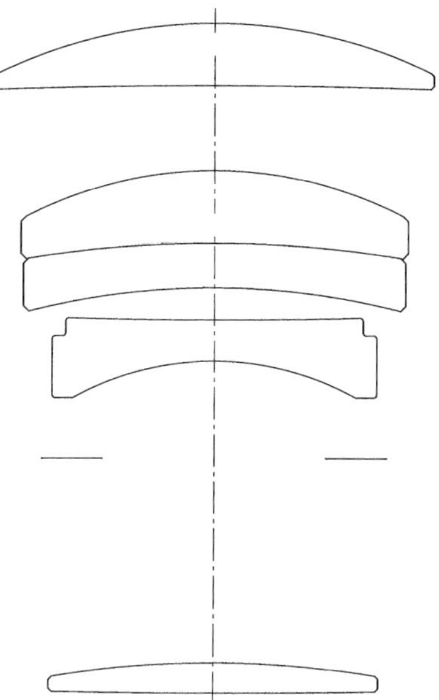

Apo-Teylt-M 135mm f/3.4
Apochromatic correction and elements made from glass with extreme and anomalous characteristics give this lens outstanding imaging characteristics in all disciplines: it defines the new standard for 135mm lenses!

does not often have the opportunity to close the lens to is minimum aperture, even with ISO 100/21° film in the M6. The shutter speed to avoid camera shake is much more important than a few metres of depth of field. If one can achieve the desired depth of field with a moderate aperture and a bit of effort, leave the aperture open! One can achieve more than the required short exposure time. With a 135mm lens, the shutter speed should be at least 1/125s, or to be safer 1/250s. Even the least bit of vibration will consign a picture to the waste basket! At fast shutter speeds, one has a limited depth of field as a compositional tool at no charge. Light shining on the subject from the side also lends an accent that separates such a shot from the average. Long focal lengths and shallow depths of field train the eye to see the important, guides the art of omitting, feeds the passion for an unusual style of picture. One cannot evaluate the effect of the narrow depth of field in the viewfinder of the Leica M6 TTL unlike on the ground glass of the SLR. The image therefore has to be created in the mind of the photographer as that is the only place where he or she will see how the image will appear on the film.

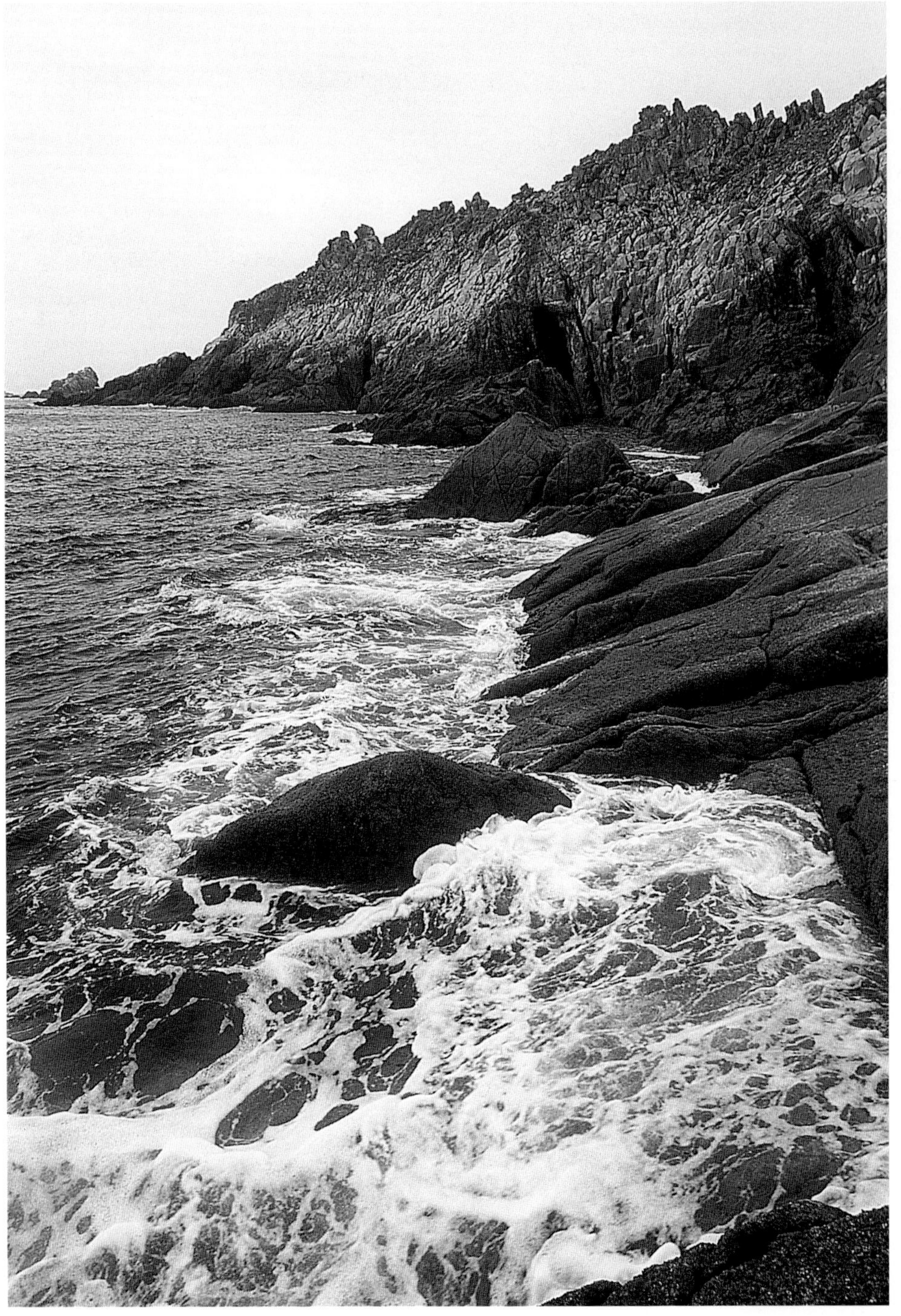

The new long-focal length Leica lenses mark an end to an era. Their lens heads cannot be unscrewed from their bodies to be attached to reflex housings for distant and macro shots. The Visoflex I, II and III reflex housings with which one could convert a Leica M-camera into a reflex for long-distance shots or macro work have long since been discontinued. We will discuss this shortly.

Three = One = TRI-ELMAR-M 28-35-50mm F/4 ASPH

This little Leica sensation is not a zoom lens. The Tri-Elmar offers the freedom of modifying the focal length to 28mm or 35mm or 50mm. Audible, manual click stops protect the optical system very well from unintentional adjustments. One cannot select intermediate focal lengths. A complex system connected to the focal length ring projects the appropriate format frame into the M6 TTL viewfinder in which one can control focus and exposure as usual.

Two of the eight elements in the Tri-Elmar-M 28-35-50mm f/4 ASPH have aspheric surfaces. Five are made of glass with very high refractive indices. The Tri-Elmar-M offers good to very good optical quality with good detail resolution and contrast at all focal lengths, even at maximum aperture. Stopping down to f/5.6 or f/8 increases the imaging qualities further.

Thanks to the most modern optical construction and precision

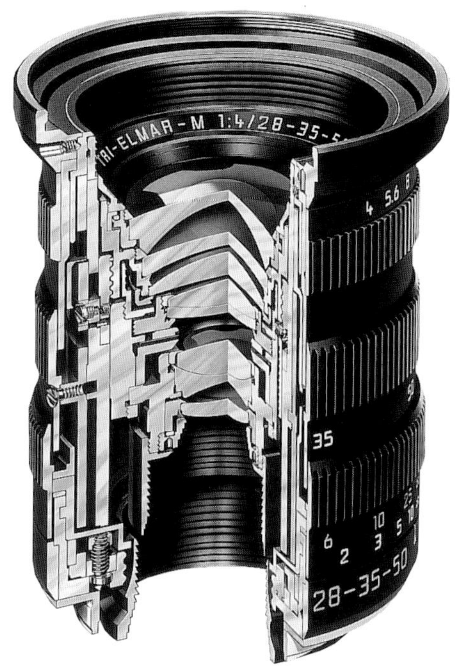

Tri-Elmar-M 28-35-50mm f/4 ASPH
One lens—three focal lengths with consistently high imaging qualities—simply top performance! The focal length ring also controls the projection of the format frames for the 28mm 35mm and 50mm focal lengths into the Leica M-camera's viewfinder. Combined with the Elmarit-M 90mm f/2.8, it is the ideal pair for any trip—as long as one does not need fast speeds.

II *For a landscape shot taken with a super-wide-angle lens it is absolutely essential to have a large subject element in the foreground—otherwise it is boring.*
Super-Angulon-M 21mm f/3.4.

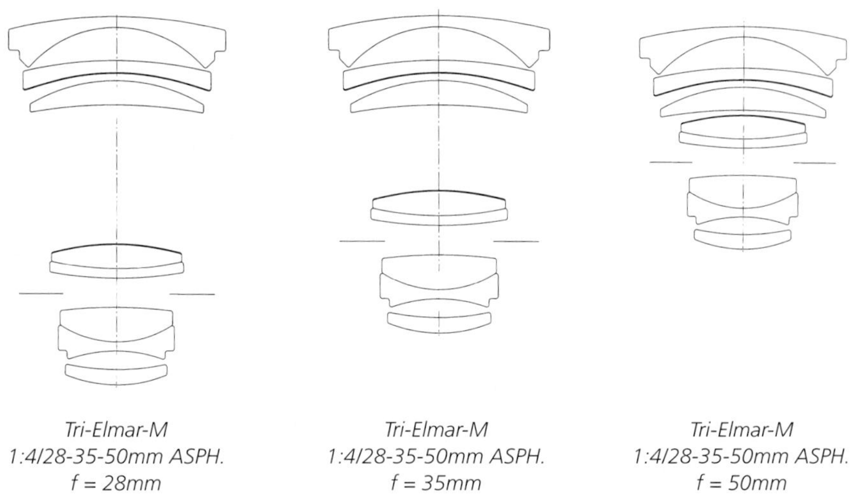

Tri-Elmar-M 28-35-50mm ASPH: a complex, high-precision and robust mechanical system moves the elements and groups to form the three focal lengths. The heavier lines indicate the aspheric surfaces on two elements.

engineering, this compact, 300g light-weight Tri-Elmar-M 28-35-50mm f/4 ASPH is the ideal lens for a photo stroll as well as a vacation with minimal photo luggage—if one does not need fast lenses. Together with the Elmarit-M 90mm f/2.8, the Tri-Elmar makes the perfect pair for just about any subject on long or short trips.

Freedom of Choice

Eight focal lengths, four shorter and three longer than the 50mm normal focal length, with a definite emphasis on the wide-angle end, a variety of speeds at the same focal length—this makes the question of which lens should one, must one, have very difficult to answer. As old as Leica photography is, the time-tested trio of 35mm + 50mm + 90mm has survived the test. The most recent version of it is the Tri-Elmar-M 28-35-50mm f/4 ASPH with the Elmarit-M 90mm f/2.8 or Apo-Summicron-M 90mm f/2 ASPH. If the 28mm focal length is not wide enough for you, you can expand the classic trio with the Elmar-M 24mm f/2.8 ASPH or, if you like it really wide, the Elmarit-M 21mm f/2.8 ASPH. Lovers of the longer focal lengths will buy the Apo-Telyt-M 135mm f/3.4 rather than the 90mm lens—but they should partner it with the M6 TTL with the 0.85x viewfinder magnification: focusing accuracy and subject control are simply better on the larger view-finder image. But the gap between a

45° angle of view of a 50mm and the 18° of a 135mm can be too large at times.

The quartet of 24 + 35 + 75 + 135mm focal lengths, angles of view of 84° + 64° + 31° + 18°, is a very good combination. The Summilux-M 75mm f/1.4 is a good replacement for the 50mm lens. In any lens combination, the Elmarit-M 21mm f/2.8 ASPH assumes the role for wide landscapes, impressive architecture, confined spaces. Someone who, for whatever reason, must have the Noctilux 50mm f/1, will also choose the faster versions of the other lenses in their trio or quartet, as far as possible. The Leica-M focal lengths of 21mm, 24mm, 28mm are only available in f/2.8 and the 135mm only with a maximum aperture of f/3.4.

The Summilux-M 35mm f/1.4 ASPH, Noctilux-M 50mm f/1 and Summilux-M 75mm f/1.4 are the team for subjects and scenes at the edge of darkness. After months of practice with the Noctilux-M 50mm f/1, I will happily assert that subjects it allows one to capture under low light conditions do have their appeal. On the other hand, as I learned in my long experience of Leica photography, even an aperture of f/2 is sufficient for the twilight hours of the day, for the dimness of the romantic cafe. A maximum aperture of f/2.8 is a little tight, but one can manage with a bit of skill. The photographer stressed out by a zoom with a nominal aperture of between f/4.5 and f/5.6 (and this is by no means the actual light transmission of the complex optical system) will be surprised by what can be shot handheld at the end of the day with an aperture of f/2.8. My Leica palette is the following: Super-Angulon 21mm f/3.4, Summicron 35mm f/2, Summicron 50mm f/2, Summicron 90mm f/2, Elmarit 135mm f/2.8 and the Telyt 200 f/4 on the Visoflex II. I use the head of a Hektor 135mm f/4.5, which can be unscrewed from its long barrel, on the Visoflex with a bellows unit for macro and product photography. Since I use the Leica lenses for the features included in their price, namely their first-class imaging quality even at maximum aperture, I have shot happily with ISO 50/18° films or slower. The Leica M6 TTL has a sync. socket and control contacts beside the X-sync. contact in the hot shoe. But I have the feeling that the Leica-M, designed for unobtrusive shooting in low light conditions with fast lenses, does not fit well with electronic flash units—right up to the situations where flash illumination is the only way to get a shot: this is where opposing philosophies collide.

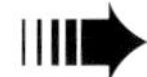

Lenses fo

Lens	Angle of view	Smallest aperture	Elements/ groups	Closest focusing
Elmarit-M 21mm f/2.8 ASPH	92°	f/16	9/7	0.70
Elmarit-M 24mm f/2.8 ASPH	84°	f/16	7/5	0.70
Elmarit-M 28mm f/2.8	22°	f/22	8/7	0.70
Summilux-M 35mm f/1.4 ASPH	64°	f/16	9/5	0.70
Summicron-M 35mm f/2 ASPH	64°	f/16	7/5	0.70
Noctilux-M 50mm f/1	45°	f/16	7/6	1.0
Summilux-M 50mm f1.4	45°	f/16	7/5	0.70
Summicron-M 50mm f/2	45°	f/16	6/4	0.70
Elmar-M 50mm f/2.8	45°	f/16	4/3	0.70
Summilux-M 75mm f/1.4	31°	f/16	7/5	0.75
Apo-Summicron-M 90mm f/2 ASPH	27°	f/16	5/5	1.0
Elmarit-M 90mm f/2.8	27°	f/22	4/4	1.09
Apo-Telyt-M 135mm f/3.4	18°	f/22	5/4	1.5
Tri-Elmar-M f/4 ASPH		f/22	8/6	1.0
28mm	76°			
35mm	64°			
50mm	45°			

* = rounded-off value
** = to bayonet flange
*** = weight in grams for black anodised finish, followed by silver-chrome and titanium finishes.

Notes to Lens Table

1. For all Leica M cameras
2. Aperture setting ring with click-stops at half stop intervals
3. ASPH = one or more elements with one or both surfaces aspherical
4. 21mm bright-line finder needed for M1, M2, M3, M4, M4-2, M4-P, M5, M6
5. Push-on lens hood
6. Distance setting by camera rangefinder
7. 24mm bright-line finder needed for M1, M2, M3, M4, M4-2, M4-P, M5, M6
8. 28mm bright-line finder needed for M1, M2, M3, M4, M4-2, M5, M6 0.85

M-Cameras

Smallest object field cm*	Length mm**	Diameter mm	Weight grams***	Filter mm	Notes
105 x 70	46.0	58	300 410	E55	1,2,3,4,5,6,15 9
95 x 63	45.0	58	290 390	E55	1,2,3,5,6,7,15 9
80 x 53	41.4	53	260	E46	1,2,5,6,8
63 x 24	46.2	53	310 415 414	E46	1,2,3,5,6 9 10
63 x 42	34.5	53	255 340	E39	1,2,3,5,6 9
62 x 41	62.0	69	600	E60	1,2,6,11,15
42 x 28	46.7	54.5	275 380 380	E46	1,2,6,11 9 10
42 x 28	43.5	53	240 335	E39	1,2,6,11 9
42 x 28	37.6	52	170 245	E39	1,2,5,6,12,15 9
29 x 19	80	68	560	E60	1,2,6,11
33 x 22	78	64	500	E55	1,2,3,6,11,13,15
33 x 22	76	56.5	410 560 560	E46	1,2,6,11 9 10
33 x 22	105	58.5	460	E49	1,2,6,11,13,15
 120 x 80 99 x 66 72 x 48	70	58	340	E55	1,2,3,6,11,14,15

9. Also available in silver-chrome
10. Also available in titanium
11. Built-in telescopic lens hood
12. Length from bayonet flange when retracted 21.6mm
13. APO = Apochromatic correction
14. Lens can be set to three different focal lengths
15. Lens contains elements made from glass with anomalous dispersion

The M6 TTL and the Visoflex

They still exist, the M-photographers, who are interested in and use the reflex housing (officially: Visoflex mirror-reflex attachment) on their M3/4/5/6 with long focal length lenses, or for close-up and macro photography with a bellows unit or universal focusing mount, extension tubes and lens head, despite the SLR option. The Leica M6 is 2.5mm taller than all other M-cameras but this does not signal the end of a chapter in Leica photography. The first mirror reflex housing for the Leica was offered in 1933: for focal lengths longer than 135mm, for close-up and macro photography with magnification ratios better than 1:1. The reflex housing was practically unavoidable for serious Leica photographers. As late as 1980, when the Leicaflex, Leica R3 and R4 had already made SLR photography available to Leica users for 15 years, the Visoflex III and its lenses, the Telyt-V 200mm f/4, 400mm f/6.8, 560mm f/6.8 and the Telyt-S 800mm f/6.3 were still in the Leica catalogue. One could also find short focusing mounts, a bellows unit and extension tubes on which one could use the unscrewable heads with focal lengths of 50, 90, 135 and 200mm. The Visoflex "died" in 1983, but the Telyt 400mm, 560mm and 800mm with an R-bayonet stayed in the catalogue until 1994.

Anyone who owns a Visoflex I, II or III can use it with some limitations on the 2.5mm higher M6. The Visoflex I fits with all the magnifiers that were available for it. The Visoflex II does not fit with the 90° prism 4x (16460 T), only with the vertical, inverted-image 5x magnifier (16461 Q)! The Visoflex III, the one that locks onto the Leica with the rotatable bayonet ring, can be used with the 90° prism 4x (16499) and with the vertical 5x-magnifier (16498). The aligning screw on the release lever on the Visoflex II and III is long enough to be fitted onto the camera's release such that the mirror flips up out of the way before the shutter releases.

Anyone who wishes to use focal lengths longer than 135mm on their M6 TTL or use the camera to photograph small things has to rely on second-hand offerings in Leica stores or magazines. They are still available there, the Visoflex I, II and III and the lenses for them: the TELYT-V 200mm f/4 or the.TELYT-V 280mm f/4.8. Made of four individual elements in a relatively weak telephoto construction, their performance can hold its own against that

The 135mm lenses for the M6 can be focused down to a close-focus distance of 1.5m and a reproduction ratio of 1:9. A spotted flash from behind though a translucent material and white Styrofoam reflectors as frontal illumination were used to light this English tea maker. Elmarit-M 135mm f/2.8.

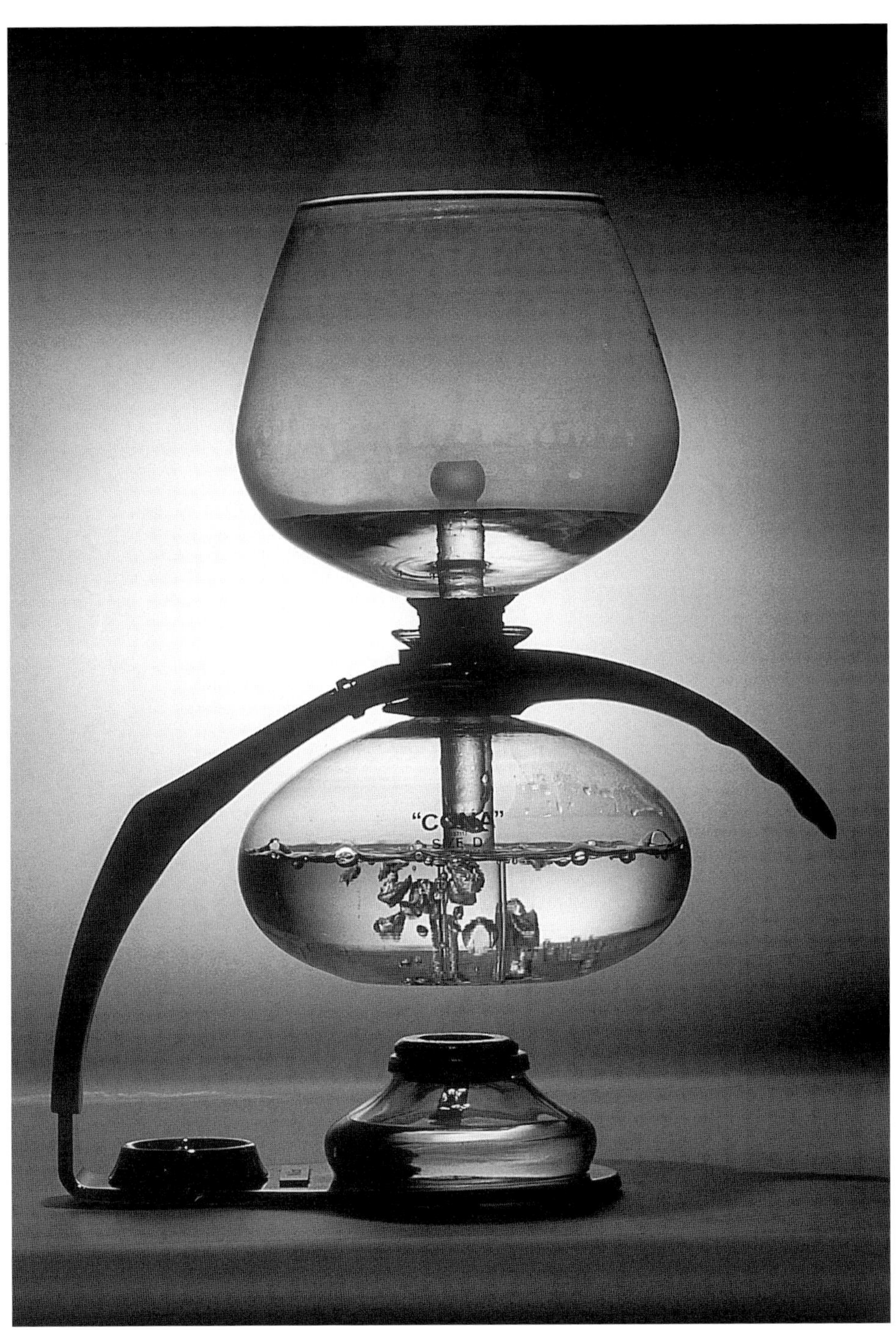

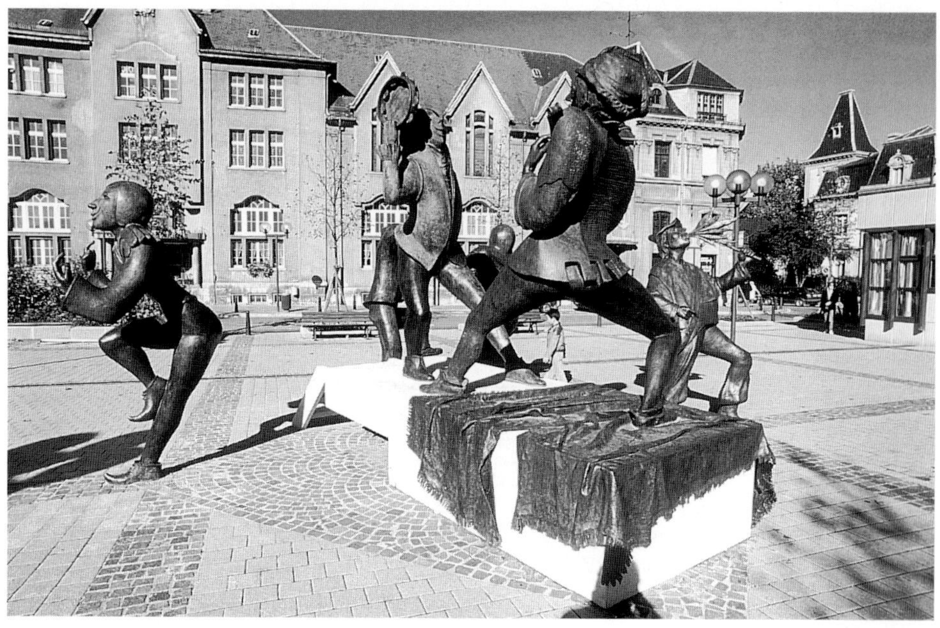

Jesters in a wide-angle shot that encompasses practically the entire square in front of the theatre in Luxembourg. Elmarit-M 21mm f/2.8 ASPH. (Photo: Jean-Alexandre Delattre)

of more modern lenses. Or the TELYT-V 400mm f/6.8, TELYT-V 560mm f/6.8 or TELYT-S 800mm f/6.3, achromatic lenses made of two, and in the case of the Telyt-S 800mm f/6.3, three elements cemented together. These elements are made of glass developed by the Leitz glass laboratories. The two-element 400mm and 560mm focal lengths offer very high detail rendition, good sharpness and colour accuracy. Thanks to their relatively simple construction, they show field curvature at maximum aperture. Focusing a few millimetres off the centre of the viewfinder image places the focused object in about the middle of the curvature and the blurring of the corners is lost in the depth of field.

The three grouped elements in the Telyt-S 800mm f/6.3 are made of glass with anomalous partial dispersion designed in the Leica glass laboratories. They are blessed with high light transmission, high imaging contrast, extensive sharpness and high resolution. With a secondary spectrum reduced to one third, it demonstrates excellent apochromatic imaging characteristics. One can only take full advantage of it if one supports it at the back with a sturdy tripod, preferably made of forearm-sized oak, and an additional tripod at the front attached to its purpose-designed tripod-mount ring.

And taking a step closer?

Leica lenses hit their close-focus limits at reproduction ratios of 1:2 to 1:9. The high quality of low-speed black-and-white and colour films enables magnifications of ten-times from the slide or negative without serious consequences—but one might, on occasion, want something better.

If you have a reflex housing for your M, you know the pleasure of exploring the world of small things with it. I encourage anyone who adds a well-preserved Visoflex to his or her M6 TTL to attempt the step into close-up and macro photography with it. Using a short focusing mount, an extension tube—again from the second-hand department—and a head unscrewed from an older 90mm and 135mm Leica lens, for example. Or with the Elmar-V 65mm f/3.5 and its focusing bellows 16464 which focuses it from infinity to a magnification ratio of 1:2.4 and is mounted directly onto the Visoflex. Or with the Leica bellows-unit II with the M-bayonet for the Visoflex II and II. It offers a thread for the adapter rings for the Leica lens heads, other manufacturer's macro lenses and for enlarging lenses with focal lengths of 80 or 100mm, which offer excellent imaging qualities for close-up and macro photography. Any instrument mechanic should be able to produce adapter rings for you.

Another way is to use the Novoflex universal bellows unit "Baluni" with the requisite adapter rings to connect the M6 TTL, Visoflex, Baluni and lens head. The best thing is to contact Novoflex office in Memmingen, Tel 08331/ 88888.

One can use the Visoflex in conjunction with the exposure meter in the Leica M6 with a long focal length lens or in a macro shot. After arranging the subject on the Visoflex's ground glass, flip its mirror up and use the arrows in the M6's viewfinder as usual to match the aperture to the previously selected shutter speed—at least 1/250s for the telephoto lens, 1/125s for the macro shot. Then return the mirror to its lowered position for a last check and release the shutter. This all naturally works better on a tripod than hand-held—and not as quickly as with a Leica SLR camera, but the results are comparable.

Chapter 5

The Flowchart: Idea—Subject—Image

At first glance it seems easy: grab the camera, wait for nice lighting over the subject, match the shutter speed and aperture so that the film gets exactly the right amount of light, defined by the exposure value, and a depth of field appropriate to the subject produces the correct effect in the image. But as is usually the case with the first glance: it fails to see the characteristic niceties, freedoms and expressions of the user.

The Elmarit-M 21mm f/2.8 ASPH can easily capture the entire grandiose panorama of the Roman amphitheatre in Orange from the first balcony, in which the few visitors look like ants, to the distant rock face of Mont Ventoux. Using the Apo-Telyt-M 135mm f/3.4, you can isolate the resting wanderer in front of the stage, or the young couple taking pictures of each other, or the cat dozing in the sun in front of you. This optical exploration of the subject area is the one argument in favour of photography with interchangeable lenses. The second argument is the relationship between focal length, angle of view and perspective.

Focal Length—Angle of View—Perspective

There are only indirect variables that affect the angle of view determined by the focal length of the lens and the perspective in the image. The fixed size is always in the background: the diagonal of the film format. In 35mm photography it is 43.3mm long. The angle of view is above it. It is enclosed by the

The distance to the most important element in the subject and the focal length determine the size-relationships between the foreground and background. If one changes one's distance from this element while changing the focal length such that it always appears the same size, the proportions between it and the background change remarkably!
Leica M6 TTL, Elmarit-M 21mm f/2.8 ASPH, Summicron 50mm f/2, Summicron-M 90mm f/2, Apo-Telyt-M 135mm f/3.4.

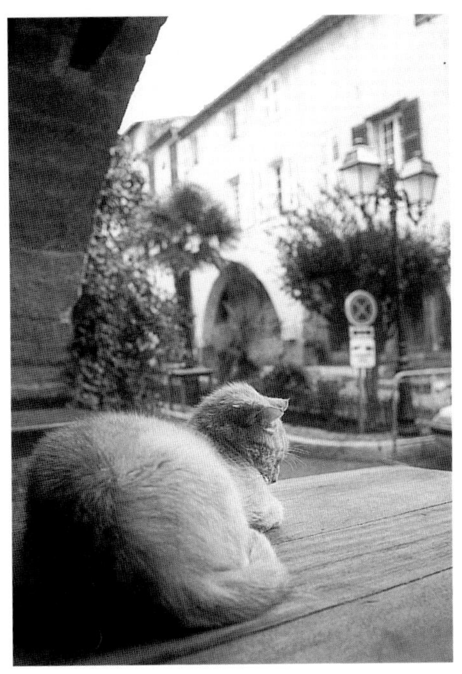

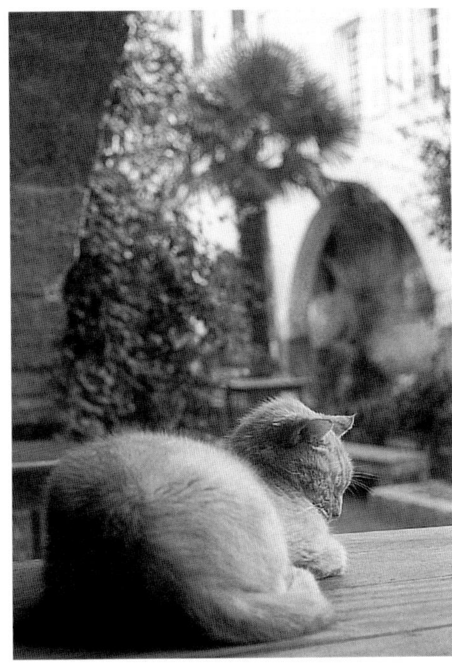

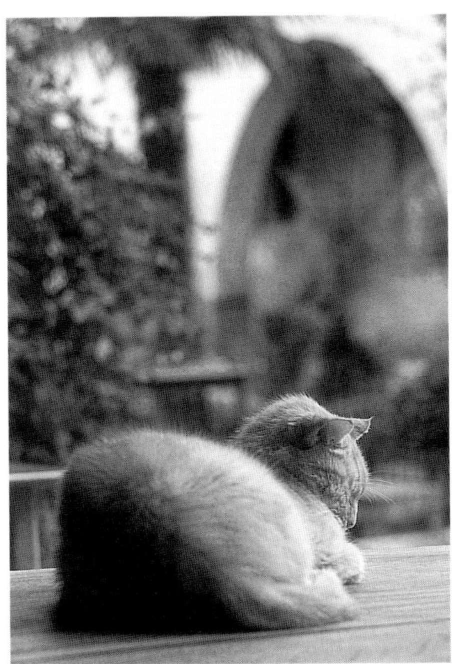

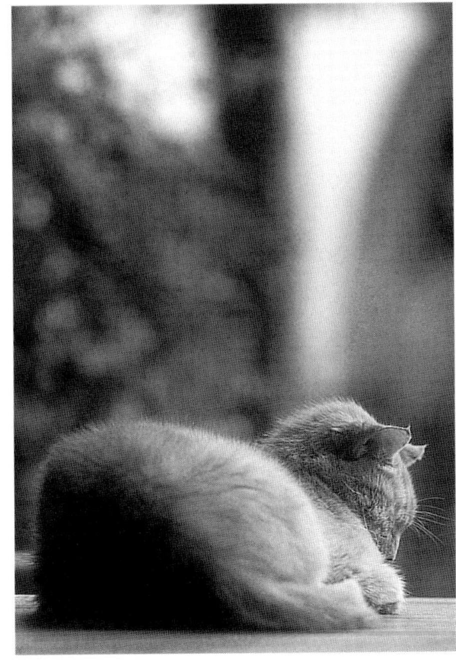

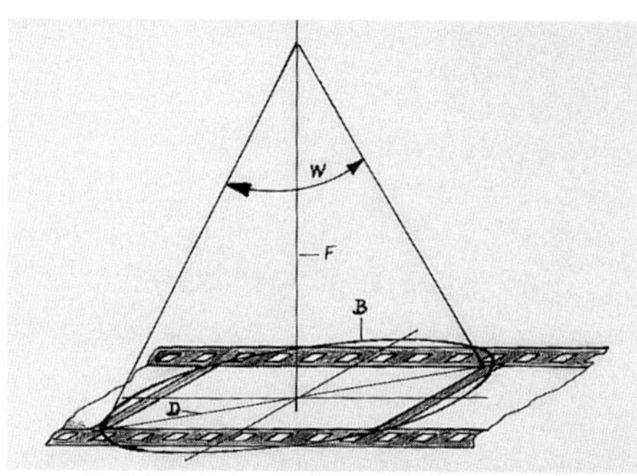

The angle of view "W" is subtended by the frame diagonals "D" which are about 43.5mm long with small format film. The width of the angle of view is determined by the focal length "F". The image circle "B" is the area that a lens has to project in focus and without distortion. For 35mm photography, it has to have a diameter of at least 44mm. Repro with M3, Hektor 135mm f/4.5 on the bellows unit.

imaginary lines that connect its endpoints with the origin of the focal length which intersects the film at its centre. If the height of this triangle, the focal length, is as long as the format diagonal, the angle contained by the connecting lines is about 53°. Nature varies the angle of view of our eyes anywhere between 45° and 50°. This is why we consider images taken with a 50mm lens "the same as the eye sees it."

If one takes as a reference the panorama image that encompasses the amphitheatre wall, roofs and mountain ranges, taken with the Elmarit-M 21mm f/2.8 ASPH, and uses longer focal lengths to isolate elements out of the scene while standing at the same spot, the size ratios of the foreground to background elements remain the same. Only when you change both the focal length and your position in the image do you change the proportions between foreground and background. Taken from up close, the bowsprit of the sailboat seems to tower over the houses on the other side of the harbour. Now using the 50mm and moving to a point where the bowsprit appears the same size as it did in the wide-angle shot, the perspective in the shot is the same as you see it. Using the Apo-Telyt 135mm f/3.4 to photograph the bow from a distance so that it appears exactly the same size as in the other two shots, a very small section of the house-background appears in the slightly blurred background. The details of the carved figurehead stand out dramatically. If then the low sun lights the subject from the side, this image might be a real eye-catcher. Even in small 10x15cm prints of the three shots, you will see that it is not the focal length that creates the perspective, but the relationship between the angle of view determined by it and your distance from the subject!

You can prove this by trying the reverse of this test. Shoot the subject using the Elmarit-M 21mm f/2.8 ASPH from the same distance as that used when you shot with the Apo-Telyt-M 135mm f/3.4. Enlarge the section with which the 135mm filled the frame out of the resulting negative to 10x15cm. You will not see any difference in the perspective between the foreground and background. The proportions in the subject area, the size ratios between the foreground details and the background only change if you also change your position in the image space when you change focal lengths. This flexibility in composition of the image is perhaps the biggest argument in favour of photography with interchangeable lenses. The theory that wide-angle lenses produce a more marked perspective in the image than longer focal lengths is thus debunked. It came to be because one gets so close to a subject with a wide-angle lens that even a small foreground seems to overpower everything else.

Focus and Depth of Field

For a cook, sharpness is the indispensable characteristic of a knife, for us photographers, it is what we value most in our lenses. But one cannot define it in numerical terms. The sharpness value distilled by physicists and opticians in the laboratory are more for scientific purposes than for our photographic tasks.

We all know how "not sharp" looks in a picture from our own bad expe-

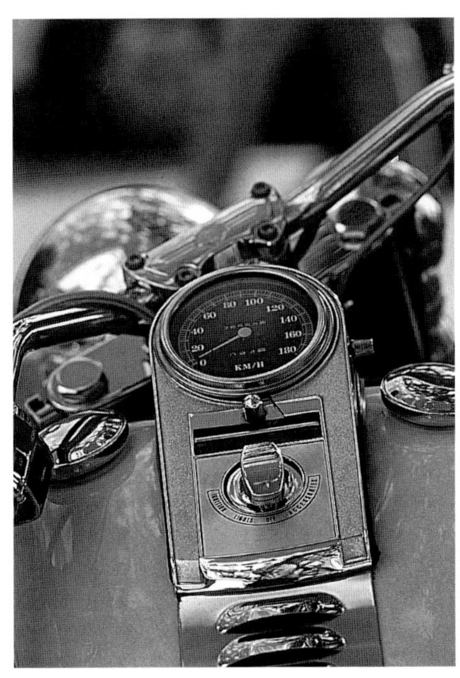

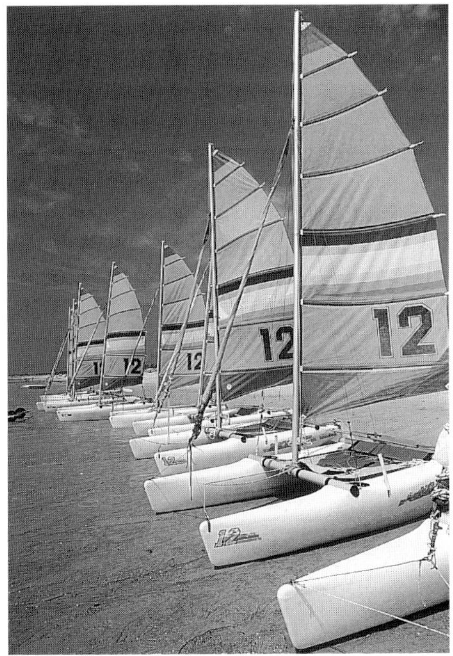

Depth of field as a compositional tool:
The narrow depth of field offered by maximum aperture (left) separates the details from the surroundings in a very eye-catching manner. Summicron-M 50mm f/2, at f/2.
Small aperture and short focal length (right) provide this depth of field that encompasses the entire image area. Super-Angulon-M 21mm f/3.4, at f/11.

riences. We can also determine whether a "not quite sharp" picture is still acceptable or has to be thrown out without the aid of numbers and measures. The reasons for out-of-focus pictures are well-known:

- The lens only has moderate imaging characteristics; but this is never true of a Leica lens!
- The shutter speed was not fast enough to overcome the vibration of the camera.
- The exposure time was too long to freeze the movement in the subject.
- The lens was not set to the correct focusing distance for the subject.

The cures are:

- To prevent camera shake, particularly with longer focal length lenses, faster shutter speeds and/or a tripod under the camera.
- A short exposure time appropriate to the movement of the subject prevents motion blur.
- The Leica M6's rangefinder guarantees very accurate distance setting of the lens, even in low light—so be more careful.

But even this does not adequately define what we photographers call "crisp focus." The only thing that remains is the definition formulated by Oskar Barnack over 70 years ago that also has a physical-optical basis.

The wave-nature of light and the minimal aberrations, which affect even the best lenses, mean that even those lenses cannot capture the dimensionless black dot the way it appears on a piece of white paper. Even when focused exactly on this dot, the image transmitted by a lens onto film shows a microscopic transition from the dot's black to the paper's white that does not exist in the original. The width of this transitional zone also depends on the overall imaging characteristics of the lens—but one cannot judge the quality of a lens system on this edge effect alone! The further a photographed dot is from the plane of focus, the wider this grey area, the more "diffused" the dot will appear on the picture. If the transitional zone is so wide that one can see when looking at a 24x30cm enlargement from a distance of 30cm, the image appears out of focus. Enlarge the image to 90x60cm and regard it from a distance at least equal to the diagonal of the image, one has the same perception of sharpness as with the 24x30cm image. The closer one is to the large image, the more the appearance of sharpness will decrease.

Using this as a starting point, Oskar Barnack came up with his definition for the boundary between an image that is "still sharp" and one that is "not quite sharp". Anything that is to be perceived as sharp in an 18x24cm enlargement of the entire 35mm negative, can only have a circle of confusion with a diameter of 0.033mm on the negative. With an eight-time magnification to 18x24cm, they grow to 0.26mm and are therefore just below the

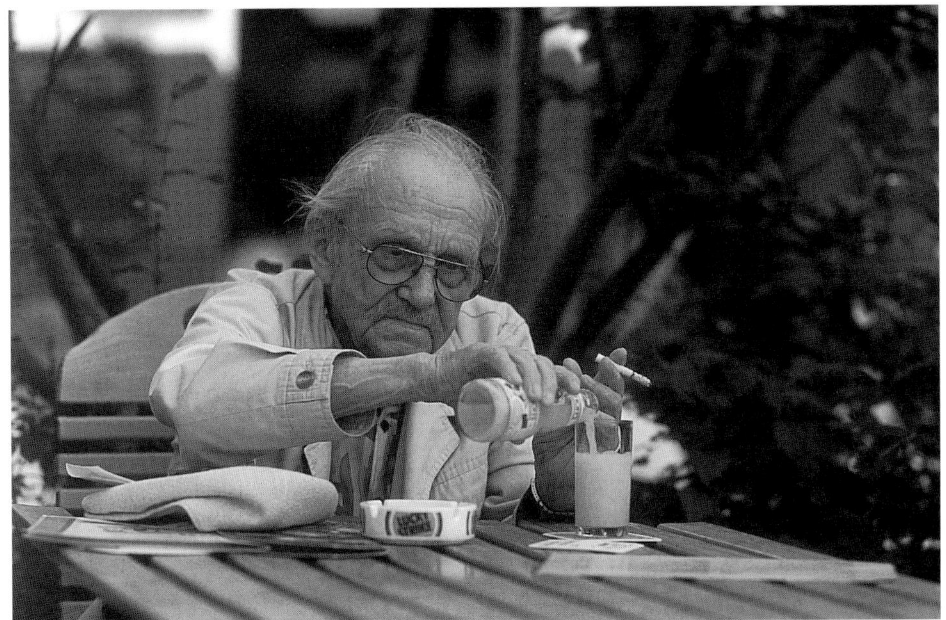

Unperturbed by the bustle of big-city life, he enjoys the cool shade of the pavement bar. The long focal length eliminates the unwanted surroundings. Elmarit-M 135mm f/2.8.

One needs a long focal length for this balcony scene.

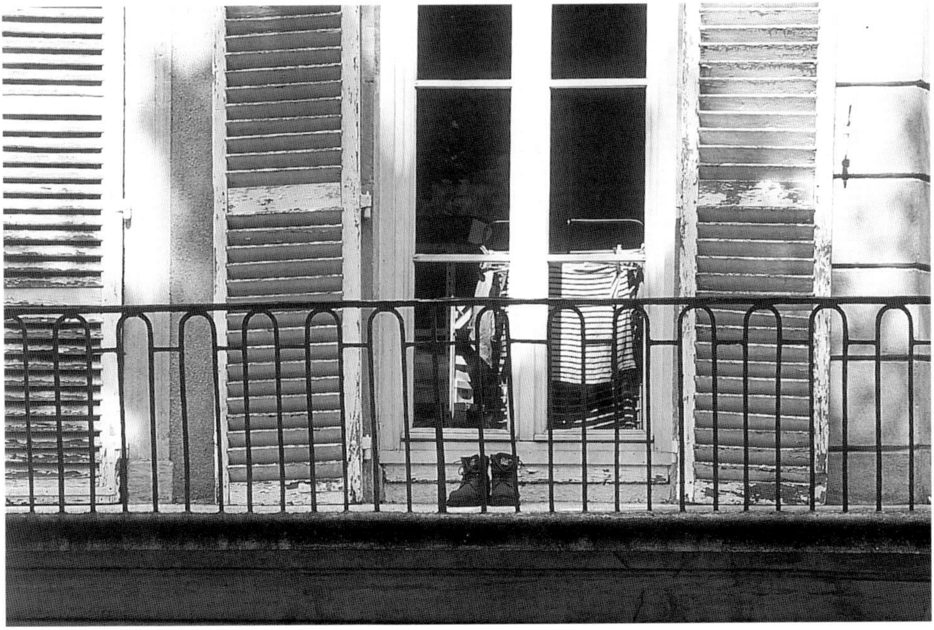

resolving power of the normal eye at the 30cm viewing distance.

The 0.033mm value also defines the boundary of the depth of field. The maximum-aperture depth of field which encompasses, say,only the eyes and mouth in a unique portrait is the one extreme, the all-encompassing harbour panorama in which the depth of field stretches all the way from the ketch in front of you to the far-distant horizon is the other. Playing with depth of field is the tool for photographic image composition. The shutter speed is now in a secondary roll—as long as it is not too slow for camera stability and the dynamics of the subject. The 0.033mm boundary still separates the sharp from the not-sharp. Depth of field corresponds to the amount of space in front of and behind the subject that is still in focus. It depends on the size of the aperture. Closing the aperture increases the depth of field, opening it moves the 0.033mm boundaries closer together. In the close-up range, the same aperture will always offer a much narrower depth of field than over larger distances. A longer focal length will offer a narrower depth of field at all apertures than a shorter one.

Recipes which prescribe how much depth of field is required with which subject and where it should be placed are just as successful as trying to nail a pudding onto the wall. You see the subject and you determine the depth of field that you think is right for the subject and you place the plane of focus where it corresponds to your idea of the image composition. The deciding factor is what you want the resulting picture to look like. Shooting diagonally along the post-and-beam wall at maximum aperture to capture the Madonna in the minimal depth of field is just as correct as using minimum aperture from the same spot to capture the first beam to the last in crisp focus. Use the freedom to choose this or that depth of field, to experiment, analyse and identify your style of shooting to capture the images you want. Depth of field is not an invariable constant like focal length or shutter speed. It is the major element of image composition. A penchant for needlepoint planes of focus between blurred foregrounds and backgrounds can be detrimental, an addiction to maximum depth of field likewise.

In the Leica M6 TTL viewfinder, you will always see the subject in focus from front to back. How the depth of field affects the image can therefore only be seen in the finished print or the projected slide. This is where the photographer's imagination is required. Despite my 35 years or more of photographic experience, my depth-of-field imagination is merely mediocre, but the thing that I miss least on the camera is the depth of field preview button. You can depend on it that no-one will ever ask you why you placed the depth of field here rather than there if the image is impressive.

Static Sharpness

The depth of field of an Elmarit-M 21mm f/2.8 ASPH reaches from 130cm to just about infinity at f/5.6 when focused at 2.5m. Even with an ISO 50/18° film, one will seldom run into camera-shake problems under our typical lighting conditions. The Elmarit-M 28mm f/2.8 has to be stopped down to f/8-11 for the same results. But whether one is using the 21mm or the 28mm to shoot the group of teenagers gathered around the ice-cream vendor from such a close vantage point that he stands out as the central character in the image—the disturbing element in this picture is that he blends in with the plethora of masts, walls and stuff in the background. The more expansive depth of field of a wide-angle lens sometimes makes photography easier, but the image is not always an eye-catcher. Should one wish to photograph this scene from further away using a 90mm lens, one would have to close down to f/32 to achieve the same depth of field. Neither of the Leica 90mm M-lenses offer an aperture of f/32, as it causes noticeable diffraction. Even f/16, compared to f/5.6, produces an eight-times longer, and often camera-shake critical, exposure time. Blurred shawls can be attributed to the light summer breeze—but a shaking pier cannot realistically be attributed to an earthquake.

So one should divorce oneself from thoughts of depth of field, open the aperture until the shutter speed is right and focus precisely on the actor. Depth of field from front to back has to be in as crisp a focus as shallow, and cannot be plagued by the effects of shake. Rather than hand-holding when focus from front to back is required, put your trust in a tripod—and one that is generally one level heavier that you want. After all, you never know when the light one with its multitude of spindly leg extensions will quiver under the weight of its burden. Tripods of more solid design are more exhausting to carry as they are more reliable. A monopod is an occasionally useful compromise between hand-held flexibility and the restrictions of a tripod.

Sharpness that encompasses the entire subject area, or a narrow depth of field placed strategically on the subject, are two equally valid compositional methods—only your ideas, moods and preferences can choose between them.

Crisp Motion

Fast moving objects should normally appear sharp on the film, so the lens will constantly have to be refocused. Experienced photographers will keep the two partial images in the viewfinder on top of each other all the time by constantly adjusting the focus ring and then swivel the TTL just before the exposure so that the moving person or object will have more space in front of them in the picture. Select exposure and aperture in advance, so you can concentrate completely on the focus operation.

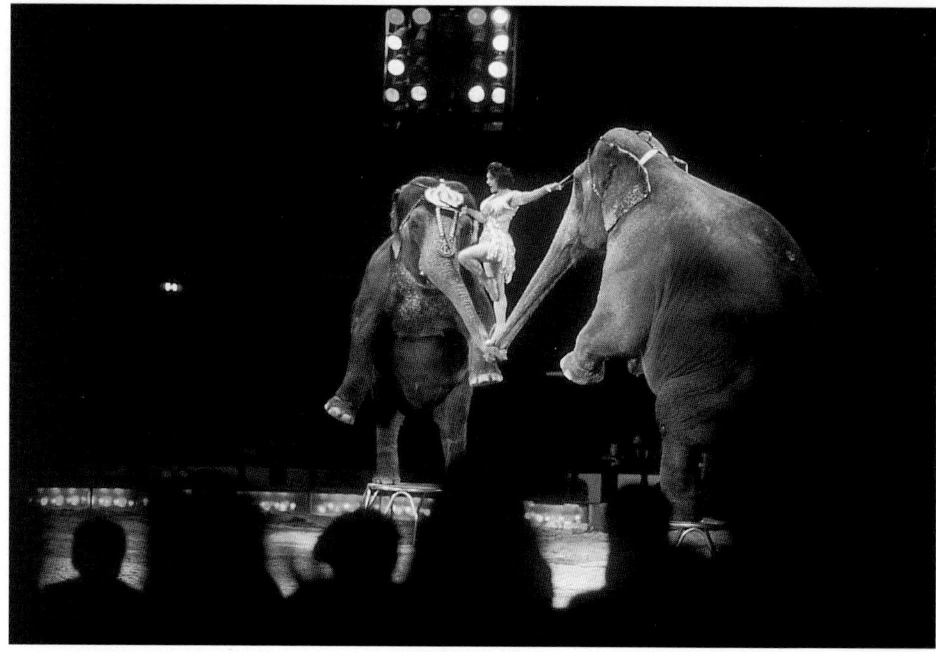

A balancing-act on elephant trunks—definitely a more difficult task for the artist than for the M6 TTL with Summicron-M 50mm f/2 and high speed film.

In order to be able to focus precisely, one has to be able to see the viewfinder image clearly. If you cannot, you need a Leica correction lens on the M6 TTL eyepiece. They are available in half-dioptre increments from –3 to +3. If you wear glasses, you can hold the eyepiece right up to them. A small, rubberised ring on the eyepiece prevents the glasses from getting scratched. If you are successful in setting the focus precisely with your glasses on and can see the entire viewfinder image, you can spare yourself the expense of a correction lens and the trouble of glasses on, glasses off, glasses on, when alternating between direct examination of the subject and looking through the M6's viewfinder.

Or, for example, focus on the chalk-mark that the hurdler is about to reach and press the release when he is one step away—a favourite reporter's trick. The shutter release delay with the M6 TTL is only about 10 milliseconds!

Or, another example, place yourself with the Leica M6 TTL fitted with the Elmarit-M 90mm f/2.8 about 15m away from the edge of the water hazard, focus on the other bank and wait for the runners. Seventy seconds for the last 400m are probably not world-record material. But does 1/250s match this speed? 400m in 70 seconds equals 5.7 m/s. Multiplied by the magnification ratio, the image of the runner travels across the film at a rate of about 33m/s. Now the 0.033mm-limit comes into play: combining it with the 33m/s of the runner, one arrives at a shutter speed of 1/1000s! Those who only want 9x13cm prints can risk 1/250s. Aperture f/5.6 or f/8 and 1/1000s—quite a bit of sun has to be shining on the subject even with a ISO 100/21° film. With an overcast sky, an ISO 400/27° film is necessary to capture the pumping legs crisply while still affording the requisite depth of field. If you place narrow depth of field right at the take-off point, you might survive with ISO 100/21°.

If light and film are too weak for f/4 and 1/500s, try it this way. Focus on the edge of the water hazard, select a speed of 1/60s or 1/125s and adjust the aperture accordingly. Track the runners in the M6 TTL viewfinder, pan the camera along and fire when the first runner is getting ready to jump. If you have a winder under the M6, leave your finger on the trigger for a series of two to four shots. The runners appear partially in focus but with blurred hands and feet in front of a markedly diagonally striped background. The longer the exposure time, the more the background will turn into a blurred scene. From at least f/8 on, the unavoidable jerks in freehand panning will appear as vertical streaks in the horizontal structure. At such a slow shutter speed, only the bodies of the runners will appear in focus as they do not move relative to the panning camera.

Alternatively, mount the M6 TTL on a tripod, set the shutter to exposure times between 1/30s and 1/4s and adjust the aperture accordingly. Fire as soon as the first runner lifts off to jump. At 1/4s and 1/15s, the athletes float through the image as coloured streamers. With exposure times longer than 1/4s, they leave only lines on the film: they cover almost 6m in one second which is more than half the distance that a 90mm lens covers in its horizontal angle of view over a distance of 13m.

Fast movements bring another element into play. The shutter delay of the Leica M6 is about 10 milliseconds. The command "fire!" takes, depending on the person and their condition at that moment, between 1/5s and 1/15s of travel from the brain to the fingertip. Adding the "reaction times" of the human and camera, one comes up with 125 milliseconds. The following table contains some subjects and the distances they move in that 1/8s that it takes the signal to leave the brain and the shutter to move.

One therefore has to send the signal an appropriate amount earlier in order to capture passers-by, athletes and cars at the precise point in the image where one wants them. Up to about the speed of a recreational cyclist at 15km/h = about 0.5m in the 125ms this

Distance Moved by a Subject in 1/8 sec.—the Response Time between Brain and Shutter Release	
a pedestrian at 4 km/h	about 0.14m
a recreational cyclist at 10 km/h	about 0.35m
a fast cyclist at 30 km/h	about 1.04m
a car at 50 km/h	about 1.74m
a water-skier at 65 km/h	about 2.26m
a bus at 80 km/h	about 2.78m
a car at 100km/h	about 3.47m

difference does not play a significant role. A winder under the M6 TTL does not help much here: at three frames per second, about 300ms elapse between shots. You can multiply the distances given above by 2.4 in order to determine the distance these subjects will cover in that dark time.

Light and Film

A photographer can only control light if he produces it himself using a flash or other artificial light. He has to accept daylight the way it is. Reflector boards can be used on dull days to bounce light and reflections onto the subject, but dull light does not become more exciting. The sun and the sky always radiate the same light mixture. They should arrive at earth at a colour temperature of 5600K (degrees Kelvin). But daylight is an incalculable wonder. A little bit more moisture in the air gives the light a slightly different feel than it had yesterday. In the half-hour after sunrise, it has a different colour nuance than it does in the half-hour before sunset. Depending on the height of the sun, water vapour, mist, dust and other things in the air give light very different colour balances.

Colour films are calibrated for the 5600K of average daylight. Colour in temperature degrees? An invention of physicists. They heated up an ideal black body and found: at certain temperatures, the colours it gave off were the same as those of our artificial lights—hence the colour temperature of our light in degrees Kelvin. Important colour temperatures are:

Those who do not want to accept the variations in daylight can use a colour temperature meter and use filters to convert the ambient light into average daylight. One can thus capture subjects as close to reality as possible on film—but the appeal of the baroque facade illuminated by the evening sun will get stuck in the filter. The path of the sun determines the illumination of the subject. If its best side faces south, i.e. towards the sun, one has sidelight from the right

Colour Temperature of Illumination Sources	
Household incandescent bulb 100W	about 2700K
Conventional photofloods	3100 to 3400K
Halogen lights	3200 to 3400K
Clear flashbulbs	3800 to 4000K
Blue flash bulbs	about 5000K
Pure sunlight	about 5400K
Average daylight	5500 to 4000K
Pure sky light without sun component in the shade	12,000 to 18,000K

in the morning, frontal illumination at midday, and in late afternoon sidelight from the left. Is the morning or evening sidelight that emphasises structure the better illumination? Or should one wait until a thin, white cloud provides diffused bright, accentuating sunlight? Light coloured ground reflects diffuse sunlight into the shadows created by horizontal architectural structures and lightens them up. The not-particularly exciting frontal illumination becomes more interesting if one shoots from an angle to it into the subject. Photography is more important than theory when it comes to light! One has to invest some time and effort if one wants to turn often-photographed subjects into new pictures using light (see for example the colour plate on page 112).

Absolute backlight for cutting images is only afforded by a lowering sun or a bright-white wall in the background. At midday, its light hits the camera from above, which makes it too steep in summer to create attractive backlight.

Any type of light creates different accents. Landscape and architecture photography swing between patient waiting and seizing the moment, particularly when flashes of sun and cloud make for rapid changes in illumination in 20-second intervals.

The Film—A Multi-layered Secret

Only after it is developed does it reveal what it captured of the subject. The most important characteristic of a film is its sensitivity to light. The ISO-value of its sensitivity indicates the amount of light that has to strike it in order to produce a negative from which good enlargements can be made or a brilliant slide once developed. The ISO-value of the film sensitivity that you have set on the back of the M6 and the amount of available light are used by the M6 exposure meter to calculate the correct exposure value.

Their sensitivity to colour divides films into three groups: black-and-white films capture even the most colourful of subjects in shades of grey. The colour negative film, the precursor of the colour print, shows the subject in inverted colours. Colour reversal films leave the lab as slides ready for projection. Colour films not only register the significant difference between incandescent and day light, but even their finest nuances. Those who shoot under incandescent light with daylight balanced slide film have to accept an unpleasant yellow-red cast in the slide. Incandescent-balanced slide film reacts to daylight with strongly blued images. Even colour negative films register the difference between daylight and incandescent light. A good lab can filter out most of the effects. But when best results are required, one should use the appropriate film.

Images in Black-and-White

Famous and less-famous photographers have worked in this medium since the first days of the Leica and have helped it and photography reach widespread acceptance through their impressive images. This, in turn, has encouraged the development of black-and-white films of ever-higher performance. Those who desired similar images, furnished their own darkroom, often improvised: 50 sheets of 18x24 black-and-white paper were generally more important at that time than a well-equipped darkroom. New films and papers with excellent characteristics are generating renewed interest in black-and-white photography. What used to be friendship-threatening themes of fine grain, fine grain or surface developer and contour sharpness are now merely side-discussions. Although increased sensitivity in black-and-white films still leads to larger grain and results in loss of fine detail.

The absolute top in contour sharpness, resolution and fineness of grain is Kodak Technical Pan. Developed in Kodak's Technidol or in Tetenal Neofin-doku, one can use it for any application. New technologies led to new middle and high-sensitivity B&W films with fine grain structure and contour sharpness that was once only possible with slow films. Classics like Kodak Tri-X or Plus-X were improved, Ilford Pan-F Plus, FP-4 Plus, and HP-5 Plus replaced the earlier versions with higher quality. With equally improved developers, one can enlarge negatives from any of these films to poster-size without any difficulty. But anyone who changes film and developer every two weeks will not get to know either very well and will only achieve the high-quality results of B&W photography with great difficulty.

The raked seating in the Roman amphitheatre in Orange is a wonderful place to rest and photograph—and to be photographed. Elmarit-M 135mm f/2.8.

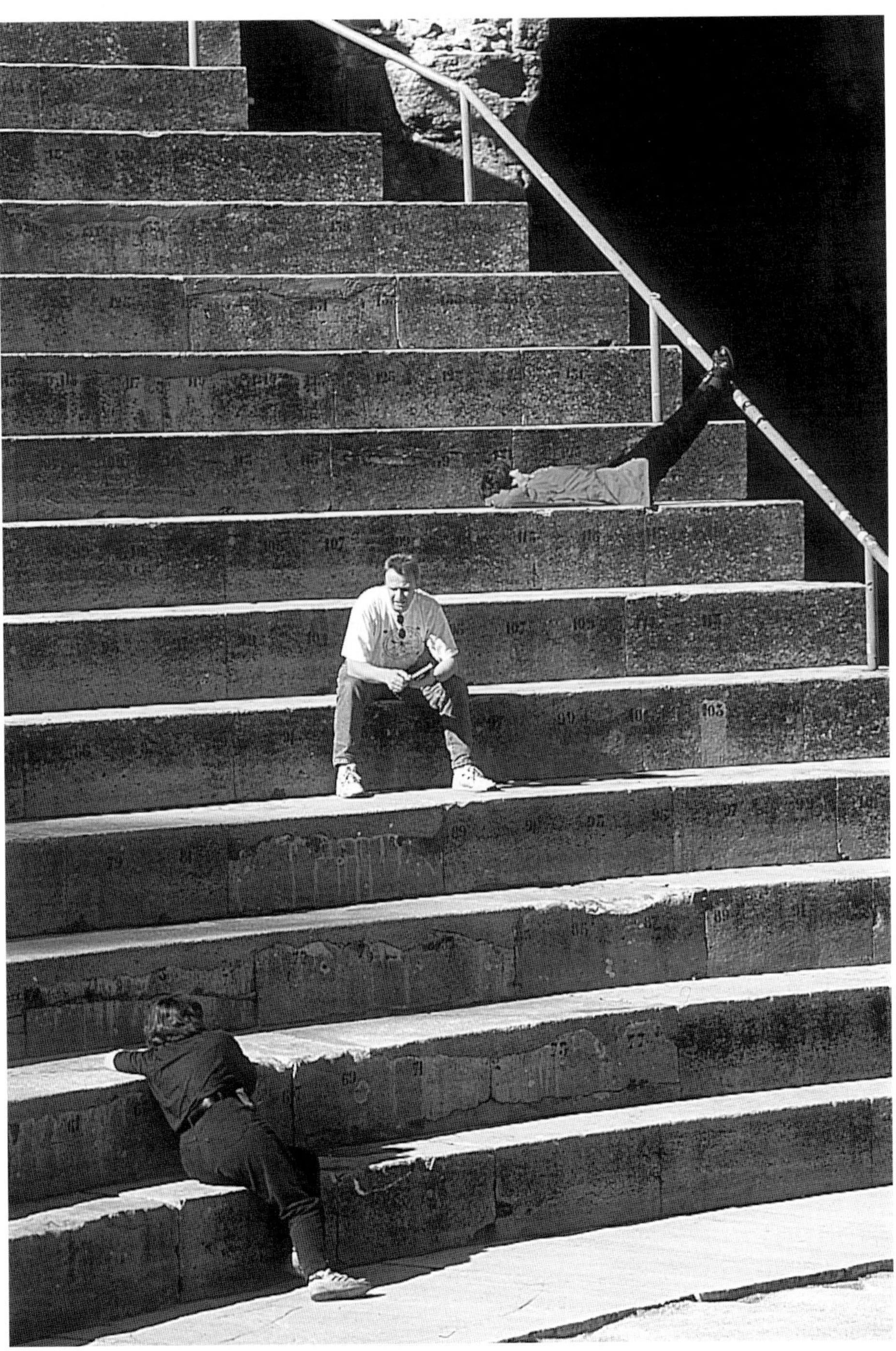

To translate colours into equally-bright grey tones is no longer the aim of B&W photography. It excels with its old and new qualities in the realms of product and sport photography and photo-journalism. Light and shadow, structures and areas make wonderful fine-art prints.

Colour On Paper

What colour negative films of 16-18 DIN used to offer in terms of colour accuracy, colour rendition and grain, films today of ISO 100/21° and ISO 200/24° beat easily. Even the relationship between increasing sensitivity and coarser grain, which was also true for colour films, seems to be defeated. Only in the ISO 3200/36° films designed for very low light is it still apparent. They don't have quite the same brilliance as the ISO 100/21° films, and the colours are often not exactly as they were in the original—but which colours under low light—and particularly under neon—are right? The Kodak C-41 process is the international standard for the developing of colour negative films. But each manufacturer's product has its own characteristics. Those who wish to exploit these characteristics for their pictures cannot avoid their own darkroom—and the nights spent in it! Loading the best of films into the M6 and then entrusting the film to the cheapest printer for 29-cent prints simply wastes the potential of the film and the Leica. The alternative is to take the five best shots of the quarter and take them to the professional lab for large enlargements to hang on the wall.

Brilliant Colours—The Slide

Most slide films are sold including processing. Those who buy Agfachrome, Ektachrome or Fujichrome without processing included either have a regular lab they can rely on, or do the processing themselves. This makes sense if one regularly exposes five films a month. Colour reversal films are only processed using Kodak E-6 which is by now almost as easy as B&W developing. Despite E-6 standards, slide films have their own dose of individuality. One appears a little "cooler" in projection as it is more sensitive to the blue in the atmosphere, the other, being a bit more sensitive to yellows and reds, gives a "warmer" result. If you don't like the colour characteristics of your slide film, try another kind. The range of colour slide films extends from ISO 50/18° to ISO 1600/33°. The M6 TTL ISO scale ends at 6400/39°, meaning that one can use it to push even the most sensitive films by two stops. Under the low light for which the fastest films were designed, colours appear a little dull even on a slide. So don't expect the usual display of colours on the screen.

Colour slide films are generally calibrated for average daylight. Only subjects photographed under this light will appear with their actual colours on the film. They react to lamplight with an un-

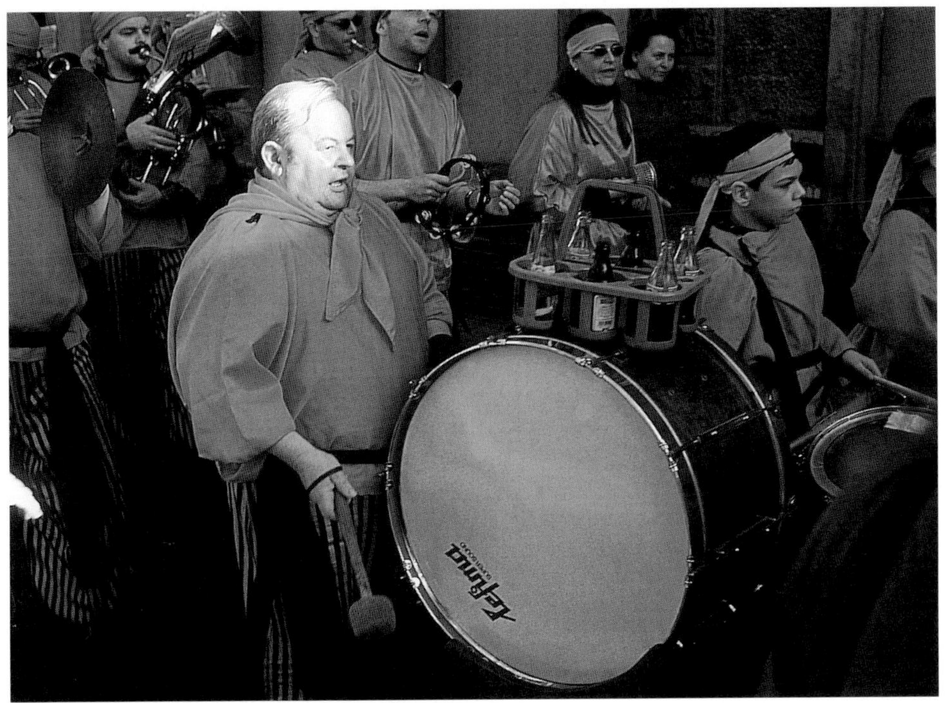

The cool drinks prevent overheating. The exposure was balanced for the sun-lit skin. Summicron-M 50mm f/2.

pleasant yellow-red cast. It usually ruins the slide. It cannot be corrected after the fact and can only be prevented at the outset by using a class 80 A/KB 15 blue correction filter in front of the lens. It absorbs about two-stops of light, meaning that an ISO 1600/33° film becomes ISO 400/27° and instead of a safe 1/125s it may require a shaky 1/30s. But don't expect a perfect correction: incandescent lights become increasingly red as they age. Since one cannot know how old a bulb is, one cannot be sure if the 80A filter is good enough. Fluorescent lighting is even more difficult. Special filters called FL-D and FL-W are available, but there are at least six different colours of fluorescent tubes, each of which has a different gap in the spectrum they produce—one has to use test shots to try to get the right shot.

Incandescent-balanced slide film fits better than daylight film, but even it is not perfect for 2700K light. If halogen spotlights are used in conjunction with somewhat older incandescent bulbs to accent interior architecture, correction filtration becomes a game of chance. One's only hope is to experiment to get the right shot.

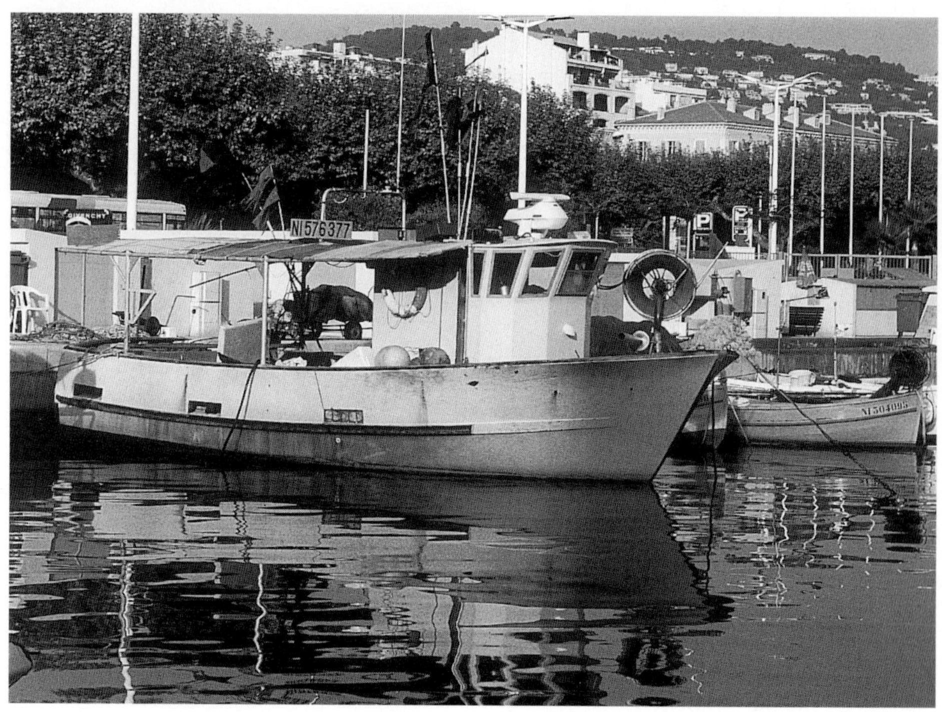

Only a long focal length could capture this old tug and its reflection in an interesting manner. Elmarit-M 135mm f/2.8

First-class paper prints from a slide are no longer a question of price or quality. If the colours on the print do not match those on the slide, one can ask for a refund more easily: the proof of how wrong they are is evident on the light-table. One has to accept small deviations though, because the the best paper print will never look the same as.an illuminated slide.

If you project slides taken with the M6 TTL through a cheap projector onto a crumpled bed sheet, you are wasting image qualities just as much as the buyer of cheap paper prints, and be disillusioned about the necessity for creative effort. Not only Leica users know that the Leica Pradovit projector is the best that one can buy. Whether it is the P150, P30, P600 or the pro-projector P2002—all offer impressive image sharpness, very bright, even illumination of the slide, mechanical precision and reliability and a comparatively moderate temperature in the image chamber which does not damage a slide, even during prolonged projection. A true professional unit of the highest calibre is the Pradovit RT for horizontal circular magazines that hold

80 or 140 slides and with 300W lamps—a bit too much for the average living room. You should spend an afternoon at your local Leica dealer's to compare the characteristics of the various Pradovit projectors. For a slide-show in the living room over a distance of 3m (10ft), you probably do not need the 250W bulb—used in econo-mode it will last almost for ever. If you subsequently splash out for 2m-wide projections—2x2m screens are still almost affordable—250W in econo-mode will still be more brilliant than 150W at full-power—and you also will not need a pearl or alu-effect screen. The money saved as a result is well-invested in the next level of Pradovit.

Chapter 6

The M6 TTL and Flash

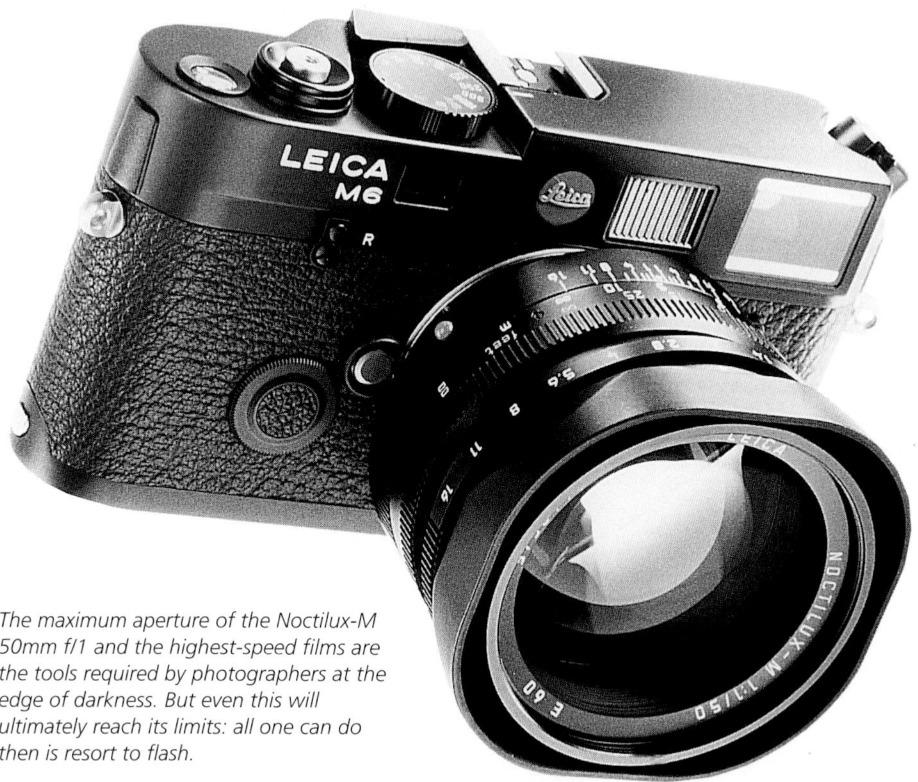

The maximum aperture of the Noctilux-M 50mm f/1 and the highest-speed films are the tools required by photographers at the edge of darkness. But even this will ultimately reach its limits: all one can do then is resort to flash.

Fast lenses with excellent imaging qualities at maximum aperture, uncomplicated handling, a brilliant viewfinder image even in low light, light-touch release, extremely low-vibration and quiet shutter, all make the Leica M6 TTL an ideal available-light camera with which one can risk hand-held shutter speeds that one would not dream of with a reflex camera. But even with the most sensitive film and an aperture of f/1.4, one will run into the end of hand-held shooting at some point.

Halogen spotlights are one solution, to get through the darkness,flash illumination another

The Leica M6 TTL offers two contacts for flash units: a normal sync. socket on the back and a centre contact in the hot shoe as well as, and this is new compared to the "old" but by no means obsolete M6, signal and control contacts for TTL flash control via direct metering of subject illumination off the film surface. Normal sync. socket and centre contact establish the communication with the Leica SF-20 or to any other flash from minis to full-blown studio systems. You can use both contacts at the same time, but not in TTL mode!

The typical characteristics of flash illumination set the rules for working with it. The duration of its illumination is always orders of magnitude shorter than the time the shutter takes to travel over the film gate. The aperture is therefore the only device that can control the amount of flash light striking the film. TTL flash control loosens this restriction, sometimes more, sometimes less, but cannot overcome the limited range of the flash illumination and the reduction of its intensity by the square of the distance to the subject. Both characteristics are contained in the guide number equation:

aperture = guide number ÷ distance

or

guide number = aperture x distance

The distance is always the separation between the flash and the most important part of the subject. The guide number corresponds to the power of the flash and is usually given with reference to ISO 100/21°.

The time it takes the shutter to move across the image window is always longer than the flash duration. It follows that the flash can only illuminate the entire film format if the shutter blinds have opened the entire width. Since the M6 TTL shutter blinds move relatively slowly over the film gate in order to reduce noise and vibration, this condition is only met at exposure times of 1/50s, marked by a flash symbol on the shutter speed dial, and all slower ones, as well as "B." With times shorter than 1/50s and with the shutter speed dial in the "OFF" position, the flash does not fire.

If the Leica M6 TTL battery is so weak that the display in the viewfinder does not illuminate, or if there is no battery in the battery compartment, the flash will not be fired by the sync. socket or the centre contact!

Since the guide number, and hence the flash power, cannot be changed, the distance to the subject determines the aperture and hence the depth of field—there is hardly any latitude for image composition using depth of field.

An electronic flash unit offers freedom for composing an image using depth of field if it offers

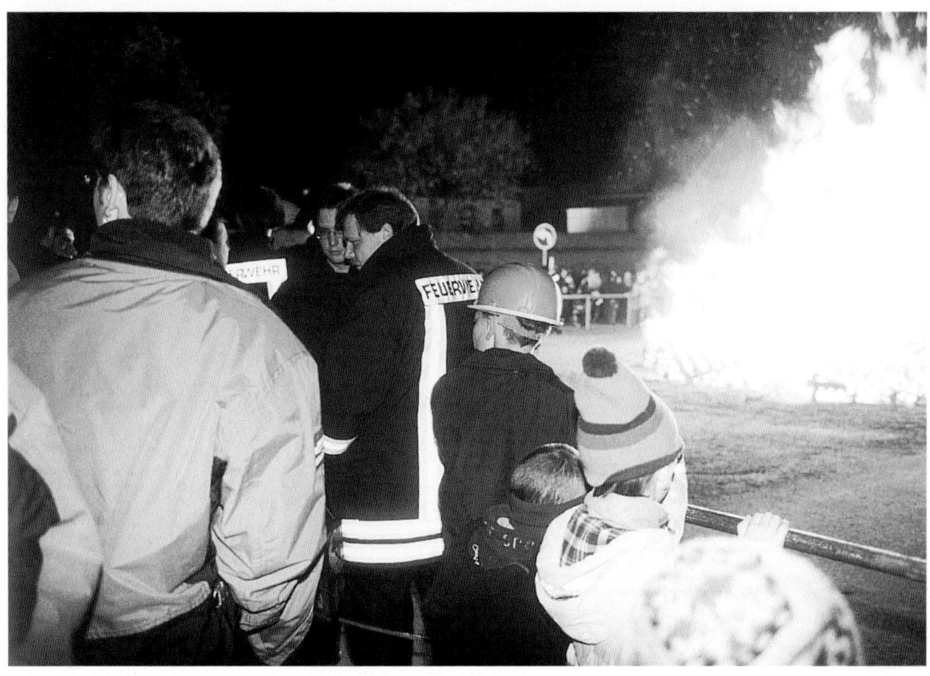

Even at the bonfire, the M6 TTL and the SF 20 control the flash illumination correctly via the TTL system.

various power settings. They and the film speed then determine the required aperture. Illumination control is assumed by the silicon photocell and the flash's thyristors. The silicon-photocell measures the increasing amount of light on the subject produced by the firing flash and converts it into an electronic signal. If it reaches the reference value determined by the power output, the thyristor turns the flash tube off. The unused energy remains stored in the flash's capacitors. The sensor control takes the subject-flash distance into account as well as colour filters, gels and other accessories mounted on the flash and even effectively controls indirect light bounced off an umbrella or reflector board onto the subject. The electronic flash's sensor cannot take into account filters on the lens, the lens's effective aperture or additional light required due to extensions used for macro photography. These factors can only be compensated for by selecting a larger aperture than the one corresponding to the flash's power setting.

The TTL flash control of the Leica M6 TTL allows full control over the aperture and hence the depth of field—as long as the flash's power is appropriate. You choose the aperture that produces the desired depth of field: from the maximum aperture for effective limited depth of field to the smallest for the greatest possible depth of field. But here the power of the Leica SF 20 flash unit sets limits to the possible.

Once the first shutter blind clears the film gate, it gives the fire signal to the SF 20—the flash fires. The silicon-photocell on the floor of the M6 TTL measures the subject illumination as a reflection off the film. Once this metered value reaches the reference determined by the film sensitivity, the computer system turns the SF 20 off and pulls the second shutter blind over the film window. TTL flash control considers the distance from the flash to the subject, filters and reflectors in front of the flash, the brightness of the subject, the effective aperture, the increased light required by long extensions in macro work, filters in front of and converters behind the lens. Even indirect light from an umbrella or light bounced into the subject off a reflector is controlled precisely by the TTL system—but one soon reaches the performance limits of the flash with these devices.

Part of the M6 TTL flash control system is stroboscopic flash. Prerequisite is a compatible SCA-3000 flash and the 3501/M SCA adapter.

SF 20—The System Flash Unit for the M6 TTL

This approximately 180g lightweight midget really has it all, as you will see from the table on the next page.

What the SF 20 Can Do

A guide number of 20 with reference to ISO 100/21° indicates a range of only three and a half metres at f/5.6; at ISO 50/18° it shrinks to 2.5m—but the way one can play around with the power of the SF 20 is fun.

In TTL mode, the light given off by the SF 20 is controlled solely by the amount of light reflected off the surface of the film. Standard light output does not always lead to a balanced relationship between ambient and flash illumination, for example the busker in the increasing twilight and shop window illumination. The aperture is no longer a light-controlling element as any change in aperture in TTL mode simply results in a change in flash output. You can select light output that differs from standard using the plus/minus buttons in third-stop increments between –3 and +3 EV. Rules for how much one should correct to plus or minus do not exist. So one should expose a few variations—if the subject holds still long enough. You can only control the manner in which the background appears in the final image by using shutter speeds slower than 1/50s—as long as they are still reasonably shake-safe. A big help from the intelligent SF 20 is if you touch the aperture button briefly in TTL mode, an aperture blinks on the LCD monitor at the same time as the range of the flash. Using the plus or minus

SF 20 Flash Unit Technical Data	
Guide number for ISO 100/21° with diffusion screen	20 14
Operating modes	**TTL** via built-in SCA 3501 adapter, **A**utomatic via sensor **M**anual
Apertures in Automatic mode	f/2.8 – f/5.6 – f/11
Flash illumination times in **TTL** & **A** in **M** with full flash	1/30,000s to 1/400s 1/400s
Charging time in **A** & **TTL** in M	ca. 0.5s – 6s ca. 6s – 8s
Exposure correction in **TTL** in **A**	+/– 3EV in 1/3 steps 0 – 3EV in whole steps
Flash light output stages in **M**	1/1, 1/2, 1/4, 1/8
Flash control	flash success display in viewfinder of M6 TTL and R8
Photo sensor metering angle	25°
Colour temperature	ca. 5600 K
Illumination angle with diffusion screen	covers 35mm focal length covers 24mm focal length
Film speed in **A** & **M** modes in **TTL** mode	ISO 25/15° – ISO 800/30° ISO 12/12° – ISO 3200/36°
Number of flashes per set of batteries	ca. 250 at full output
Batteries	2 x Lithium DL 123A or CR 123A
Dimensions (WxHxD)	109 x 66 x 40mm
Weight	approx. 180g

buttons, you can now determine the flash range for apertures from f/1 to f/45.

In A-mode, the SF 20's light sensor takes over the control of the flash illumination with its electronics. It can be set to apertures f/2.8, f/5.6, f/11. Use and functionality of this system is identical to that of other electronic flashes. In order to customise the flash illumination according to the subject, you can now only use the minus button up to a correction corresponding to ISO 80/30°. The other control method is to select a different aperture from the power level set on the

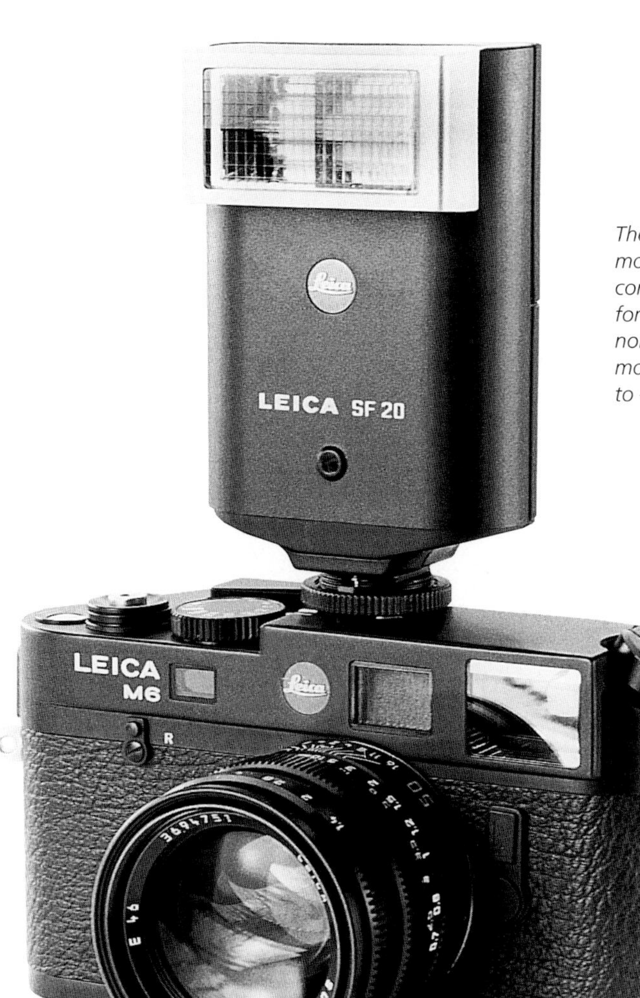

The Leica SF 20 flash unit in TTL mode with the M6 TTL offers a correction range of –3 to +3 EV for fine-tuning light output. In the normal computer-controlled mode, it offers corrections to –3 EV.

SF 20. The same is true here: experiment, experiment, experiment in order to gain experience. How bright the background appears is controlled by selecting shutter speeds slower than 1/50s—but a camera-shake blurred background does not always produce an impressive result.

In M-mode for manual, you are working with the guide number formula alone. Since one cannot always select the distance to the subject and since controlling the flash illumination with the aperture alone does not always lead to an optimal result, the SF 20 also offers power settings in "M": from guide

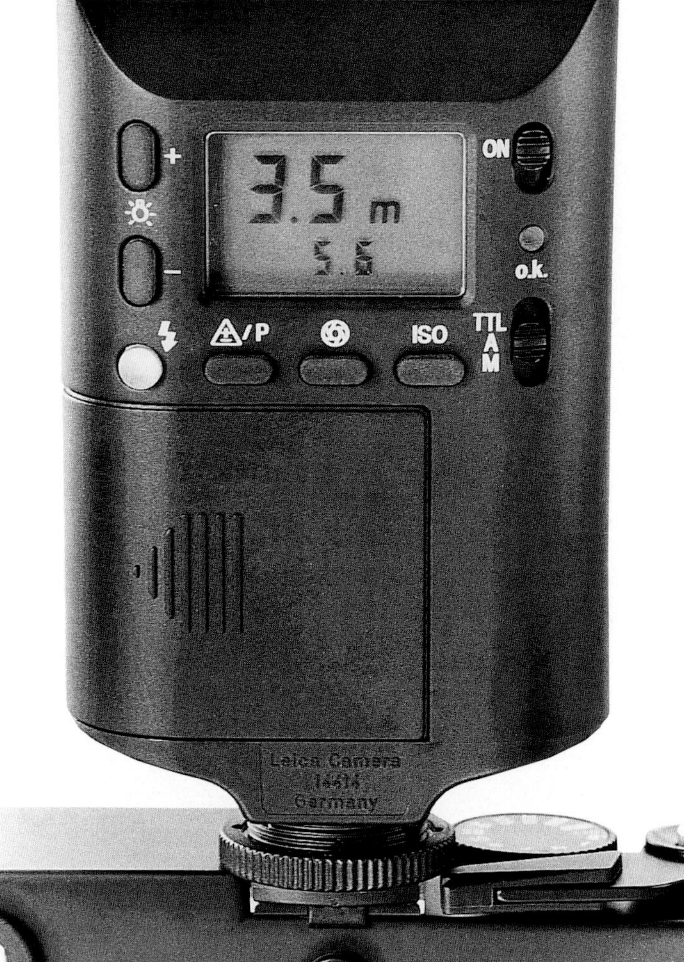

The information and control centre on the back of the SF 20 Leica flash unit, whose output can be controlled in three ways: TTL control with the M6 TTL, computer control and manual.

number 20 to 1/2 = GN 14, or 1/4 = GN 10 or 1/8 = GN 7, each for ISO 100/21°. You can obtain guide numbers for other ISO values if you multiply using these values:

for ISO 25/15	times 0.5
for ISO 50/18	times 0.7
for ISO 200/24	times 1.4
for ISO 400/27	times 2.0
for ISO 800/30	times 2,8
for ISO 1600/33	times 4.0

Since the SF 20 produces the same amount of light in any of the power levels in "M", you can only control the illumination of the main part of your subject in very narrow bounds using the aperture—you do not want to over- or under-expose it. Use shutter speeds slower than 1/50s to determine how brightly the background is captured on film.

From Flash Light to Flash Illumination

The smaller or larger amount of frontal flash illumination is evidently the photographic style of our time. True, there are situations in which one can only bring the image home by using flash. But even as carefully as one can control the SF 20, it is still frontal illumination. It is not the best way to bring light into the subject. One would like a 2m long coiled cord between the M6 TTL and the SF 20 so that one can hand-hold it off to the side or bounce the light off a white ceiling while still transmitting all TTL signals. Sometimes wishes are heard and even fulfilled—maybe this is one of them.

One-handed operation of the M6 TTL is something both you and I have practised often—it is absolutely no problem because one has set aperture, shutter speed and distance in advance. If one does not have a cable for the SF 20, one can use this work-around. Mount a centre-contact adapter on the SF 20 and attach its short cable to a longer, regular sync. cable which is then connected to the sync socket on the back of the camera. Control and dosing of the flash illumination, which can now strike the subject from above, below or the side, is assumed by the SF 20's sensor and computer. But: flash illumination coming in from the side is, from the camera's point of view, reduced by a factor of the angle of incidence. It is reduced to 0.75 for 45° and to 0.6 for light coming from 75°. The performance limit of the SF 20 is soon reached. One should not be content with just one shot here either! This method is not recommended for indirect bounce flash as the SF 20 will meter the white ceiling or the umbrella and not the subject!

For flash illumination from the side, and particularly for bounce flash, one needs powerful units. Freedom to compose with light is possible with an external sensor mounted on the M6 TTL hot shoe which is, in turn, connected to the flash via a long cable. It transmits the fire command to the flash and controls the subject illumination from the same direction as the lens sees it.

There are no correction factors to prevent shadows that are too dark in areas that the flash does not reach. Even TTL flash control gives up. Fill-in is required. Use the projection screen, white Bristol board, white Styrofoam, crinkled aluminium foil glued to a piece of cardboard. For a portrait, you should use 90x90cm, for an entire person 130x200cm. Position the reflector as close to the subject as the angle of view of the lens will allow.

For indirect flash, one will seldom have too much, but often too little, light. The flash should have a minimum guide number of 40 for

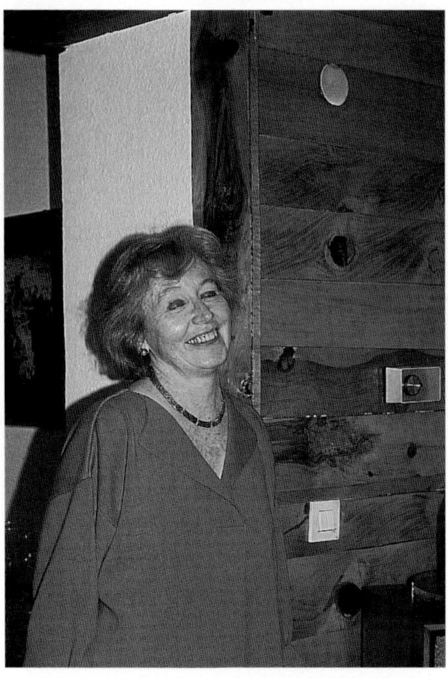

Three examples using only one flash—and yet three different pictures. The Leica SF 20 certainly is a versatile, multi-function flash unit—but mounted on an M6 TTL, it still remains frontal light with a small reflector with all its disadvantages.

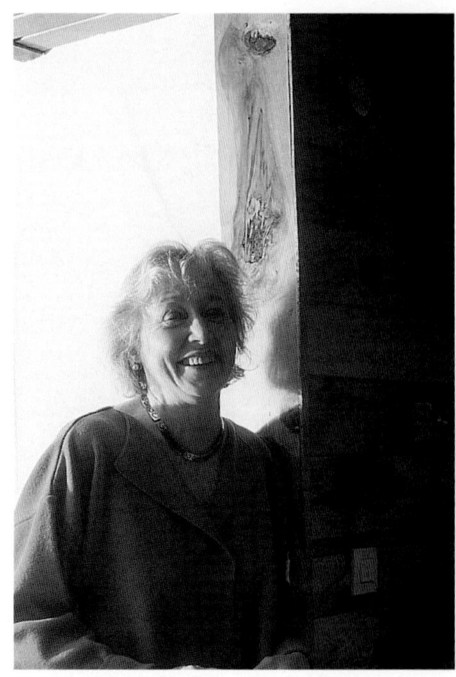

Shot from an adjoining room at f/2.8/f4, illuminated by the SF 20 under computer control and set to f/5.6, the same scene looks quite different.

ISO 100/21°—even if you create a small system out of three individual flash units. Use only flash units from one manufacturer in order to avoid electrical surprises when you connect them together. An external sensor connected to each flash via at least a 3m-long cable, which allows at least four stops of control, saves you a great deal of calculation and test shots. If the external sensor offers more non-sensor controlled power settings as well, you are well-equipped for photography using flash. As well as you can be when using flash units with a guide number of 40.

You think you have too much light with three GN 40 flashes at ISO 100/21°? Flash illumination coming in from the side is, from the camera's point of view, reduced by a factor of the angle of incidence: reduced to 0.75 for 45° and 0.6 for light coming from 75°. Two identically powered flash units do not double the guide number, but raise it by a factor of 1.4—if they illuminate the subject from the same angle and the same

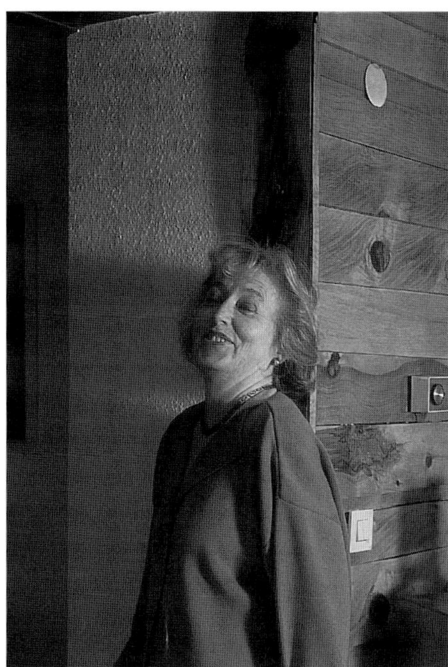

The light coming from the studio flash system's 40x40cm soft box, the flash illumination is much softer.
All images with the Summicron-M 50mm f/2.

distance. Also, a guide number of 44 for ISO 100/21° becomes GN 22 for ISO 25/15°. An angle factor of 45° reduces it to merely 17! At a distance of 2m, however, one can still attain f/8. An umbrella or a diffusion screen for softer illumination demands two stops of light—and one is at f/5.6 or f/4—and hence too narrow a depth of field for most subjects. In my experience, two or three units with guide numbers of 60 are not a waste of energy but rather a comforting power reserve for shooting products at a small aperture on low-speed film, as an example. A flash exposure meter and a multi-level control sensor belongs to this class of power output with options including a flash duration of 1/10,000s to "freeze" motion. The cat's cradle of cables around the shooting table provide a plethora of toe-catchers for amazing side-effects. You should therefore only connect one flash to the M6 TTL via a cable and control the others via radio slaves.

Regardless of how you control flash production, rules for balancing front, side and effect flash are, at best, guidelines. Experiment, take test shots and record the settings in order to gain experience and confidence. With complex and/or non-repeatable situations, one should shoot a series of exposures, changing the flash settings each time. But two problems typical of flash-illumination remain unaddressed. You cannot judge the distribution of light and shadow in the subject before the exposure, and the light bounced off small reflectors often creates hard lines and shadows that are too dark. The remedies are as follows.

Clip-on Lamps And Lighted Surfaces

There is always room on the tripod beside the flash for a small clip-on lamp with an incandescent bulb. 150W with an illumination angle of 50° or 60° is adequate to assess light and shadow in the subject and, above all, to see how and where the second and third flash units create shadows or hot-spots in the subject where there were none before. It will

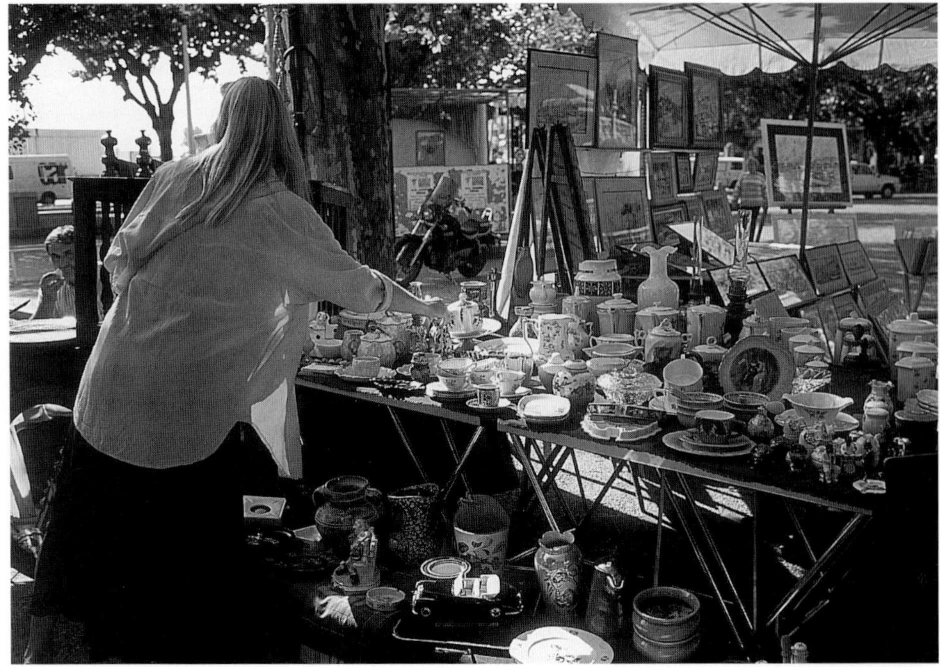

Lying under the thick, leafy canopy of trees, the flea market is blessed with very contrasty lighting—one will probably have to bracket this shot to arrive at the correct exposure.

also show you where you will need to strike this or that surface with a fill-light so that it does not appear "dead."

Shadows thrown onto a subject from a hard source remain harsh even when lit with fill-in because the 4.5x9cm small reflector of the hand-type flash is still a point light source. So one should transform this point light into a larger surface using diffusers and umbrellas to create soft, practically imperceptible transitions from light to shadow. Furthermore, your favourite model will feel better in front of an 80x80cm lighted surface than in front of a harsh, point light source. Many product shots even look better in a soft flood of light. If the light surface is very close to the model or object, it sends more light into the shadows the bigger it is. It smooths out the sharp edges. A 2m high and 150cm wide diffusion screen illuminated from one metre behind by three flashes, 50cm apart, creates a very flattering flood of light. Heavy translucent material produces the same effect.

Or one can flash against an umbrella or a reflective surface such as pure-white Styrofoam or wrinkled household aluminium foil.

Umbrellas are available in diameters from 70cm to 180cm. Reflecting surfaces are best made oneself using appropriate materials and matched to the dimensions of the room. Umbrellas and reflectors cannot be that close to the subject because the flash has to be between them and the subject.

The M6 TTL And The Studio Flash System

Studio flash systems are not acquainted with computers and TTL flash control and they need ready access to power from a wall-outlet. But studio flash units offer two big advantages over any other types of flash.

Firstly is the integrated modelling light whose brightness one can select over a range of many stops. Using it and fillers, one can determine the exact position of light and shadow over the subject. One can also match the contrast to the capabilities of the film. Proportional control of the studio flash unit ensures that the flash illumination is always a fixed multiple of the modelling light's intensity. One can therefore use an exposure meter to determine the differences between the highlights and shadows with the modelling light.

Secondly, one can change the reflectors on a studio flash unit as easily as one changes the lenses on the camera. In order to compose an image with flash illumination, one has to be able to steer it and shape it. The assortment of reflectors available for my studio flash system range from a snoot with a diameter of barely 10cm and a length of 25cm, through the normal reflector which has a diameter of 25cm and is 17cm deep, right up to a one-square-metre light box from which 75° of softly diffused sunlight-like illumination emanates. The halogen modelling light is situated in the centre of the circular flash tube and shows the differences in light characteristics produced by the normal reflector, effective output area of 490cm2, the snoot, output 78cm2 and the 75x75cm soft box, output 5.625cm2.

Since the reflectors for the studio flash systems have widely different illumination angles and effects, it does not make sense to quote the power of such a flash as a guide number. The guide number always refers to the size and shape of the normal reflector with which it was created. One can therefore only compare the studio flash's guide number relative to the normal reflector to the guide number of a compact flash with caution. The 25cm normal reflector for a 200 watt-second studio flash produces light with a guide number of 40 at ISO 100/21°. But despite the same angle of illumination of 50° as the compact flash, the light produced by this reflector is very different from that produced by the smaller flash's 4x6cm reflector.

A guide number for the big soft box that can even be remotely compared to the compact or hand-type flash cannot be given. This is why the power of a studio flash unit is only quoted in watt-seconds (Ws). One can only compare them with hand-type flashes with values measured in practice.

My 500Ws flash unit, fitted out with the 25cm normal reflector, produces a calculated guide number of 65 at ISO 100/21°. This corresponds to the highest class of two-part hand-type flashes such as the Metz Mecablitz 60 CT 1/4. Two metres in front of this reflector, there is enough light for f/32. Two metres in front of the snoot, there is enough for f/45, two metres in front of the 40x40cm soft box f/16, two metres in front of the 1x1m soft box only f/11. Those who use large soft boxes with low-speed films will soon run out of power with 200/250Ws flash units. 500 or 600 watt-seconds offer enough reserve power to illuminate larger subjects and macro shots on the other side of the 1:1 magnification ratio. Careful use of large and small reflectors along with two 500Ws units are enough to handle just about any situation. I never had too much light with my two 500Ws units because I can reduce their power to 120Ws, or three stops. It makes one breathe easier to know the power is there.

A flash exposure meter belongs to a studio flash system as gas to a car. It should be able to read reflected and incident illumination in flash and ambient light and should offer correction possibilities for the use of filters and macro extensions. You need only connect one of the units gathered around the subject to the Leica M6 TTL, the others can fire via their built-in slaves. Anyone who does a great deal of studio flash work with the M6 TTL should bear this in mind: it will not fire the flash with a weak or nonexistent battery!

If the balance between light and shadow shown by the modelling lights matches your ideas for the image and the abilities of the film, the flash exposure meter will give you the requisite aperture with a few test flashes. Whether one should use the big soft box or the small reflector is part of creating the image using light and shadow. There are no rules here. The only aids are experience and your own creativity. You can earn both while training on the job.

A more recent Nautilus model on the Canal du Midi. The narrow angle of view of the longer focal length removes the unwanted surroundings from the shot. Elmarit-M 135mm f/2.8.

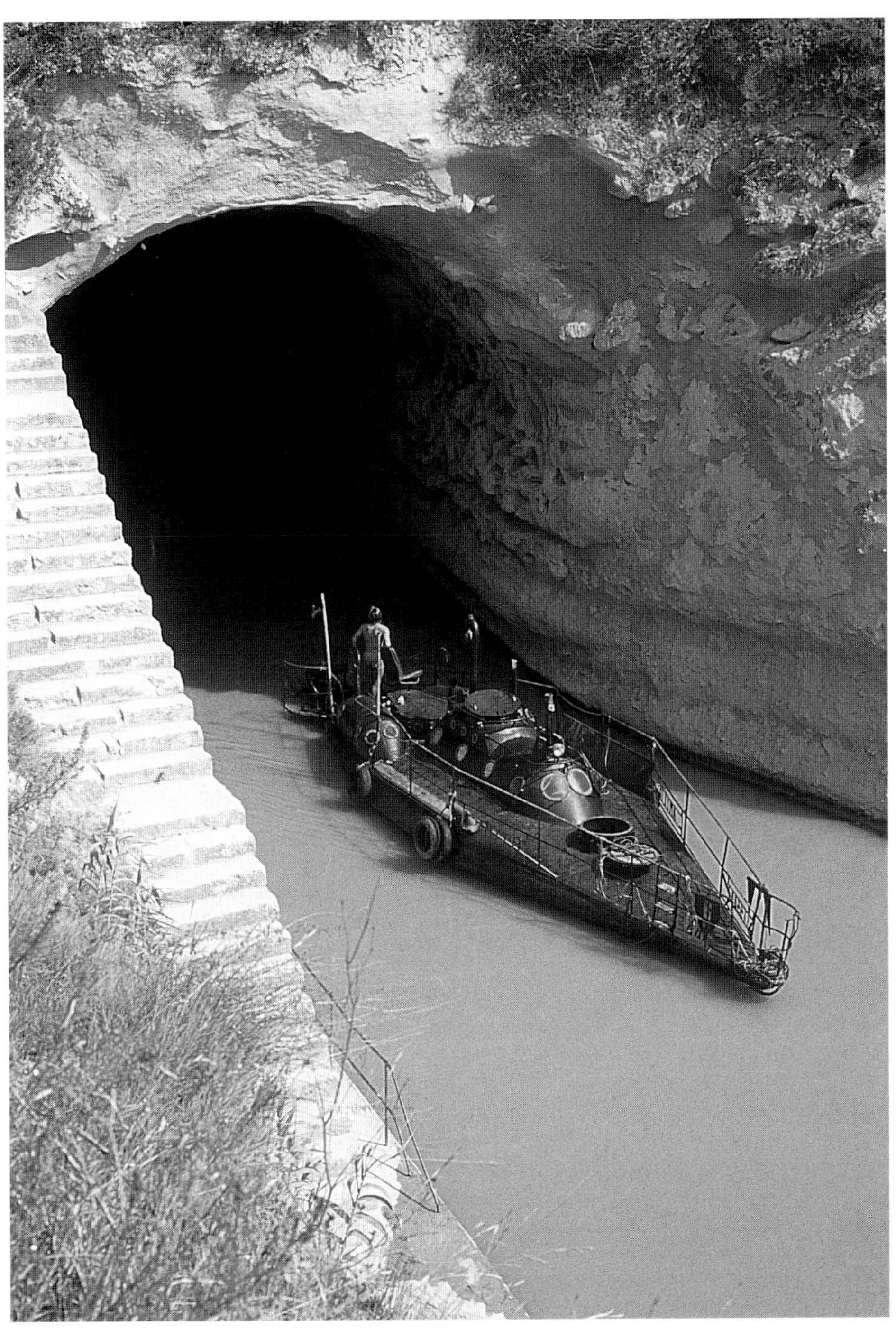

Index

L

M

W

Z

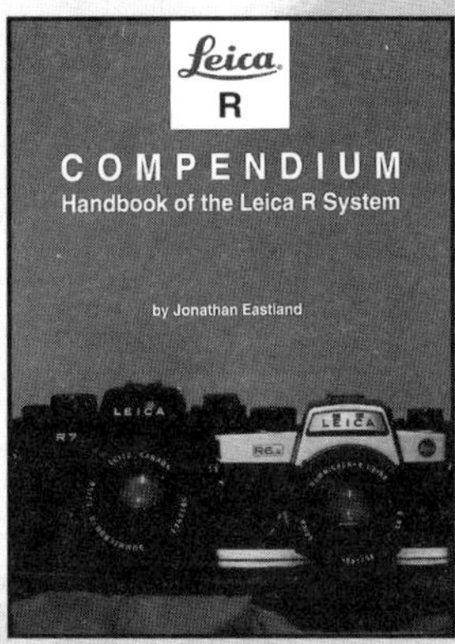

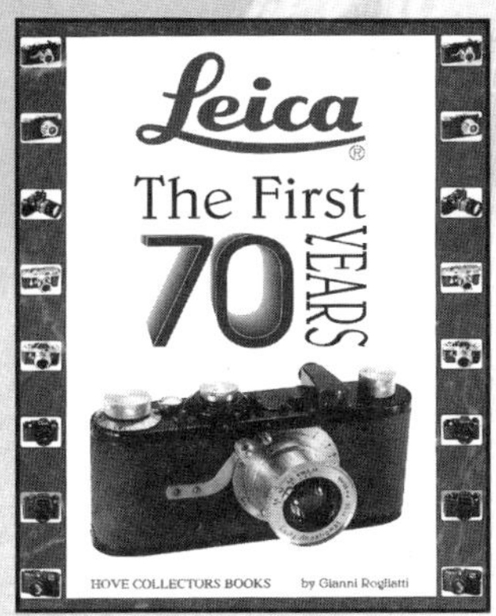

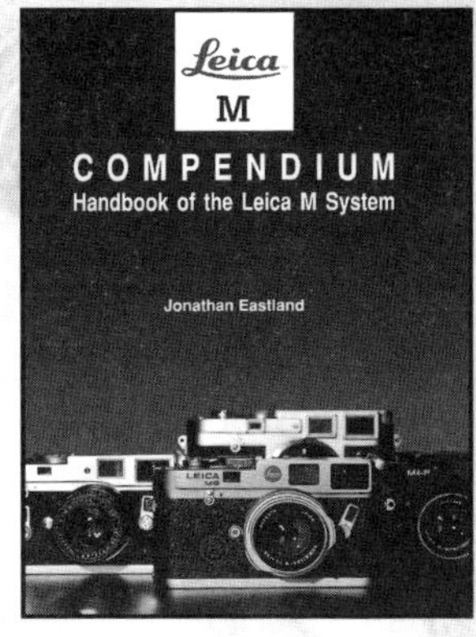

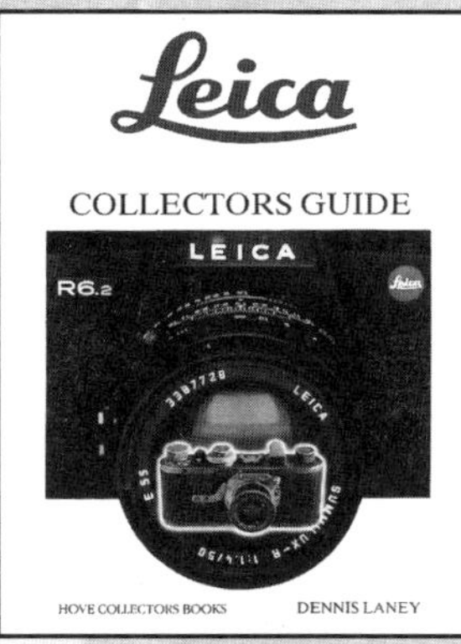

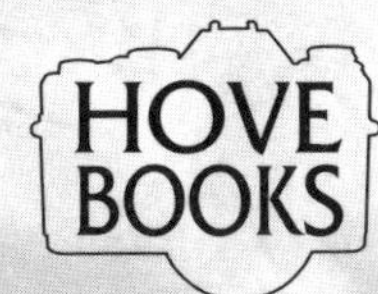

Telephone or Fax
for a copy of our
FREE
colour brochure
Tel: +44(0)1273 495757
Fax: +44(0)1273 494992

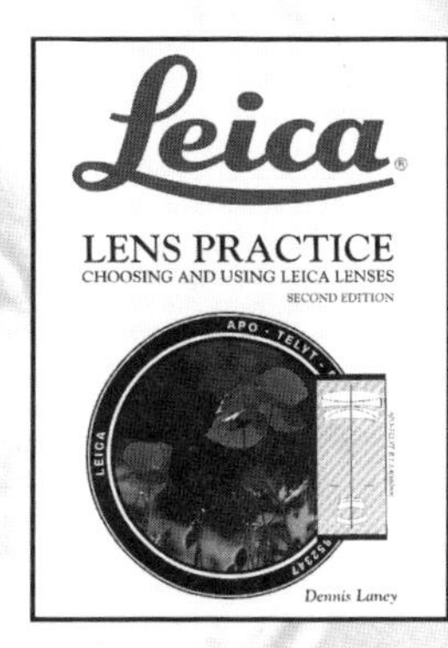

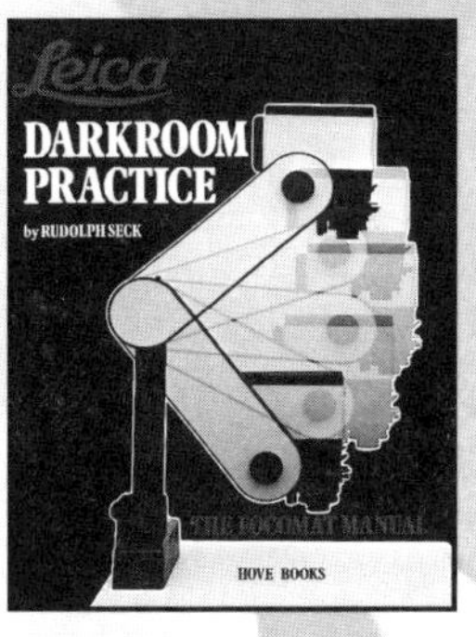

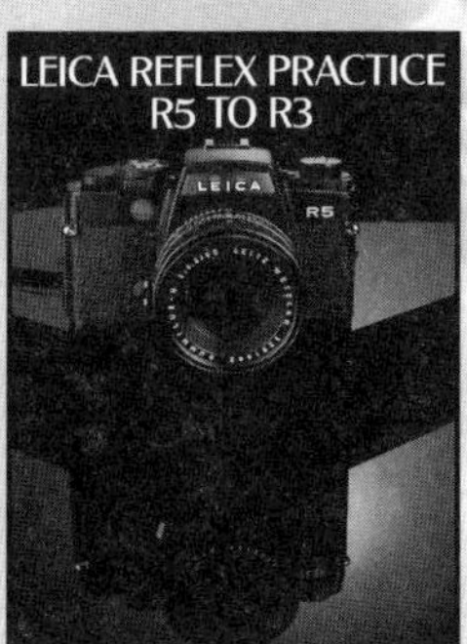

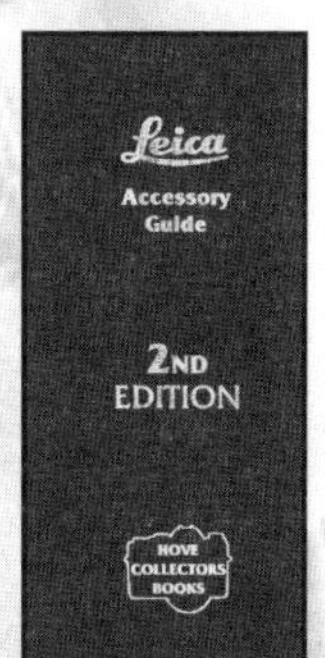

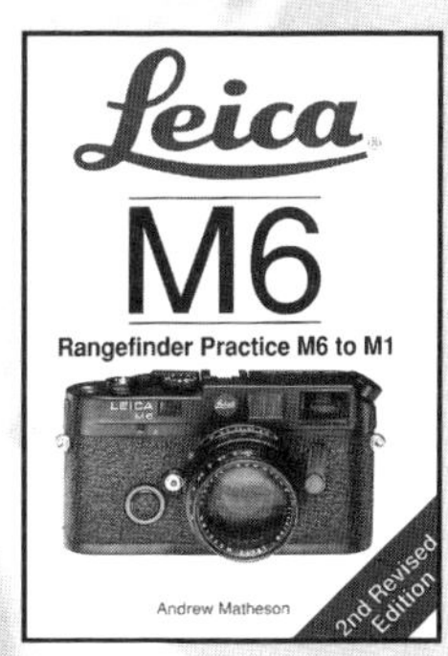

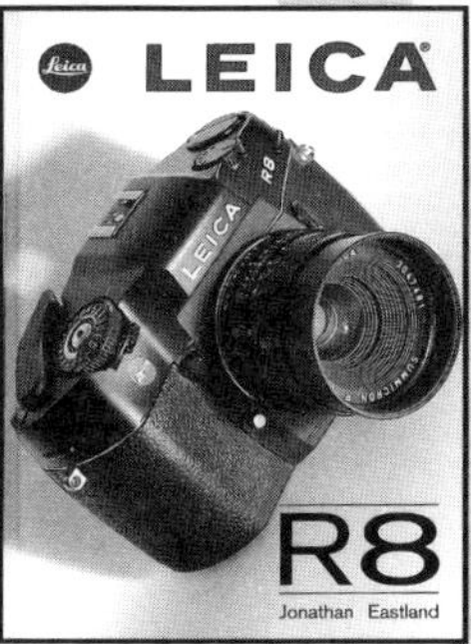

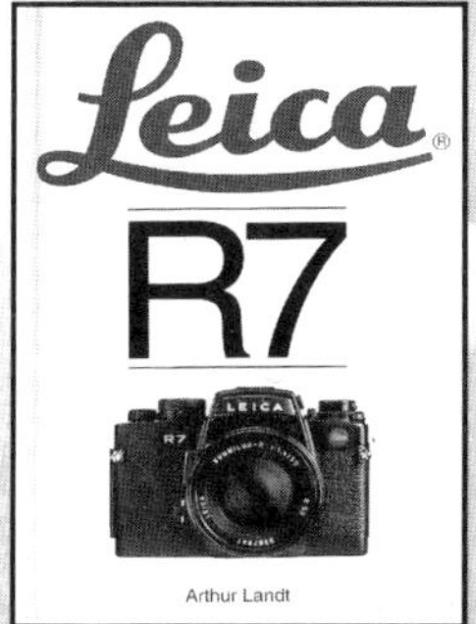

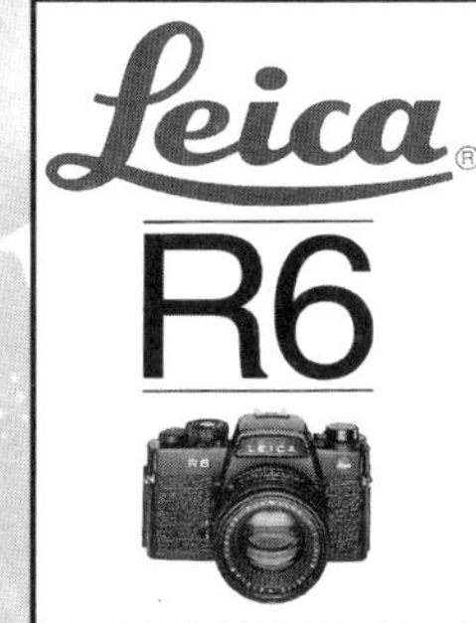

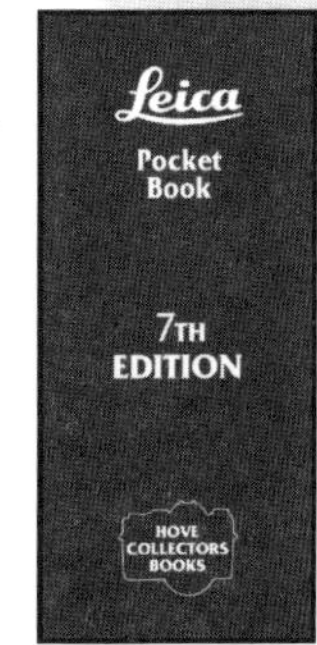

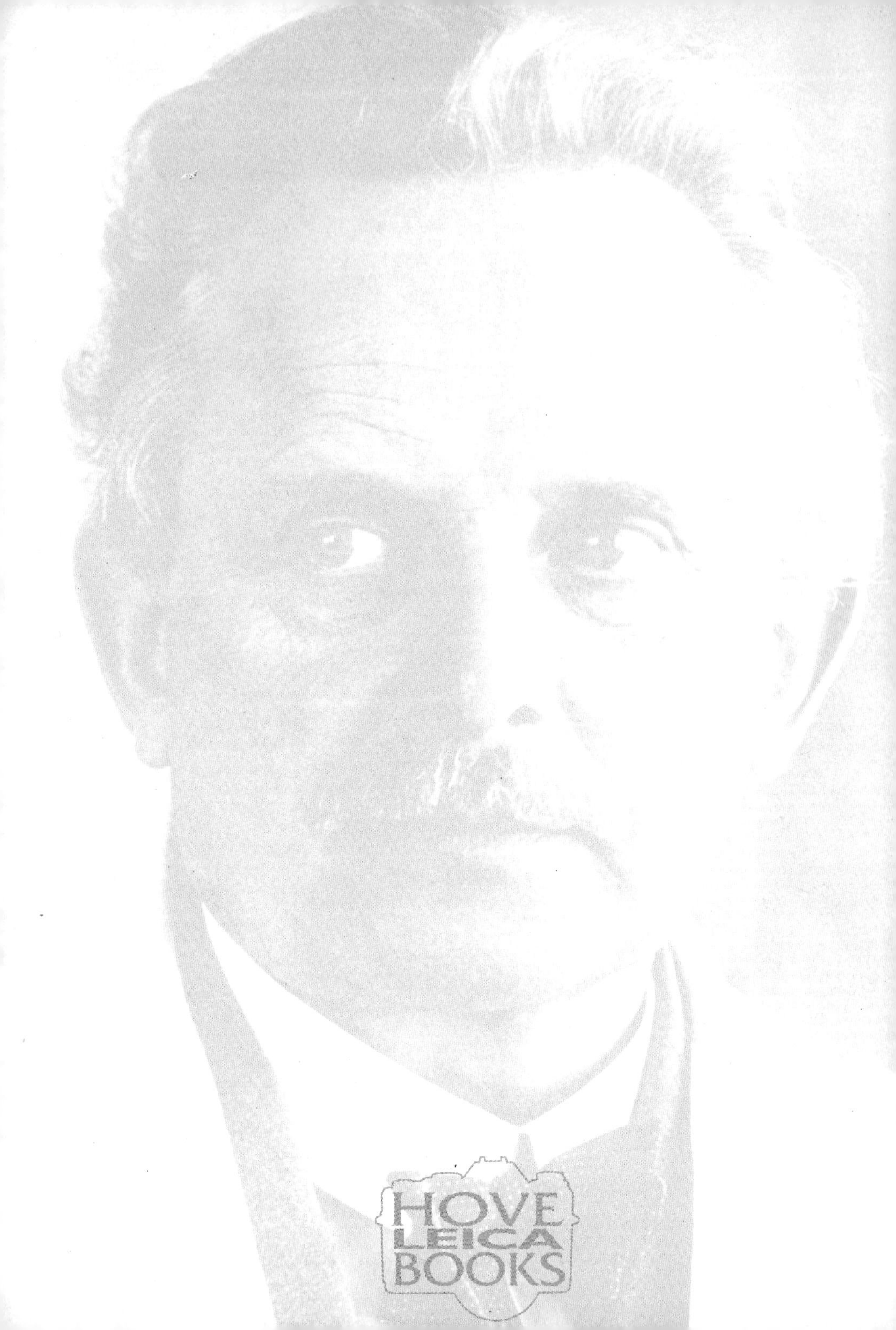
HOVE
LEICA
BOOKS